Facilitating
the Socio-Economic
Approach
to Management

Results of the First SEAM
Conference in North America

A volume in
Research in Management Consulting
Anthony F. Buono, *Series Editor*

Facilitating the Socio-Economic Approach to Management

Results of the First SEAM Conference in North America

edited by

Henri Savall
ISEOR, IAE Lyon, University Jean Moulin

John Conbere
University of St. Thomas

Alla Heorhiadi
University of St. Thomas

Vincent Cristallini
ISEOR, IAE Lyon, University Jean Moulin

Anthony F. Buono
Bentley University

INFORMATION AGE PUBLISHING, INC.
Charlotte, NC • www.infoagepub.com

Library of Congress Cataloging-in-Publication Data

A CIP record for this book is available from the Library of Congress
http://www.loc.gov

ISBN: 978-1-62396-667-6 (Paperback)
978-1-62396-668-3 (Hardcover)
978-1-62396-669-0 (ebook)

CONTENTS

PART I

THE SOCIO-ECONOMIC APPROACH TO MANAGEMENT

PART II

WORLDWIDE EXPERIMENTATION WITH SEAM

PART III

BRIDGING SEAM WITH AMERICAN PERCEPTION

PREFACE

Anthony F. Buono

This book is the 20th volume in the *Research in Management Consulting* (RMC) series and the sixth major collaboration with Henri Savall, Veronique Zardet, and their team of intervener-researchers from the Socio-Economic Institute for Firms and Organizations (ISEOR) in Ecully, France. It is hard to believe that it has been roughly two decades since I was first exposed to Savall's insightful work on the challenges of intervening in organizations and the need to more explicitly integrate the qualitative, quantitative, and financial dimensions of organizational life if those interventions are truly to make a difference. Beginning with a thoughtful introduction to the ISEOR paradigm—the Socio-Economic Approach to Management (SEAM)—in the first volume in the RMC series (Savall, Zardet, Bonnet, & Moore, 2001), the stage was set for myriad contributions from my French colleagues and their associates.

Much of the content in the series' second volume, *Developing Knowledge and Value in Management Consulting* (Buono, 2002), was based on the first European conference of the Academy of Management's (AOM) Management Consulting Division, which was hosted by our Lyon-based colleagues. That volume focused on the processes and challenges involved in developing knowledge and creating value in management consulting, especially amid the unprecedented changes taking place in the industry. Those first two volumes launched a concerted international effort to reduce the mystique and ambiguity surrounding management consulting—enhancing the

Facilitating the Socioeconomic Approach to Management, pages ix–xi
Copyright © 2014 by Information Age Publishing
All rights of reproduction in any form reserved.

dialogue between applied scholars and scholarly practitioners in the consulting field, capturing innovative empirical and conceptual research and field experience, and disseminating the resulting insight to a broad range of practitioners, academicians, and organizational executives.

Savall and the work of ISEOR have continued to be a core dimension of the RMC series since that time—from updated translations of his earlier works in French, *Mastering Hidden Costs and Socio-Economic Performance* (Savall & Zardet, 2008), *Work and People* (Savall, 2010), and *The Qualimetrics Approach* (Savall & Zardet, 2011), to his more recent insights into *The Dynamics and Challenges of Tetranormalization* (Savall & Zardet, 2013) and a coedited volume on SEAM interventions that was one result of a month-long sabbatical stay at ISEOR (Buono & Savall, 2007). Through these interactions and exchanges I continued to become increasingly immersed in the ISEOR paradigm, which to date have also led to another upcoming sabbatical visit (Spring 2014) in Ecully and plans for a second edited volume with Savall's group of intervener-researchers.

While ISEOR's intervener-researchers were also highly active in AOM meetings and the Management Consulting Division's other European conferences over the next decade—Lausanne, Copenhagen, Vienna, Amsterdam—2013 marked the first time that ISEOR cosponsored a conference on its SEAM paradigm and methodology in the United States. This volume captures the ideas, applications, and exchanges of that meeting hosted by the University of St. Thomas in Minneapolis, Minnesota. The book attempts to bring the reader into the conference itself. The different chapters include the contributors' presentations ("Chapter Prologue: Conference Remarks"), revised conference papers, and the question and answer dialogue for the session. Conference presenters are identified in these exchanges, though in many instances those raising questions are simply identified as "Conference Participant." For those interested in delving further into the SEAM approach, the volume also contains a general bibliography on the development, critique, and application of the framework.

As Savall and Michel Péron note in their introductory chapter, two University of St. Thomas professors—John Conbere and Alla Heorhiadi, who also served as coeditors of the volume—were sufficiently intrigued by the SEAM approach that they worked diligently to become "SEAM practitioners." After participating in a number of ISEOR conferences in Lyon, Conbere and Heorhiadi played an active role in ISEOR's first English-based consultant training program, focusing their work and contributions on the cultural differences and nuances that raised knowledge transfer related challenges in bringing SEAM to the United States. As a way of further developing and testing their understanding and expertise with the SEAM approach, they integrated the framework in their classrooms, working with the next general of intervener-researchers in ISEOR's ongoing internationalization and entry in the United States—and provided the impetus for the conference on which this volume is based. I would like to add my personal thanks to my ISEOR and University of St. Thomas colleagues, as well as all the conference participants and chapter coauthors, for their contribution to one of the RMC series core objectives—our ongoing efforts to capture the true blending of theory and practice in our interventions in organizations.

REFERENCES

Buono, A.F. (Ed.) (2002). *Developing knowledge and value in management consulting.* Greenwich, CT: Information Age Publishing.

Buono, A.F., & Savall, H. (Eds.). (2007). *Socio-economic intervention in organizations: The intervener-researcher and the SEAM approach to organizational analysis.* Charlotte, NC: Information Age Publishing, 2007.

Savall, H. (2010). *Work and People: An Economic Evaluation of Job-Enrichment.* Charlotte, NC: Information Age Publishing.

Savall, H., & Zardet, V. (2008). *Mastering hidden costs and socio-economic performance.* Charlotte, NC: Information Age Publishing.

Savall, H., & Zardet, V. (2011). *The qualimetrics approach: Observing the complex object.* Charlotte, NC: Information Age Publishing.

Savall, H., & Zardet, V. (2013). *The Dynamics and Challenges of tetranormalization.* Charlotte, NC: Information Age Publishing.

Savall, H., Zardet, V., Bonnet, M., & Moore, R. (2001). A system-wide, integrated methodology for intervening in organizations: The ISEOR approach. In A. F. Buono (Ed.), *Current trends in management consulting* (pp. 105–125). Greenwich, CT: Information Age Publishing.

INTRODUCTION

Henri Savall and Michel Péron

This book represents one further step in our various attempts at disseminating our socio-economic theory of organization worldwide. In fact, with regard to the United States, we asked ourselves whether this was not tantamount to bringing coal to Newcastle or trying to sell ice to Eskimos. However, one of our colleagues, Rickie Moore, a professor of entrepreneurship and management at the EM Lyon and a member of our research team, convinced us that there was a permanent need to re-evaluate organizational performance and a lack of an appropriate methodology to implement large-scale change in American enterprises. This task is exactly what SEAM is aiming to accomplish: to deal with enterprise operations as a whole, in order to facilitate the emergence of sustainable, effective, and innovative solutions for a successful mastering of change as opposed to a quick-fix, short-term, and ultimately limited approach. SEAM intervention differs from action-research due to its holistic side.

As French professors in management as well as consultancy experts tend to pledge allegiance to U.S. management specialists and consultancy moguls, we thought it was necessary to open their eyes to the existence of other methods in different parts of the world. Our research center, for example, has already launched initiation and development operations in numerous countries and on several continents leading to the creation of a Laboratory of Socio-Economic Management in the Universidad Autonoma Metropolitana of Mexico. We were perfectly aware that such a breakthrough into our

Facilitating the Socioeconomic Approach to Management, pages xiii–xvi
Copyright © 2014 by Information Age Publishing
All rights of reproduction in any form reserved.

scholarly world would require some sort of prior acceptance or recognition of the SEAM methodology by the U.S. business community and academic circles, especially in the wake of Savall's *Work and People: An Economic Evaluation of Job Enrichment*, initially published in 1981 by Oxford University Press and updated in 2010 with Information Age Publishing. The ISEOR team thus found itself facing a number of assignments.

First, the challenge of developing academic cooperation with American business professors. We initially sought out colleagues who were keen on positioning the contributions of the socio-economic method through sharing of experience. This initial move was made possible by Central Michigan University academics working alternately in the United States and at ISEOR in France, concomitantly with attending the annual Academy of Management (AOM) Conference and participating in a series of Professional Development Workshops with AOM's Management Consulting Division.

The second task was to organize a series of international colloquia in Lyon with the participation of various AOM divisions, including Management Consulting, Organization Development and Change, Research Methods, and Social Issues in Management.

A third set of ventures focused on additional publication, contributing to a special issue of the *Journal of Organizational Change Management* that was dedicated to the socio-economic approach through the invaluable intermediation of Professor David Boje, and collaboration on a book on SEAM intervention, carefully edited by Professor Anthony Buono. This work led to an ongoing relationship in which Buono also edited a series of books coauthored by Henri Savall and Véronique Zardet, opening new perspectives for research in the field. The most recent development in this work is this volume, which captures the presentations and papers presented at the first U.S. conference dedicated to SEAM hosted by the University of St. Thomas in Minneapolis.

The collaboration with Therese Yaeger and Peter Sorensen from Benedictine University has also triggered off many opportunities to discuss and compare Appreciative Inquiry (AI) and SEAM, leading to our conclusion that both methods could be easily reconciled. The faithful and enriching contributions of Yaeger and Sorensen have considerably helped in making our method better known, and more especially the illuminating article they jointly published with ISEOR focused on a provocative comparison between AI and SEAM (see Sorensen, Yaeger, Savall, Zardet, Bonnet, & Péron, 2010).

After having regularly attended the International June Conferences held in Lyon, John Conbere and Alla Heorhiadi "decided to learn to become SEAM practitioners" and took an active part in the consultant training program in English set up for the first time in 2008. As very demanding and insightful participants, they contributed to the fine-tuning of some recurring concepts in our SEAM methodology, clarifying some cultural specificities that might cause problems in front of an American audience, and challenging our opinion on the short-termism of U.S. managers as they insisted on the fact that they are no longer short-term focused but on the contrary ready to take time for change. They mentioned the ongoing monthly coaching of the manager as critical for the change process, but lamented the lack of proper development on this point. Conbere and Heorhiadi broke new ground when they decided to "get down to brass tacks" when appropriating the SEAM method and teaching it in their classrooms. It is worth mentioning that courses about SEAM that have been taught in a few U.S. universities have led to intervention-research projects by students with their professors or some carried out by the students themselves. These interventions, however, did not integrate all the components of the SEAM methodology and were limited to partial references to the holistic approach. In essence, these projects were deprived of part of their significance. None of these attempts were aimed at setting up a completely relevant implementation of the SEAM methodology and, consequently, could not expect quality control assessment from ISEOR.

The knowledge transfer that occurred in the Minneapolis Conference was instrumental in facilitating and helping participants understand the nuances of the SEAM process. As Conbere puts it, language should be considered an important vector of such transfer, with regard to the integrity of the concepts. As an example, after a careful reading of Alanna Kennedy's contribution on "SEAM and the TFW Virus" (see Chapter 3), it became obvious that the developed acronym should be the "Taylorism, Fayolism, Weberism virus," since it refers to the distorted view of their henchmen rather than to the authors' genuine stance. If the measure of success for the industrial philosophy that is encapsulated in two words—Scientific Management—consists of an increase in productivity, efficiency, and profit, it must be difficult to persuade St. Thomas students that these are not also the major indicators of performance with SEAM. In this connection, Conbere and Heorhiadi found the right formula when they posited that problems came from "the fundamental oversight of the power of the individual," while underpinning that the organizational bottom line remains the actual value that drives decision making in most U.S. enterprises. Insisting on the essential concept of human potential, Conbere and Heorhiadi find it easy to combine competitiveness with creating future potential and reducing dysfunctions within the framework of an innovation project that includes improvement actions for both social and economic performance.

The different contributions to this book underscore that the major challenge for the ISEOR team in the United States is to successfully train scholars and managers to become reliable, full-fledged intervention-research practitioners and to devise ways to operate efficiently in terms of cost and time for American students.

REFERENCE

Sorensen, P., Yaeger, T., Savall, H., Zardet, V., Bonnet, M., & Péron, M. (2010). A review of two major global and international approaches to organizational change: SEAM and Appreciative Inquiry. *Organization Development Journal, 28* (4), 31–40.

PART I

THE SOCIO-ECONOMIC APPROACH
TO MANAGEMENT

CHAPTER 1

THE HISTORY OF SEAM

Marc Bonnet and Henri Savall

CONFERENCE REMARKS
Chapter Prologue

Marc Bonnet

We are going back to the genesis of this method, which was created 40 years ago by Henri Savall. In order to develop his theory, he needed a research center. The aim was to document all the interventions, making sense of the learning through conceptualizing ideas, and then teaching the SEAM approach. ISEOR stands for Socio Economic Institute for Firms and Organizations. It is a nonprofit association created in 1975 and associated with the University of Lyon 3 and IAE Business School. The former dean of the business school, Gilles Guyot is present today with us.

The theory draws on experiments and consists of 1.6 million hours of intervention research. Two thirds of the time involved with this research was spent within the companies. This emphasis is different from traditional research in the field of management, where researchers send questionnaires, use structural equations and then come to conclusions.

The conceptualization process, the learning process is very slow and it should be necessary to bring evidence to all the conclusions. Before writing

Facilitating the Socioeconomic Approach to Management, pages 3–12
Copyright © 2014 by Information Age Publishing

3

a paper it might take years. An untraditional aspect of the research is the rigor of the documenting process.

At the ISEOR research center, there are students of the doctoral program who are intervener researchers—and to date 126 doctoral theses had been defended, and doctoral students are working through the SEAM approach.

INTRODUCTION

This chapter briefly reflects on the genesis of the Socio-Economic Approach to Management (SEAM), which was created roughly 40 years ago by Henri Savall. In order to fully develop this theory, Savall needed a research center, with an aim to documenting the interventions, making sense of the learning through conceptualizing ideas, and then teaching the SEAM approach. The result was ISEOR—the Socio-Economic Institute for Firms and Organizations, a nonprofit association created in 1975 and associated with the University of Lyon 3 and IAE business school.

The SEAM theory is based on a series of experiments, consisting of 1.6 million hours of intervention research. Two thirds of this time was spent within the companies—which is a significant departure from traditional research efforts in the field of management where researchers send questionnaires, use structural equations, and then come to conclusions. The underlying conceptualization and learning process in SEAM is relatively slow, based on the understanding that it is necessary to bring evidence to all the conclusions. It might take years of research before writing a paper, which is a reflection of the rigorous nature of the documenting process. The ISEOR Research Center is also composed of doctoral students, who are referred to as intervener researchers. To date, 126 doctoral theses had been presented defended by these intervener-researchers working with the SEAM approach.

THE EPISTEMOLOGICAL FOUNDATION OF SEAM

The ISEOR Research Center is more than its research team and there learning that takes place intimately involves companies we work with. The Center is a reflection of the epistemology of the research method—trying to create robust learning through the interaction between researchers and companies (see Figure 1.1). This particular principle is referred as *interactive cognitivity*. We create knowledge through interacting with real cases.

Another guiding concept in each and every intervention is the *contradictory intersubjectivity principle*, which enables the creation and formalization of robust management knowledge based on a lengthy process of engagement

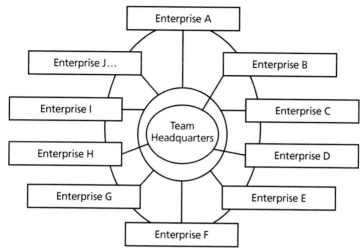

Figure 1.1 The Laboratory of Investigation of ISEOR.

that enables comparisons through different point of views. All the results of interventions in these companies are replicated in different countries, sectors, and industries. Emphasis is placed on those factors that cut across interventions, enabling us to create scientific knowledge. We continually examine and question each intervention—which of the factors are invariant? Which ones context specific rather than generic in nature?

Through the conceptualization process, our goal is to reach what we refer to as the *generic contingency* principle. There are two kinds of learnings involved in our interventions—one is contingent, specific to the context. For example, in an assessment of a public transport company one might learn how to better manage this type of company, but at the same time the researcher can also formalize more generalized ideas about management and organization, such as the importance of enhancing concerted delegation. This is the process we utilize to compare results across different cases.

There are two concepts of *generic contingency*. Henri Savall and Veronique Zardet founded the qualimetrics approach from these principles (for further elaboration on this approach see Savall & Zardet, 2011). In qualimetrics, in order to reach conceptualization you have to overarch the different natures of qualitative, quantitative and financial variables. Qualimetrics is aimed at creating bridges across those three different kinds of variables.

Intervener researchers need to gather a large amount of data, which raises the challenge of keeping track of that data. ISEOR has a huge volume of archives where all documents are coded and stored. Analyzing the content of these archives makes it possible to compare different cases—ranging from the service sector such as transports nonprofit organizations, to industrial companies—creating a learning process. With regard to a number of various sectors, 37 countries have been so far the object of 1,300 interventions that took place in Africa, Europe, and America, including Latin America. These experiments enabled us to bring evidence of the efficiency of the intervention. Much like a vaccine against the flu, SEAM can be thought of as possible medicine for the organizations. Such comparative analysis may lead to a specific point (contingency) or it may suggest generic contingency.

Treating the Organization as a Nonstatic Structure

Underlying the SEAM method is the idea that organizations should not be looked at as something static, as in accounting or management control. Organizations are living entities. The research is focused on organizational metamorphosis—it may look like an organization development (OD) process, but one of the phenomena that facilitates the ability of companies to survive is that we organize their change process overtime. The learning is that management tools are most focused on commoditizing people. Usual management tools analyze the organization as if it was something rigid—like a case—but it is not a case, in fact it lives, a reality that must be taken into account. The results of these experiments are like in the field of biology or medicine, they result in innovative tools that can be used both by practitioners and by scholars.

SEAM AND ISEOR RESEARCH

One of the images of the origins of SEAM refers to the early research projects carried out at ISEOR during the 1970s. At that time, accountants and financial managers assumed through the balance sheet that an account of profit and loss showed the health of the company. In essence, the underlying belief was that through financial analysis alone one could assess how well the company was doing.

The SEAM approach, from its very origin, questions this assumption. It is based on the understanding that there are *hidden factors* underlying organizational performance. These hidden costs and performances are related to human potential and to the quality of interactions within the company. SEAM intervention acknowledges the existence of these hidden costs and performances, and the challenge of overcoming the underlying difficulties through participative projects, which must involve all managers, including the CEO and top management teams. The project teams need to be trained to be aware of the hidden performance features of the project and the hidden costs of not implementing the project. The challenge is that designing such projects can be costly, but not designing one can prove to be even more costly considering the hidden costs involved, which include lost opportunity costs.

Hidden Costs and Performance

We therefore need "new glasses" to be able to successfully calculate the hidden costs that exist in all our organizations, often ranging from 50% to 200% of the equivalent of the firm's payroll. The economic balance of socio-economic projects shows that innovative action plans are far less costly than inaction, and they can be both socially and economically efficient when all organizational members are involved.

As an example of this approach, the case of a glasswork company, the amount of hidden costs was 806,000 euro per year, while the investment in the project, aimed at weeding out dysfunctions and hidden costs, was only 123,000 euro. This calculation illustrates the high cost of inactivity. The enhanced performance in the first year amounted to 463,000 euro, which was the equivalent of 8,000 euro per year and per capita. The assessment thus illustrated the cost of not undertaking the innovative project, which was brought to light as people became more aware of the need to prevent dysfunctions and create innovative solutions rather than becoming accustomed to such dysfunctions.

One of Henri Savall's assumptions at the early stage of the SEAM was the "ostrich" behavior concept (see Figure 1.2). In this image, the organization is compared to an ostrich putting its head in the sand, and not being aware of the importance of the hidden costs and the untapped potential that exist in virtually all companies.

CONCLUSION

There is a need to accompany an organization's managers, in order to help them shift from a silo and specialized approach to a more systemic approach based on a heuristic way of thinking. The fundamental hypothesis underlying the SEAM method is that performance results from the dynamics and quality of interaction between the different structures of the company (physical, organizational, technological, demographic and mental structures) and the behaviors of the actors (at individual, team, activity group, categories and collective levels). Like in a recipe, management has to be successful in creating good food. They have to organize and synchronize the processes to prepare a dish as a cook does in a restaurant.

Figure 1.2 The organization as ostrich: Ignoring hidden costs.

The issue raised by managerial practices is that, most of the time, managers only focus on one set of structures or behaviors, such as technology, organizational structure or individual behaviors. This results in lack of coherence, just as if a chef was preparing a pie and proceeding in independent steps: you first bake the flour, and then you bake the sugar and then the eggs. Once all ingredients have been baked separately, you mix everything together—which results in a pie that is uneatable. By comparison, we need synchronization in the management of the companies, an approach that requires integrated managerial training within the context of a socioeconomic intervention. That is the essence of SEAM.

In looking at the origins of SEAM, the process was developed to counter the separation between the action-research stream and the limits of financial analysis. The need to expand these perspectives had become increasingly evident—and SEAM emerged as a much needed system-wide approach to organizational metamorphosis.

REFERENCE

Savall, H. & Zardet, V. (2011). *The qualimetrics approach: Observing the complex object.* Charlotte, NC: Information Age Publishing.

APPENDIX:
CONFERENCE DIALOGUE

Peter Sorensen: Have you, with your colleagues, developed this epistemology as an educational opportunity, to wear the glasses of or consider the perspective of critical theory transforming learning and the research? What are its effects on the sociotechnical organization development (OD) tradition? To what extent do you have been engaged with this challenge by critical theory in development?

Marc Bonnet: SEAM is a critical theory aimed at contributing to the redesign of traditional organization theories as well as action-research in the field of management. The objective is to bring an emphasis on Human Potential as the most important factor of sustainable economic performance of the organization.

Peter Sorensen: My concern is the question of human emancipation. The health and the development of individual is an outcome of change.

Marc Bonnet: The SEAM assumption is that traditional approaches to management are characterized by specialized and partial analyses of the whole system. It may have been successful for a certain period of time, but proves to be toxic in an environment that becomes more and more complex.

  By comparison with medicine, one can observe the impacts of viruses on health. In the case of management, Henri Savall and the ISEOR team have observed organizational viruses. The Taylor-Fayol-Weber virus is one that creates dysfunctions and fragmented decision-making processes. It calls for a vaccine that helps organization come back to synchronization and integration.

  SEAM is a complete process aimed at enhancing organizational metamorphosis. You don't have to limit it to the analysis of the dysfunctions. Nevertheless it starts from an imbalance aimed at releasing the untapped potential through shading light on dysfunctions.

Therese Yaeger: In your presentations, I could see more economic than social evidence. When I look at the diagram (Figure 1.2), I am wondering if I am naïve. Do you see as many social aspects as economics ones?

Marc Bonnet: The main aspect of the SEAM approach is not social or economic, it is definitely both—integrating both of them opposed to a conflicting concept between those approaches. It is filling the gap.

Conference Participant: I think part of it is close to the classical idea that the participative element in the process is part of the social signs. I think that the fact that everybody participated is blowing away managers who are not participating. You are modeling a key point. This has a strong flavor of change when it is needed.

Conference Participant: It is important to say that coming from economic approaches and moving to a social focus, it helps for the social-oriented approaches to create a relationship with the economic approach.

Conference Participant: Those seems to me a positive inquiry, about appreciating the spirit of the company and SEAM is about growing the spirit that created the company and the process that is attached is about recognizing the human spirit in this company. In SEAM you have unified that, I would say that we are looking at different parts of the element, that approach says that.

Henri Savall: Are you breathing or are you speaking? In this moment, do you breathe or do you speak?

Alla Heorhiadi: It is a rhetorical question. I am thinking of love. It comes down to your title because until today I thought it was a socio-economic balance but I know that it is not a balance.

Henri Savall: In a movement, you don't need that socio or economic aspect. You breathe without thinking that you are speaking. It is a dynamic theory. And time resolves the problems.

Marc Bonnet: By working in the United States, what has been learned? We assume that what is value added is not the spare part of the SEAM: American companies and academic associations are full of tools. But SEAM is an integrative model.

SEAM integrates theories and metrics stemming from economic or financial theories. It pays lip service to the social science of organization. SEAM tools demonstrate that Human Potential is at the core of performance. This factor is considered as a key even if it does not create immediate results on a daily basis but also increases creation of potential which means long term economic performance.

Sometimes you may find methods that improve performance in the short term. By looking closer to those effects, you could see that they result in downsides—that is, it results in loss of skills and so on. When you want to cut costs, it only improves short-term performance for a few months. It is the shadow side of traditional performance management. A lot of experiments have been carried out in the United States, for example, in Minnesota by John Combere and Alla Heorhiadi, in New Mexico with David Boje and Grace Ann Rosile, and in Michigan with Larry Lepisto and Randy Hayes, the latter of which is illustrated in the "Able Plasties" case study published in the IAP book on SEAM interventions.

Conference Participant: In the city of Los Angeles, California, Hewlett Packard hired student interns who focused on SEAM. A special issue of the *Journal of Change Management* was released back in 2003 about SEAM.

Marc Bonnet: Five books about SEAM experiments have been published by IAP and coedited by Anthony Buono, current chair of the Management Consulting Division of the Academy of Management (AOM). Nine international conferences have been organized in Lyon by the Academy of Management (AOM) and the International Institute of Costs (IIC): the AOM is focused on the social side and the IIC on accounting. We know the importance of developing in business schools both social figures and financial metrics.

Another example is the journal published by ISEOR—*RSDG-Management Sciences: Ciencias de Gestion*—which listed on Cabell's. It is published in English, Spanish and French and it may be considered as a silo breaker between the specialized approaches to management science.

What we have learned through these cooperative endeavors is that SEAM does not contradict management methods that are already used in the United States. They confirm that SEAM has potential to integrate methods into a system-wide framework.

When we compare the SEAM approach with other methods, colleagues say that it sounds like SEAM is the most integrated of them. It is both top down and bottom up as had been mentioned in the presentations. And, as a sign of break up, SEAM enables interaction between different domains of management science: Human Resource, Accounting, and Quantitative management. Through SEAM, some colleagues at Central Michigan University created a common language between HR and accounting strategy. SEAM is a kind of engineering method.

In another aspect, SEAM combines economic performance and social objectives: performance metrics consist in qualitative, quantitative, and financial. This helps to make visible the hidden performance of organizations, and differentiates SEAM from the triple bottom line approach, which downplays financial figures in the social and environmental performance of organizations. The key is the economic balance of projects: there is a limit to all the projects. Implementing short- and long-term projects for developing the Human Potential transcends OD and action research projects through scoring the economics spaces and bringing evidence of the positive impact.

Socio-economic logbooks integrate both immediate results and creation of potential. It might be compared with glasses that look both at long term, creation of potential, and short term, immediate results. Through discussion with colleagues in this seminar on SEAM, we observe the need for more integration and interaction in the field of management sciences, such as Human Resources, accounting, finance and so on. SEAM is a contribution to meeting this need.

CHAPTER 2

THE TAYLORISM-FAYOLISM-WEBERISM VIRUS

Vincent Cristallini and Henri Savall

CONFERENCE REMARKS:
Chapter Prologue

Vincent Cristallini

I would not have been allowed to cross the border into the United States borders with a physical virus. When the custom agents questioned me upon arrival, I had to explain that the vaccine I was importing to America was SEAM, invented by Henri Savall—and spreading SEAM in America may prove to be a major contribution to U.S. businesses and organizations and their management.

INTRODUCTION

The inception of the Taylor-Fayol-Weber (TFW) virus metaphor in 1973 stemmed from Henri Savall's critical reflection on the management sciences. Savall's early work criticized the world-wide dissemination of flawed management analysis and decision-making models that were shaped by a

Facilitating the Socioeconomic Approach to Management, pages 13–18
Copyright © 2014 by Information Age Publishing

particular mindset. This mindset, which reflects much of what still happens in today's society and management practice, is deeply rooted in this TFW virus. Basically, this virus is an ideology that has contaminated structures and behaviors in every kind of organization. And it is all that more serious when one considers the myriad ways through which it is inoculated, from training programs and management education and practices, to mentoring.

THE NATURE OF THE TFW VIRUS

Although the TFW metaphor reflects a mix of the initials of Frederick Winslow Taylor, the TFW virus refers to three key promoters of a certain ideology—Taylor, an American engineer, Henri Fayol, representing French engineers, and Max Weber, a German sociologist. These individuals had a common and probably unconscious approach to people at work, envisioning a particular type of organization design that could have been partly relevant at the very beginning of the twentieth century. They set three ideas that form the basic principles of this virus. First, they assumed that hyper-specialization was efficient. They also assumed that design and execution at work must be separated, assuming that workers were not clever enough to be involved in the design process. Eventually, they thought that job design had to be depersonalized. The resulting virus is based on a basic assumption that people would be slavish and that throughout the world people would obey management.

There are two postulates behind these ideas that are wrong. The first postulate is that people would sell their work and that selling their work leads them to accept rather than criticize the system and their managers, in essence leaving their problems at the door of the organization and giving their good ideas to management. The second popular postulate is that there is a wall between work and personal life. At the same time, this view also means incidentally that work-related problems should be separated from people's personal mood.

In SEAM, science means *authentic* observation. Scientific observation totally contradicts the subordination postulate of the TFW virus because people are clever—including being strategists and tricksters, and often disobedient—so they will only buy in if they want and if they know how to proceed.

IDENTIFYING THE TFW VIRUS

There are four main symptoms of this virus. The first set of symptoms is a lack of interest in one's work, without any hope of developing one's life. One can observe boring work—no versatility, no learning, no responsibility, and no decision making—because management assumes subordinates are not sufficiently intelligent to take on those responsibilities. It is accompanied by a lack of recognition on behalf of management and the popular idea that people are disposable.

The second set of symptoms of the virus concerns the separation between persons, areas, territories, categories, functions, and trades. This separation hides a false logic. The systemic science assumption that the organization is a whole is not true because there are separations everywhere that create misunderstanding, through language, concepts, and tools. People often do not understand each other and conflicting objectives prevail. When people show their contempt or their arrogance, one can conclude that the virus has developed a sense of superiority, a lack of consideration, and some ostracism. We can observe the extensive focus of the virus on intellectual capacities and sometimes, particularly in France, on diplomas. We can observe communication gaps in management practices, as well as an absence of dialogue and a lack of cooperation.

The third set of symptoms is, in a way, a set of consequences of the virus. Many dysfunctions appear at the interfaces of organizations: delays, misunderstanding, errors, lack of interest in quality control and in the customer service, conflicts between people and between organizational territories, and barriers to active cooperation.

The final set of symptoms concerns the lack of an individualistic approach—in which management views its employees as a herd of cattle for which "you just need barking dogs." It assumes that people must fit with their job description and be obedient. It stereotypes people within the organization and sets some egalitarian persistence, meaning that everybody should be the same, although it is recognized that some would work less or harder than others. Practically, a single supervisor manages an unreasonably high number of people—our worst record is one supervisor for 170 persons. Moreover, the client management is sometimes excessively technocratic. There are nonflexible procedures and standards doubled by a cold technocracy where there is no one to listen or to talk to the client. Some changes are made without consultation, without explanation and without training when it impacts people's activity. The lack of interest in persons, professions and areas also prevails. Means and resources are also inequitably distributed. The virus is a serious issue.

SEAM VERSUS THE TFW VIRUS

The SEAM approach addresses the virus as a whole. It is based on a belief shaped by our experience in which we consider that the innovative paradigm in management is the consent commitment. Performance must be negotiated. It depends on the capacity of negotiation between actors (employees) and managers. Managers need specific sets of skills to educate and influence employees. As a second belief, reinstating people is needed within the organization. It means that sharing is at the base of cooperation and it needs to be stimulated. Acknowledging that the entire virus has contaminated the whole organization, an intense integrated training and a system of communication–coordination–cooperation need to be enhanced.

There are four principles that can help an organization move forward to socio-economic management and get rid of the virus:

- An organisation needs to achieve a product or activity as completely as possible from A to Z.
- Responsibilities are great sources of motivation. SEAM turns down the paradigm that claims that some persons are responsible while others are not. Everyone is in charge of responsibility.
- An efficient organization needs teamwork and a balanced and versatile competency, as opposed to hyper-specialization.
- The organization must be client-oriented—inside and outside the organization.

In contrast the TFW virus claims that:

- People can be submissive and exploited—but people are creative, geniuses through their activities.
- People would be subordinate, but SEAM claims that people do what they want. They are clever strategists, tricksters, and disobedient. The virus assumes that if people do not obey, management must sanction or replace them. SEAM asserts that people can generate an important amount of hidden costs that cannot be addressed without their cooperation.
- Performance happens due to competencies and specialization, but SEAM assumes that performance happens because of diversity and cooperation.
- People would sell their work and resources, which would then belong to the organization, but SEAM assumes that human potential has to be nurtured, and that work effort belongs to the individual.
- Conflict is an anomaly and should be hidden. SEAM brings evidence that conflict is natural and that it is a main source of energy and change.
- Finally, efficient work means breaking down the job into pieces, and SEAM shows that the efficient organization is based on system integration and the quality of cooperation.

Finally, the metaphor of the virus allows us to understand that two major paradigms of management compete in all types of human organizations, and determine, in the sense that they permeate, strongly how people and activities are managed, and the results of all orders made under it. In the paradigm of submission subordination carried by the TFW Virus, confidence in the human—his or her intelligence, energy, creativity, commitment, and capacity exceeded . . .—is simply denied. In this perspective, the generation of performance is a kind of techno-economic mystery, in which the system seems to more or less work without anyone really understands the springs. In the paradigm of the agreed commitment promoted by the socio-economic approach to management, taking into account the human as a true potential, raises the issue of performance as an ability to lead and negotiate the performance with the actors. An outcome is the result of a set of interactions, and not the result of a good stable and sustainable organization, equally providential and illusory. The difference between the two models lies in the genuine consideration, and respect that results, for people.

APPENDIX:
Conference Dialogue

Conference Participant: According to your experience, do you think that Lean and Six Sigma implementation nurture the virus?

Vincent Cristallini: To answer, I would say that, with the virus, you do not listen to people or personalize work. Every norm or rule should be negotiated whatever management system is set up. It is the case with SEAM.

Conference Participant: As an observation, among a lot of critical social theories, SEAM is certainly concerned with the dignity and sovereignty of the individual. It has been well expressed by many people.

Conference Participant: Why do you use the term "actor" when referring to employees instead of using the word "employee" itself or "organizational member"?

Henri Savall: In SEAM, we use the metaphor that "an institution is theatrics." We are not people, we are actors who have a part in a play, like in a theatre. This metaphor sheds light on many phenomena in management.

Conference Participant: Why did SEAM spread out of France?

Henri Savall: I am Spanish, and I was born in Spain. SEAM is a geopolitical project that spreads in a broader place than France. All our conferences in France are held in French, English, and Spanish because we think that the world's positive values imply in-depth diversity, and I think that U.S. values imply diversity in language. A few years ago, someone told me that we had to speak Spanish in the Academy of Management because there is a great lack of it. We have made some progress in that direction and our strategic patience will be fruitful in three or five years. SEAM may be the only democratic concept in management, freed from any political implication. Regularly listening and answering to people results in ongoing and collective learning. This conference held at Saint Thomas University is a great latter-day achievement of the Lafayette ("La Fayette" in French) Cooperation.

Marc Bonnet: The idea of the Lafayette Cooperation refers to the 18th century when American insurgents needed cooperation with the French to rid themselves of British domination. Accounting for the recent period of complexity—the financial crisis and the need for restructuring or re-creating organizations—and drawing on the genuine American value for getting rid of viruses, it may be helpful to cooperate again. The Taylorism-Fayolism-Weberism virus presents us with that type of challenge.

CHAPTER 3

TAYLOR'S ILLUSION

An Historical Account
of the Progression of the "TFW Virus"

Alanna G. Kennedy

CONFERENCE REMARKS:
Chapter Prologue

Alanna Kennedy

I was interested in comparing SEAM with the classic factory systems of Frederick Taylor and the more contemporary Japanese lean factory system. To address the issue, I looked at the genesis of these approaches and also reflected on Vincent Cristallini's paper about how the Taylor-Fayol-Weber "virus" contagion spreads.

Basically, Taylorism's principles can be summarized as the search and analysis for the "one best way." Taylor was notorious for analyzing the best way to perform a manufacturing operation. This best way included the best materials, the best tools, the best machines and the best sequence of the work using the least amount of time. He diligently worked at perfecting this

Facilitating the Socioeconomic Approach to Management, pages 19–32
Copyright © 2014 by Information Age Publishing
All rights of reproduction in any form reserved.

concept throughout his career and it became the foundation of his book *The Principles of Scientific Management.*

Taylor was born into a privileged Quaker family in Philadelphia. He initially was fated to go to Harvard to study law, and he actually sat for and passed the entrance exams. But by that time, he had become an apprentice in a factory and discovered his passion for manufacturing. He thrived in his career. At age 20, he was a shop foreman. By the age of 30, he advanced to chief engineer and he was notoriously known as an efficiency expert by the age of 40. After the age of 40, he never charged a fee for his services. He dedicated his time to further develop and promote the principles of scientific management without financial reward.

Taylor believed in the far reaching positive societal effects of his work. Business owners would be rewarded with increased profit and employees would have steady employment and be paid a fair wage. Ultimately society would benefit by the availability of cheaper goods as prices fell due to gains in efficiency as the application of the principles of scientific management spread. From its inception, Taylorism was controversial—and that controversy became global as the principles of scientific management became well known and were applied.

In 1911, Taylor published the *Principles of Scientific Management.* He did not intentionally write a book but rather he wrote a series of five articles that he published in a magazine which he later organized into a book. The book, approximately 100 pages in length, takes little time to read. It is ironic that such a small, thin book could have such lasting global impact.

As fate would have it about the same time that *The Principles of Scientific Management* was published, World War I was declared. With the world at war, the demand for goods and war materials skyrocketed. Taylorism proved to be a promising model for achieving the productivity improvements required to fulfil the increase in demand for goods and war materials. Quickly, scientific management gained visibility and became the global guide to increase productivity and profitability. As Taylorism spread, it gained further visibility based upon its role in other key historical events, such Stalin's Russian revolution and the political turmoil of Germany's new Weimar Republic. However, the quick rise of Taylorism also stimulated a global and public debate about the welfare of the worker. There were many critics and criticisms of Taylorism. Many questioned the fairness and equitable economic applicability of his principles of scientific management. Furthermore, many called Taylorism inhumane and questioned the quality of life of the worker under the system. One famous critic was Kurt Lewin. He was concerned about the application of Taylorism from an Organization Development (OD) perspective. After studying the principles of scientific management, he advocated that Taylorism be developed with a professional audit of the mental health of the worker.

World War II was punctuated by the solidification of Fordism and Taylorism in industry. Ford developed the *assembly line* but Taylorism influenced Ford. By the time World War II was over, Taylorism and Fordism had proven invaluable. The proof was the substantial differences in the productivity ratios between American, German and Japanese workers. In 1945, at the end of World War II, it was calculated that in America, the country where Taylorism and Fordism were the most advanced, the productivity of one American worker equaled that of six German workers or nine Japanese workers. At this time, there was little doubt that the Taylor system and the principles of scientific management were seen as indispensable.

As theorized, Taylorism actually helped lower prices and increase the personal wealth of the common man. A middle class emerged in the United States, and incomes increased while the prices of goods decreased. There was no question that on many levels Taylorism, especially when combined with Fordism, worked. The systemic flaws in Taylorism and Fordism did not appear until globally there was a sharp decline in demand for goods. In 1972, U.S. President Richard Nixon, signed the Bretton Woods Act and took the United States off to gold standard. Around the world, demand for goods slumped and the stock markets declined upwards of 40% between 1972 and 1974. During that period, the world became intrigued by a small Japanese company named Toyota. The world wondered why this company could remain profitable while others suffered huge losses. It was the first time that Taylorism and Fordism, the basis of our mass production system, was compared to the Toyota and Japan's use of lean manufacturing systems. The mass production system, which was based upon volume and capacity utilization, kept producing and building inventory. The Lean manufacturing system, in contrast, focused on making one piece at a time and the elimination of nonvalue-added activities or waste. The mass production system was based upon Taylorism and built upon the idea that the employees weren't smart enough to be included in the planning of work. In contrast, in the lean system employees were developed as knowledge workers, with the ability to contribute to the planning of work.

SEAM theorizes that employees will always act in their own best interest. Because people always act in their own best interest there will always be dysfunction and a gap between the current and ideal state within any organization. SEAM theory recognizes that dysfunction cannot be eradicated but must be dealt with at the level of daily work. A fundamental concept of SEAM is the investment in the creation of human potential and the resulting increased profitability.

Another concept of SEAM theory is an increase in the speed of learning. In organizations an increase in the speed of learning has the potential to create a competitive edge by minimizing dysfunctions and increasing value-added activities. SEAM, when compared to the Lean, shares an emphasis on increasing the speed of learning within organizations. When Lean methods were first developed, the job description and expectations of employees changed. The role of the employee was no longer to sit every day and do the same tasks. Rather employees in a lean system were expected to contribute and to become knowledge workers. In the Lean organization, managers do more training and actively invest in the creation of human potential. Subsequently Lean organizations are more competitive and profitable than their mass production counterparts. Lean systems seemed to be the answer to better profitability and the implementation of lean systems flourished globally in the 1980s and 1990s.

Today, around the globe, concern is beginning to appear with respect to lean method and theory. A whole terminology has been developed to describe what is referred to as "Fake Lean." This view refers to a situation where manufacturing lines are rearranged and inventories are trimmed to eliminate waste, but the integration of the manufacturing system to human activities has not been achieved. As such, it is "Fake Lean" because a culture of continuous improvement has not been developed. Some improvement occurs, but the speed of learning and the process of low-value activities being identified, eliminated, and replaced with higher value-added activities is slower than what is necessary to build true cultures of continuous improvement. The investment in the creation of human potential in "Fake Lean" systems is minimized. SEAM method and theory has the potential to provide the missing piece or foundation for the successful development of cultures of continuous improvement. SEAM theory and methods provide the bases for the integration of the human systems in organizations by comprehensively supporting the creation of human potential and the replacement of low value activities with higher value activities. Six Sigma and Lean systems are theories and methodologies in which there is a frantic activity towards implementation to reap any financial rewards. However, integration of the necessary human systems to build a culture of continuous improvement when using Lean and Six Sigma alone is questionable.

SEAM theory denies the underlying assumption of Taylorism, and highlights why the virus identified by Cristallini continues to spread. The virus embedded in Taylorism is the belief that everybody could be controlled every day and such a work system would result in a common economic win for everyone. Assumptions about the nature of the relationship between management and employees became embedded in the primary economic assumptions of the mass production system. Lean theory and methods made progress by investing in the future of employees, but it was still ill-defined by assumptions about the economic relationship between employees and management. Since SEAM is more integrative of human systems it is not restricted to the economic dimension but instead focuses on the whole person. Subsequently, SEAM has the potential to more readily support the development of cultures of continuous improvement.

INTRODUCTION

Vincent Cristallini (2011), in an article entitled "The Importance of Corporate Governance in the Fight Against the World Dissemination of the Techno-Economic Virus" (see also Chapter 2) uses the analogy of a virus to describe the prevailing techno-economic ideology that exists in many of today's organizations. He describes this contagion as an ideological pattern of corporate governance and influence that encourages the depersonalization and submission of the individual (Cristallini, 2011, p. 3). In organizations with the virus, it is acceptable to treat members of the organization as if they were intellectually inferior, irresponsible, and untrustworthy.

Cristallini (2011) emphasizes that, over the long term, the presence of the virus promotes a lack of cooperation and hopelessness among members of an organization. Within infected organizations, inclusion and joint participation are viewed as impossible. It is these perceptions that result in the hopelessness that facilitates the creation of the dysfunctions and hidden costs that the Socio-Economic Approach to Management (SEAM) theory addresses (Savall, Zardet, & Bonnet, 2008).

This chapter reviews the progression of the virus as it influenced and spread through the course of manufacturing history. The use of a historical framework is intended to give a new perspective, enabling the reader to become familiar with the course of these historical events in the context of SEAM theory. Within the confines of a book chapter, of course, it is not possible to include all historical events that facilitated the spread of the virus. The events and people included in the following discussion are meant to familiarize the reader with a basic timeline of the more important historical events and people who shaped the course of manufacturing history and the spread of the virus.

TAYLOR'S ILLUSION

Cristallini (2011) credits, in part, the origin and spread of the virus to the work of Fredrick Taylor and his development of an industrial philosophy called Scientific Management. Today, many agree that Taylor's work and philosophy created an enduring legacy of the exclusion, submission, and depersonalization of the worker (Copley, 2010/1923; Kanigel, 1997; Khurana, 2007). Many factors contributed to the rapid rise and acceptance of scientific management and its underlying philosophy and economic assumptions. However, Taylor's deeply-held philosophical belief that scientific management was to the benefit of all could be viewed as philosophy that was complementary to, and promoted the spread of, the virus.

Taylor's system, from its inception, was subject to debate and controversy. Taylor would not under any circumstances consider or remotely acknowledge that his system had the potential to be wrongly used. His failure to recognize the system's potential for misuse only served to reinforce and promote the spread of the virus by offering ready-made arguments that served to further obscure instances of misuse whenever they occurred. By only casting scientific management in a positive light, Taylor made it convenient for those who adopted the system to overlook and ignore the exclusion and depersonalization of the worker.

Regardless of Taylor's unwavering claims to the contrary, the potential for the misuse of the principles of scientific management was a concern from their inception (see Copley, 1923/2010; Kanigel, 1997; Khurana, 2007; Taylor 1911/2006). As early as 1920, Kurt Lewin, who was a student of the Taylor system, advocated that research psychologists work closely with efficiency experts in the formal study of work (Marrow, 1969). Lewin was concerned that, based upon the use of the principles of scientific management, the psychological health of the worker was at risk. His concerns were based upon the system's focus on increased productivity and the increased specialization of tasks, which often resulted in increased monotony and workplace stress (Marrow, 1969, p. 15).

Regardless of the raging public debate and no matter how potentially damaging, stressful, or depersonalizing the Taylor system may have been, this was not Taylor's perception of his own work (Taylor, 1911/2006). Taylor held an unwavering belief that his system of scientific management promoted cooperation and harmony between management and the worker (Kanigel, 1997). Once, during a speech, Taylor even argued that scientific management stood for peace and friendship (Copley, 1923/2010). Taylor steadfastly maintained, in the face of negative opinion and controversy, that because his system was based on a scientific approach to the management of work that it was a fair and equitable system and in the best interest of all (Taylor, 1911/2006).

Those who observed Taylor and his deep passion for his work often compared him to Charles Darwin (Copley, 1923/2010). Like Darwin, Taylor was perceived to have the same extraordinary singular intensity and devotion toward his work and, like Darwin, Taylor, during his life, was perceived to have changed the ideas of the common man (Copley, 1923/2010, p. 362). Taylor was passionate about scientific management because, in his view, it was for the good of all. For too long workers and their leaders had freely restricted output and productivity in the work place (Taylor, 1911/2006). Taylor believed that the scientific standardization of work not only benefitted management with increased profits, but it also benefitted labor with increased wages and ultimately benefitted society due to the resulting decreases in the price of goods sold (Kanigel, 1997). To Taylor, the best measure of the greatness of a society was its measures of productivity (Kanigel 1997, p. 479). In his view, scientific management produced results for the common good. On this point, regardless of the pressure applied, Taylor never wavered.

In 1911 a special committee was formed by the House of Representatives to investigate Taylor's system. During the hearings, Taylor was extensively questioned by the committee chairman, William Wilson of Pennsylvania, a former coal miner and labor sympathizer. The following exchange is an excerpt from the proceedings between Taylor and Wilson (Kanigel, 1997, p. 476).

> *Wilson:* Isn't the man selected by management [to be time studied] picked precisely because he would protect the interest of management? And isn't it true that the very essence of Scientific Management is that there must be one directing head who brooked no interference?
>
> *Taylor:* Yes. No interference can be tolerated, though management and the worker can cooperate.
>
> *Wilson:* But under the Taylor System, doesn't such cooperation have to conform to the judgment and direction and policy of the boss?
>
> *Taylor:* No, sir, Most emphatically no. The system imposes standards that are fair and just.
>
> *Wilson:* And true collective bargaining? In which the workman collectively help determined the wages, the task and the condition under which they shall work? Does scientific management have room for it?
>
> *Taylor:* Not in the "old sense." Under this system, workers and management join as one and collective bargaining instead of becoming a necessity becomes of trifling importance. Should some injustices arise, workers only need to protest and receive a careful scientific investigation into the case?

Taylor believed that if exploitation of the worker occurred, then it was not scientific management or the Taylor system that was being applied. In instances where misuse occurred, Taylor claimed that only the mechanism of scientific management was being applied (Kanigel, 1997). According to Taylor, what was required to implement scientific management in its entirety was "a complete mental revolution" by both the worker and management (Kanigel, 1997, p. 472). In Taylor's view, a mental revolution was encompassed by management and labor learning to use scientific fact instead of individual judgment and opinion in matters concerning productivity (Kanigel, 1997, p. 473). If this mental revolution failed to evolve and only the profit motive was present, Taylor felt he could not be held responsible (Kanigel, 1997, p. 477).

THE SPREAD OF TAYLORISM

Historically, based upon the timing and critical nature of events, Taylorism was quickly adopted in America and Europe. The rapid speed with which Taylorism was adopted was facilitated by the 1911 publication of his book, *The Principles of Scientific Management*, its translation into several languages, and further by the 1914 outbreak of World War I. The War created an unprecedented increase in the demand for the production of war materials (Kanigel, 1997; Grandin, 2009). *The Principles of Scientific Management* fast became known as the guideline and means for manufactures to meet the increased production the war required.

It must be understood that Taylorism, on some level, appeared to work. Entire industries, such as steel and metallurgy, shipbuilding, railroads, automobiles, and even the game of golf, were revolutionized and changed forever as the philosophy of Taylorism and the principles of scientific management were adopted and applied (Copley, 1923/2010). Taylorism worked in the sense that, based upon the use of experimental methods, time studies, and the standardization of work, substantial improvements in productivity and efficiency were experienced (Taylor, 1911/2006).

At the end of World War II, a mere 35 years after the initial publication of *The Principles of Scientific Management*, Taylor's system had lived up to its economic promise. In 1945, at the end of World War II, it was calculated that in America, the country where Taylorism was the most advanced, the productivity of one worker equaled that of six German workers or nine Japanese workers (Ohno, 1988). By the end of World War II, there was little doubt that the Taylor system and the principles of scientific management were seen as indispensable.

For nations around the globe, the appearance of Taylorism in conjunction with the appearance of Fordism and the assembly line became known as the mass-production system, and the system yielded enormous productivity gains (Lacey, 1986). As the mass-production system was adopted and its methodology diffused around the globe, improvements were experienced in the overall living conditions of the average individual and wealth was created for entire nations (Kanigel, 1997; Lacey, 1987).

On one level, Taylorism did help to change the world. It did so, however, at the expense and exclusion of the worker. Surprisingly, the mass-production system left industry in America and Europe vulnerable to competition from an unlikely and unexpected source. In 1950, a group of engineers from a small Japanese car manufacturing company called Toyota Motor visited Ford Motor Company in Detroit. The group was amazed to learn in the 15 years since their last visit to Detroit very few improvements had been made to the mass-production system. As the Japanese engineers returned home, they realized the mass-production system contained enormous inefficiencies and that there was still a chance to effectively compete against Detroit.

Upon returning home, the Toyota team set the ambitious goal for themselves of closing the productivity gap with the Americans in three short years. Historically, it would take more than three years, but it soon became apparent that the mass-production system could not compete in quality or price with the new lean manufacturing methods being developed by Toyota Motor.

THE MASS-PRODUCTION MODEL VERSUS THE LEAN-PRODUCTION MODEL AND SEAM THEORY

By the early 1980s, a mere 35 years after the end of World War II, Japan not only rebuilt its industrial base, but the country also became a dominant global force in manufacturing (Womack, Jones, & Roos, 1990). Although other Japanese manufacturers were initially critical, it did not take long for them to follow suit once they understood the increased profitability and competitiveness of Toyota's lean-production system. In a very short period of time, the mass-production model that Taylorism and Fordism helped create became subject to fierce competition from the Japanese and their innovative lean-manufacturing model.

As compared to the mass-production model, the primary difference in lean-manufacturing is the focus on the continuous improvement and elimination of waste from manufacturing processes rather than the focus on sheer volume per se. Further, a lean-manufacturing system differs in that there is an emphasis on the creation and preservation of value for the customer by eliminating waste in the system (Dennis, 2007). In a lean system, value is defined as any action or process that a customer who uses the product is willing to pay; therefore, lean methods focus on determining what waste will be eliminated from the manufacturing system as a means of creating value. All processes and actions in the system, except the actions and processes the customer is willing to pay for, have the potential to be reviewed and eliminated. As a result of efforts to continuously eliminate waste, production time and cost are reduced and overall profitability and quality is improved within the lean system.

Much has been written about Japan's lean-manufacturing model. There are many theories as to why the Japanese were able to develop such an effective manufacturing system so quickly. In contrast to the more conventional views and explanations, an application of SEAM theory offers a fresh perspective and insight. SEAM theory proposes that increases in productivity, efficiency, and profits are not the only measures of success for an organization (see Buono & Savall, 2007; Savall, et al, 2008). SEAM theory takes a broader view in that many costs within organizations are considered hidden and are not quantified or controlled (Savall, et al., 2008 p. 30). Hidden costs occur in organizations because each worker or actor has a subjective understanding of the problem and each will act according to what he or she believes to be in their own best interest (Savall et al., 2008).

These self-motivated actions of organizational members results in dysfunctional behavior. Dysfunctional behavior is known to manifest as hidden costs in six categories: working conditions, work organization, integrated training, communication–coordination–cooperation, time management, and strategic implementation (Savall, et al., 2008). These behaviors are theorized to be an ever-present influence in the performance of an organization. SEAM theory proposes that because of the continuous nature of such dysfunctional behaviors, a gap between the expected and actual performance is always present within an organization.

SEAM research shows that one viable and highly profitable approach to proactively minimizing dysfunctional behavior is to invest in the creation of human potential, which is defined as actions that will have a positive impact on future economic results. Although an organization must often wait for the return on investments made for the creation of human potential to be realized, such returns are often substantial. Research from the Socio-Economic Institute of Firms and Organizations Research Institute (ISEOR) has shown that the results for investing in the creation of human potential is very profitable, with returns that can range from between 200% and 4000% (Savall, et al, 2008). As Savall and his colleagues (2008, p. 60) have argued, very few, if any, technological investments deliver such profitable returns.

SEAM theory emphasizes that differences in the amount of hidden costs in an organization are not, as commonly believed, the deciding issues for the competitiveness of an organization. Rather, a competitive edge is acquired and honed based upon an organization's speed of learning. It is the speed of learning that enables an organization to reduce the dysfunctions that are always present. Within this context, being competitive is defined as creating *future potential* through developing and implementing proactive strategies that result in increasing value-added activities, while at the same time decreasing non value-added activities.

Although the mass-production and lean-production models are not based on SEAM theory or concepts, the SEAM paradigm can still be applied to these production models to gain a new understanding. When applying SEAM theory in the comparison of mass-production and lean-production systems there are notable differences in the management of dysfunctional behaviors, increasing value-added activities and investing in future potential. One of the most basic differences when comparing the two models is the management of organizational dysfunction through the job responsibilities and the activities of the assembler.

The Lean Assembler Versus the Mass-Production Assembler: A View From SEAM

Shortly after World War II, there was a period of labor unrest in Japan. During that period, in what would become landmark labor negotiations, employees at Toyota Motor were guaranteed employment for life (Ohno, 1988). Further, Toyota assemblers were guaranteed a wage system that was steeply graded by seniority rather than tied to a specific job function or bonus system (Womack, Jones, & Roos, 1990). In return for a pay system graded by seniority and lifetime employment, Toyota employees agreed to become flexible in their job assignments and active in promoting the interests of the company (Womack, Jones, & Roos, 1990, p. 53). Based upon the new labor agreement, it became part of Toyota's culture to increase worker skills and make investments in what SEAM theory terms *future human potential.* Such investments made sense in an organization where organizational members were employed for all of the approximate 40 years of their working lives.

Today, in order to continuously improve and identify nonvalue-added activities, a lean assembler fully participates and develops high-functioning working relationships, achieving high levels of group participation. It is a lean assembler's job to create new knowledge and information and to continually accumulate, reorganize, and apply production knowledge. Further, a lean assembler is trained in problem-solving techniques and continuous improvement methods and activities (Fujimoto, 1999). Highly flexible tools and strategies form the lean management system, but at the very heart of the system is the practice and philosophy of "respect for people" (Ohno, 1988).

In a lean system, as compared to a mass-production system, an assembler is not viewed as disposable or as an adversary. Rather, an assembler is considered a partner in the lean process (Holbeche, 1998; Mann, 2005). It is recognized that it is ultimately the employees that create increased value for the customer, and this in turn leads to increased prosperity for the employees and the company (Ohno, 1988). In theory, lean-manufacturing systems provide a positive outcome for all involved.

In contrast, in a mass-production environment, it is assumed that an assembler will perform only one or two simple repetitive tasks under the watchful eye of the foreman. Employees are never held responsible for making any improvements or eliminating waste—in fact, they are excluded from the process. Creating value for the customer is the responsibility of engineers.

When using SEAM theory as a framework for making comparisons, it is possible to gain a new understanding of the advantages that a lean system offers. Although unintentional in its design, a lean system appears to have fewer hidden costs and resulting dysfunction than mass-production systems. According to SEAM theory, hidden costs are incurred based upon dysfunctions that originate from the actors or employees acting in their own best interests. Employment-for-life, a pay system based upon seniority and a willingness to train employees is a positive influence that helps to minimize dysfunction and, subsequently, hidden costs within the system. Further, when compared to a mass-production system, it appears that higher levels of the creation of future human potential and a faster rate of learning are also present. A key element in this dynamic is the lean system's focus on, and constant organizing around, the concept of identifying value-added activities and eliminating waste and nonvalue-added activities from the system. Focus on identifying value-added activities and eliminating waste from the system creates an environment where creation of potential and faster learning rates are possible. These outcomes are desirable, as they are seen as a critical element for an organization to become competitive and to develop proactive strategies (Savall, et al, 2008).

It must also be acknowledged, however, that when abandoning a mass production system to implement a lean system there are also immediate financial gains. It is estimated that the average manufacturing organization immediately experiences a 100% increase in labor productivity, a 50% decrease in production time per unit, a 90% reduction in all major types of inventory, and a 50% reduction in production errors (Womack & Jones, 1996).

Sustainability Issues and Lean Systems

In spite of the competitive advantage and substantial increase in profitability that lean methods offer as compared to mass-production systems, current long-term research suggests that companies are having difficulty sustaining cultures of continuous improvement and sustaining lean-production methods over time (Dixon, 2007). Often, an organization's focus on the elimination of nonvalue activities and the elimination of waste fails to develop a sustainable culture of continuous improvement. Evidence suggests that, during the past several years, this negative trend is increasing. Except for the non-United States' Americas and Japan, the available research indicates the difficulty in sustaining lean-manufacturing methods and cultures of continuous improvement is a global trend (Schonberger, 2007).

In the manufacturing literature, the root cause of the difficulty of developing and sustaining cultures of continuous is often portrayed as, and attributed to, a lack of true commitment and support by executive management (Dixon, 2007). Prevalent in this type of thinking is an underlying assumption that lean methods and tools are complete. It is often assumed that the current body of knowledge about lean methods and tools offers executive management a comprehensive conceptual framework that successfully supports assessing and facilitating an organization's focus on eliminating nonvalue-added activities. Most often, imitation of the manufacturing policies, processes, and methods of the more successful lean organizations, is the most common approach to attempting to develop cultures of continuous improvement. Many organizations are finding it difficult to imitate the prescribed formula with lasting success and it is becoming apparent that the mere implementation of a lean system is not enough to guarantee the development and sustainability of a culture of continuous improvement.

SEAM'S ASSUMPTIONS
ABOUT THE WORKER–EMPLOYER RELATIONSHIP

SEAM theory does differ from lean theory in that the SEAM paradigm emphasizes and links the social and economic performance of an enterprise. In comparison to lean theory and mass-production systems, SEAM differs substantially in its assumptions about the development of the management–worker relationship. Methods, such as Taylorism and Fordism, which are embedded in mass-production systems, as well as lean methods assume the development of a successful worker and management relationship based upon mutual economic interests. Such an assumption is limiting in the design of systems and methods that support change and innovation in organizations. Assumptions about relationships based only upon a mutual economic interest ignores, and ultimately negates, consideration of the vast range of human behavior and creativity that is essential to change and innovation in organizations. What is overlooked by assuming and only acknowledging a mutual economic relationship between management and the worker is the presence and dynamics of the informal power that is inherent in each individual. SEAM theory acknowledges and cultivates the informal power of the individual. It is this fundamental oversight of the power of the individual, based upon our assumptions about economic relationships, that makes systems such Taylorism and the mass-production model depersonalizing and exclusionary, and makes lean systems difficult to maintain over time.

It is this lack of recognition of the presence of the informal and inherent power of each individual that has allowed the spread of the virus for the last 100 years. Unfortunately, this lack of recognition has served as the foundation of Taylor's illusion and the breeding ground from which TFW's virus was born.

REFERENCES

Buono, A. F., & Savall, H. (Eds.) (2007). *Socio-economic intervention in organizations: The intervener-researcher and the SEAM approach to organizational analysis.* Charlotte, NC: Information Age Publishing.

Copley, F. (2010). *Fredrick Taylor, father of scientific management* (Vol. 2). New York, NY: Harper & Brothers. (Original work published 1923).

Cristallini, V. (2011).The importance of corporate governance in the fight against the world dissemination of the techno-economic virus. *Maître de Conferences,* HDR, Lyon, France (March).

Dennis, P. (2007). *Lean production simplified.* New York, NY: Productivity Press.

Dixon, D. (2007). Lean in the job shop. *Fabricating & Metalworking, 6* (4), 16–19.

Fujimoto, T. (1999). *The evolution of a manufacturing system at Toyota.* New York, NY: Oxford.

Grandin, G. (2009). *Fordlandia.* New York, NY: Picador.

Holbeche, L. (1998). *Motivating people in lean organizations.* Boston, MA: Elsevier, Butterworth–Heinemann.

Kanigel, R. (1997). *The one best way.* New York, NY: Penguin.

Khurana, R. (2007). *From higher aims to hired hands.* Princeton, NJ: Princeton University Press.

Lacey, R. (1986).*Ford: The men and the machine.* Boston, MA: Little, Brown & Company.

Mann, D. (2005*). Creating a lean culture.* New York, NY: Productivity Press.

Marrow, A. (1969). *The practical theorist: The life and work of Kurt Lewin.* New York, NY: Basic.

Ohno, T. (1988). *The Toyota production system.* New York, NY: Productivity Press.

Savall, H., Zardet, V., & Bonnet, M. (2008). *Releasing the untapped potential of enterprises through socio-economic management.* Turin, Italy: International Training Center of the ILO.

Schonberger, R. (2007). *Best practices in lean six sigma process improvement.* Hoboken, NJ: Wiley.

Taylor, F. W. (2006). *The principles of scientific management.* New York, NY: Cosimo. (Original work published 1911).

Womack J., Jones, D., & Roos, D. (1990). *The machine that changed the world.* New York: Harper-Perennial.

CHAPTER 4

BRINGING SEAM
TO THE UNITED STATES

John Conbere, Alla Heorhiadi, and Vincent Cristallini

CONFERENCE REMARKS:
Chapter Prologue

Alla Heorhiadi

One of the issues facing American and French partners concerns the best way to transfer knowledge of the SEAM process. This presentation is a sharing of our lessons from implementing SEAM in the United States based on our work with two companies in the last year. Vincent Cristallini is in charge of the transfer of this knowledge and helped us understand the nuances of SEAM process.

John Conbere

Alla Heorhiadi and I learned about SEAM in 2006 in a conference at ISEOR in Lyon. We went to two more conferences and were sufficiently fascinated with the approach that we took the English seminar in 2009. It was

Facilitating the Socioeconomic Approach to Management, pages 33–45
Copyright © 2014 by Information Age Publishing

difficult to learn SEAM if you don't speak French, and we talked a lot about how to learn and teach SEAM in the United States.

Born from our attraction to SEAM, we formed a partnership—franchise —with ISEOR. We first tried to create the partnership through Saint Thomas University, but due to budget rules funds could not be carried from year to year—so we decided to create our own company, SEAM, Inc., to manage the interventions. With a modest investment, we became licensed to undertake SEAM interventions under the auspices of ISEOR in the United States. We were given constant coaching by Vincent Cristallini, and we often used videoconferencing for this purpose. We were also given access to the SEAM database so we were able to include our data into it. We thus have two interventions that are now part of the ISEOR database. The SEAM software has a number of advantages, such as sorting the dysfunctions, which make designing the mirror effect easier. As a result, "Operation Lafayette" is now growing in the United States and ISEOR oversees the quality of our interventions, insuring it is steered in an acceptable way, given ISEOR's 38-year history and process of intervention research. The key issue was to keep in line with the SEAM process, which is sometimes a challenge. As we are franchised, we get all the help that we need. Sometimes, learning SEAM feels like the cordon bleu approach—there is one way to cook, you are showed you how to do it, and to do it right you have to continually practice until you get it. In SEAM, there are principles to follow and an area of flexibility, but figuring out the limits for rigor is very difficult, especially at the beginning. We were constantly pushing against Cristallini's guidelines to test those limits.

In France, there are two models for learning SEAM. One model is studying in university. Students learn from the ISEOR staff at the University of Lyon 3, providing them with the opportunity to work with people who are masters. The other model is seminars. There are consultants from the field who learn SEAM in a series of four or five 5-day seminars. At this point there is only one 5-day seminar in English. The distance and the prohibitive travel costs created a challenge for learning SEAM while living in the United States. Learning was made even more difficult in that we sometimes see things differently. There were times when we were drawing on different mental models. However, after discussion, we often discovered these are more misunderstandings than differences. The challenge is the educational process. It is an intriguing process, but there are times when it is not efficient and, ironically, this represents a hidden cost. Translation can even be a problem. Cristallini, Heorhiadi, and I worked tremendously hard to understand each other, but, periodically, interpretation can be troublesome. Although we used videoconferencing, that medium is not yet an ideal condition for learning the nuances, given the differences in mental models with which we each began, and we found that we were creating a process for knowledge transfer in real time.

When looking back at the transfer process, there were some things that worked in the U.S. context. As an example, managers came to see the connection between the SEAM management tools. The mirror effect was a wonderful shock that unfroze systems. The expert opinion highlighted key points from the mirror effect, including the "non dit," root causes of the dysfunctions, themes about what needs correction, baskets, and projects. These tools transferred to the United States very well.

The SEAM belief that the actors of the organization can solve their own problems and have the knowledge and ability to succeed—in essence, escaping from the TFW Virus—has also worked well in the Untied States. We are not the problem solvers in the SEAM process—we intervene in order to facilitate the problem-solving process. We saw in all the organizations where SEAM was implemented, that changes began immediately, even within a week. Those changes were obvious and we did not have to wait for the project stage to see them emerge. Within a week, for example, I saw great improvement in the communication system at the Transportation Center. Also, ongoing monthly coaching of the manager was a very important part of the change process. We found that it was a critical, implicit part of the process, but regular coaching wasn't clearly stated in the readings.

Critics argue that Americans won't take time for a SEAM intervention because we are too short-term focused. That is not the real problem. Companies with a short-term approach simply need to become more desperate before they are ready to take the time. There is an assumption that SEAM chooses its customers. There are organizations that are ready to take the time for change and there are others that are not. There is no geographical difference, and it is the same in the United States as in France. The key is to find companies where this desperation is real and that are open to trying something different.

For the future, I would like to see more people training in the SEAM model in Lyon. On the positive side, one can talk with the founder, Henri Savall, as he explains his thinking. It is a rare opportunity. The apprentice model in France is very important for shaping intervener-researchers. It is where real value is created and communicated and I am envious of anyone who can go to Lyon, learn through apprenticeship, and then lead a SEAM intervention. But many cannot afford to go to Lyon for their entire training, and/or do not speak French. The challenge for us in the Unites States is to train SEAM students well, learn from mistakes, and develop an apprenticeship model here, which still includes some time in Lyon.

SEAM is definitely going to thrive into the Unites States. We have to learn to teach to intervener-researchers with the same level of quality control as exists in Lyon. If ISEOR staff doesn't have assurance that we're doing the right things in its research method, the intervener-researchers will not be acceptable partners.

Vincent Cristallini

One could assume that the ISEOR staff would want to keep its process for its own benefit. But for the most of us, we all live with SEAM—we have both breakfast and lunch with SEAM—and we teach with SEAM. It's a way of life that has to be shared.

The world needs SEAM. This type of knowledge transfer takes high energy, but this is our vocation. We are used to saying we are not consultants—we are *scientific* consultants. We want to create and transfer knowledge. When John Conbere proposed to us that we come to Minneapolis, we were forced to think deeply about who we are, drawing out our realizations and expectations. That is the reason why we modeled the question of transfer. ISEOR is a research company with the same problems and challenges that other companies face. It is a place to observe and experiment with management practices. We would not propose ideas or tools or concepts to others if we were not skilled in those concepts. ISEOR itself is self-sustainable. The Center is not subsidized, and such long-term success requires true professionalism. Our 38 years of existence are the reflection of our clients' satisfaction. A deep belief is that there is a lack of organizations like ISEOR engaging in our approach to intervention. Otherwise, it would be relatively easy for us to explain the role of scientific consultants. This void can be explained by the fact that our work is very demanding and tiring. A positive result is that we have created and capitalized on a great knowledge base. The management team of ISEOR has 150 years of collective experience in the field of intervention research. We have worked with roughly 110,000 people, producing 100,000 of pages of publication. Although the majority of this literature has been published in French, there are important publications in Spanish, English, and other languages. All this knowledge is available to anyone. It is rich and innovative. Our life with SEAM leads us to permanent interaction with actors in the organization, we respond to clients while developing our firmness and excluding complaisance. We practice change management; we do not only speak about it. It's a flexible yet rigorous protocol.

The idea is that one cannot learn SEAM through books and articles, just as no one learns music just with readings. The quality of the transfer is an obsession since the beginning of our great adventure because of our vocation. That is why SEAM has been taught to more than 100,000 individuals, including 5,000 people in residential training, 11,000 students, 500 intervener-researchers, 150 doctoral students, and 30 licensed consultants. Our other activities concern the idea and protocol transfer processes. Anyone knows that people are in search for confirmation. Everyone tries to compare new knowledge to what we already know. In fact, those comparisons typically emerge because people do not want to learn—learning requires time and patience. We are talking about practice and not only concepts. A chef, mason, carpenter, and baker are all supervised during their apprenticeship. We wondered why a similar process does not take place in management or in change management.

We also observed that, at times, when you teach SEAM to people, they want to eliminate you. There are many ways to get rid of the master. One can work on his own, criticize the master, convert the master, and pretend to ask for advice or criticize the knowledge itself. It is an unconscious tendency, but it has been observed. A property of the transfer is that partners need to "sweat" together, to be side by side, neck to neck, and an intense synchronization with mental and physical implications if they are to succeed. For example, the ISEOR team meets every week in a formal and planned meeting on each of the interventions. John Conbere and Alla Heorhiadi were clear with us at the beginning; they asked to do things exactly the way that we do it. The language is a small obstacle, but a really important vector of transferring regarding the integrity of the concepts. Those concepts, in SEAM, are often intriguing and challenging for people. For example, the concept of professional loyalty is extremely important in organizations, but rarely discussed. The geographic distance is difficult especially if you think that teamwork is physical. The quality of transfer needs patience, regularity, and determination.

Conbere often said when he deviated from the method, that there were cultural difficulties. If an ISEOR project stems from scientific intention, our concepts and methods do not involve any specific cultural area because we are looking for generic knowledge. Cultural differences are neither consistent nor pertinent in SEAM process. In a way, there is a lack of written material, because we do not have time to write everything on all our activities, so we have to transfer all our experience. The way to succeed is not a recipe. If we ask our partners to comply with norms, those norms are focused on the quality of the product and behavior of the intervener-researcher, but also on the control and cooperation within the team. Concerning the complexity and the completeness of the product, some parts of the product are considered pleasant and other tedious. For example, John Conbere talked a lot about the process of the mirror effect and project, I feel that he did not speak enough about the other tools in SEAM. Those tools are time management, priority action plan, internal and external strategic action plan, competency grid, and negotiable activity contract. These tools create a whole, which take part in the completeness of the project. One can implement SEAM, but the extensive notion of SEAM is complex so we extend our role to help make a comprehensive approach, help reflect on relationships, help decide on various improvements, to anticipate, plan, and manage the rhythms, to forecast two or three months ahead to be sure to have effective training and successful transfer. John Conbere, Alla Heorhiadi, and I have started fieldwork together, we began by orienting the action and feeling how it was going. We have intensified the integrated training in Lyon and

Minneapolis, according to needs as they emerged, and we organized quality controls. It is the best way to check whether the product complies with expectations. Quality control consists of reading every document and giving our opinion on the products.

We have to congratulate John Conbere and Alla Heorhiadi for carrying out two interventions—a first step toward the socio-economic "happiness." I wish them a lot of clients to continue their great adventure for the renewal of the management for the best satisfaction of our stakeholders. SEAM is not only for people within the organization, but it is for citizens of the world. Organizations have to function for the best of all the people. Consider the financial situation worldwide. The United States desperately need to examine it hidden costs. If you look at the example of France, there is $20,000 per capita of hidden costs. If you multiply that by the population, you have $5,000,000,000 of a hidden costs pool that could be used to improve the efficiency of France. Eliciting hidden costs is the best help; it's a way to reduce dysfunctions and to develop human potential in the country.

INTRODUCTION

In 2006 we went to Lyon to attend the June conference sponsored by IS-EOR and the Academy of Management's Organization Development and Change Division. During our stay, we were impressed by the Socio-Economic Approach to Management (SEAM) approach to organizational change. We both teach in a doctoral program for Organization Development (OD) practitioners, and we were intrigued about the way in which SEAM embodied OD's core practices. We think of these OD values as being articulated by such thinkers as Kurt Lewin, Rensis Likert, Douglas MacGregor, Edgar Schein and Chris Argyris. The books and papers from ISEOR cite such authors, and when we spoke about of them with ISEOR colleagues, it was clear that they fully understood the nuances and ramifications of their work.

Perhaps even more importantly, we came to realize that SEAM embodied the OD values that too often are not lived by OD practitioners. The OD Network for instance espouses the importance of ethical and person-oriented organizational decision-making, but too often we see the organizational bottom line as being the actual value that drives decision making in most American organizations. At ISEOR the SEAM paradigm stresses that laying off people when the organization is in financial difficulty is a foolish business plan—and unethical.

We also found the assessment of hidden costs to be useful. Similar practices have evolved in the United States, but none were as thorough or as researched and documented as the SEAM assessment. Because American organizations are so driven by financial pressures and considerations, the ability to demonstrate the financial costs of dysfunctions and hidden costs was attractive.

Finally we had come to believe that the most successful OD interventions must involve the whole system. We had experience in which we worked with organizational divisions, and found that when people in the division tried to use healthy communication processes, they were literally beaten down by superiors in the system. Undertaking an intervention in part of the whole did not allow us—or the organization—to deal with the systemic resistance to change.

We returned to the June conference each year, and in 2009 we decided to learn to become SEAM practitioners. ISEOR was very responsive. While courses in SEAM had been taught at a few universities, no one in the United States had developed SEAM into an actual on-going practice. Michel Peron chuckled as he told us that ISEOR had a plan—referred to as Operation Lafayette—to infiltrate into the United States. Just as Lafayette had gone to North America to assist the rebels in the American Revolutionary War, ISEOR wanted to infiltrate to assist American organizations.

LEARNING THE ISEOR WAY

Our training took place over two 3-day periods, one in October and one in June. In the first session, we were the only students—tutored by Marc Bonnet, Michel Peron, Vincent Cristallini, and Henri Savall. In the second, the group included a team of four from a Lebanese hospital system.

We discovered two things. One is our background as OD professors and practitioners helped us to understand most of what we were taught at IS-EOR. The other is that at ISEOR, SEAM practitioners are apprenticed into understanding. They attend seminars, and then assist on interventions under supervision until they are ready to practice on their own. In addition, the interventions are done by groups, always with supervision from ISEOR, so there is a strong safety net to insure that each ISEOR certified SEAM practitioner understands and follows the SEAM protocol.

Following our experience at ISEOR, we created two courses for our doctoral students, offered in the spring of 2012 and 2011 that introduced the SEAM approach. Vincent Cristallini and Marc Bonnet taught the courses with us, and allowed us to refresh our knowledge as well as learn how much we did not know. For instance, as we prepared to present a sample of the *expert opinion*—a technique in which SEAM intervener-researchers identify major dysfunctions—Cristallini showed us how as he led the session. This experience reinforced the way in which the practice of SEAM is taught through apprenticeship. The student watches others lead interventions, and the student then develops by taking on more and more of the work until he or she is proficient. Thus, students are shown the steps of intervening as well as the manner in which they should carry out the intervention. As part of this process, they learn to elicit and analyze information. They also learn how to develop trust, to make sure they never undercut the leaders with whom they work, to speak truth even when people do not want to hear the truth, and to always let the leaders know that they are not being judged or looked down upon.

Eventually we decided that we wanted to master the SEAM process, including the use of the SEAM software to analyze the interviews for the mirror effect—a stage in the diagnosis where the consultant presents the information gathered during interviews through the actual words used by organizational members as a way of illustrating dysfunctions. To acquire this real control on the SEAM process, we asked to be helped through a license with ISEOR, whose purpose was to help us concretely in the transfer and application of knowledge about the conduct of an intervention on the field. Part of the arrangement is a year of advice, and Vincent Cristallini was named as our advisor. The plan was for us to find one or two clients, and receive tutoring via Skype. We incorporated as SEAM, Inc., with four of our doctoral students who wanted to learn SEAM, looked for clients. We found our first client in January 2012, and our second in July 2012. Both of these interventions are described in separate chapters in this book (see Chapters 5 and 6).

The franchise cost was quite reasonable—around $7,000. For this we received the ISEOR software, and as much coaching as we wanted. Part of the franchise concept, as explained by Henri Savall, is quality control. Each step of the SEAM interventions we did would be reviewed beforehand by Cristallini, just as each step of the interventions in France under the ISEOR aegis were reviewed. The goal was twofold: to make sure that the work we did was of an acceptable quality according to ISEOR standards, and to help us be as successful as possible.

The software itself has two uses. One is to sort the dysfunctions, taking the comments from the participant interviews and categorizing them by dysfunction. The other is to record the data about dysfunctions from the Mirror Effect to be included in the ISEOR database. We were also impressed that ISEOR had the data base translated into English so that we could use it.

REFLECTING ON OUR EXPERIENCE

Using the data base was an interesting learning experience. The software is not particularly intuitive, and there are no instructions on paper to guide one. We were shown how to use the software at ISEOR, and had a program installed on our laptop. Essentially the process is to type the relevant comments into a Word document, and then cut and paste them into the software. The software then creates reports in which the dysfunctions are sorted into categories. To enter a comment one has to manually choose one of the six primary dysfunctions (working conditions, work organization, time management, communication–coordination–cooperation, integrated training, and strategic implementation) and then the appropriate subcategory. In the end the software prints the reports showing the comments as they fit into categories. Reports can also be produced showing distinctions like which comments were from top managers and which from middle managers.

At ISEOR reporting back to the client is done using overhead projectors, with the software report printed onto a transparency. We found that this approach would not work for us due to cultural expectations in the U.S. Today, most clients don't even have overhead projectors anymore, and we suspect that a proposal to use an overhead would be perceived as a sign that we are not technically proficient. As a result we created our own reporting template on PowerPoint, cutting and pasting from the software report.

The conferences confirmed that courses about SEAM have been taught at a few universities, including Central Michigan University, Benedictine University, New Mexico State University, Central Missouri, and Pepperdine University. These courses have led to student interventions in New Mexico, students/faculty interventions in Michigan, and outreach about SEAM by faculty from Missouri to China. None of the programs used the full SEAM approach however, and none of the interventions were done with quality control from ISEOR.

Struggles

The hardest part of the process was trying to do SEAM in the way that a fully trained intervener-researcher, like Cristallini, carries out the process. No amount of coaching would lead us to be able to match his vision of how to make SEAM work at its best. Part of this may be due to language—our French is *très pauvre*, though Cristallini's English is quite good—but periodically we still hit points where communication was difficult. I think this was more than words—it was the issue of conveying whole assumptions that in France are understood and do not have to be explained. Intercultural communication is never easy. More than once we told Cristallini what we had done, and were embarrassed to hear "that is not the way we do it." In one sense it was humbling. On another level, however, we felt some anger— a trying to do our best, following instructions as we understood them, and not wanting to fail with clients. While this situation is not anyone's fault, the underlying challenge is bridging the cultural divide, in terms of language as well as custom and expectations. Thus an ongoing issue is the processes through which the essence of SEAM can be transmitted to American practitioners.

There is a cultural element in how ISEOR approaches its teaching. While the leaders are quite clear that SEAM is flexible, a key is knowing when to be flexible. As a learner, this feels somewhat like the way cooking is taught in the Cordon Bleu tradition of preparing French chefs: there is one right way to prepare each dish—practice until you can cook the right way. Do not deviate. Learning how and when to adapt, to be flexible, remains something of a mystery. Knowing how and when to adapt the SEAM process is essential in effectively bringing SEAM to the United States—yet, at the time of writing this chapter, the solution is not yet clear.

Successes

Despite our concerns, in our brief experience we learned much about SEAM and affirmed that the process does work. Managers come to see the interconnection of the SEAM management tools. At first, our clients were polite, some willing to log hours with the time management tool, others politely waiting. We suspect that for some the "penny dropped" when they saw that they were living in the mode of sustaining the current level of operation and put little effort into development. To have the time to develop the organization, they needed to reduce hidden costs, and to become better able to delegate some of their tasks. That meant others had to become able to receive the delegated tasks. All of a sudden, the link between time management, the competency grid, strategic planning, and the priority action plan—key tools in the SEAM arsenal—became clear.

The mirror effect can be a shock to the organization, unfreezing the system. In our experience, this led managers to become more open to change in ways they had not imagined before they began the SEAM process. We received feedback that people appreciated the SEAM process. It is deliberately a bit slow, allowing people to adjust and learn without being unduly pressured by time. The fact that we stayed for months with the intervention, learning about the people and the organization, and serving as process managers rather than content experts, led people to trust the process. We were told that too often they experienced consultants as people who came, identified what they thought was the problem, told people what they should do, and left—all of which left a bad taste for consulting in the participants.

The expert opinion process has a logic that leads actors from the key points of the mirror effect, through the consultant's insights, to themes and causes and baskets and finally to projects. The goal here is to teach the participants how the system works, or does not work, to prepare them for short-term resolutions and the long-term confidence that they can solve their own problems.

Organizations can solve problems. Through the SEAM methodology, changes begin immediately—some after the first meeting, more after the mirror effect. In the projects, we found that people discovered that they have the knowledge and ability to succeed in organizational problem solving. We knew this in theory, and from our own earlier action-research type OD interventions, and we were reassured to see this working equally well in the SEAM process.

Coaching managers is an important part of the change effort. This challenge differed in each site, and was essential in both. Our contract called for one hour of coaching a month for five months per manager. At first we allowed managers to decide whether or not to use our coaching services. In retrospect, we are not sure if this was the best choice on our part. The more we coached managers, the more quickly they were able to make sense of the SEAM system.

There is an overarching challenge that we believe must be addressed. An important goal is to teach SEAM in the United States, with the expectation that it will create practitioners who will be able to carry out a SEAM intervention with the same level of quality that one would expect from an ISEOR intervener-researcher. How this can be done in a manner that keeps the high quality assurance of ISEOR yet is sufficiently efficient in terms of cost and time for American students and practitioners remains a work in progress.

APPENDIX:
Conference Dialogue

Conference Participant: I really appreciated the final point that was made by Vincent Cristallini, with regard to hidden costs and technology research. You've been engaged with interventions for long time and you even teach it. It just seems to be the nature of a profession to improve the tools with time, and adjusting the norms would be a good source of improvement. Can you talk about that or cite an example of something that you changed?

Vincent Cristallini: One example is the description of the TFW virus. In a way, people analyze things and the models they use to make decisions, and the virus limits the way they see problems in their decision-making. By teaching them to see things differently, you can change people, which is definitely the goal. Because people are intelligent, they will understand that they were using wrong ways to do things.

Conference Participant: Is that new to the process that that virus concept comes up? I am talking about watching agents in the SEAM process. Has there been any modification, upgrades, or other improvements in the process?

Vincent Cristallini: As SEAM is a research process, it has necessarily evolved over its history. As an example, with respect to pricing for clients, we are more direct, that's an evolution.

Conference Participant: If I learned SEAM ten years ago, would I need training in new areas?

Vincent Cristallini: To survive and to develop, you need food. SEAM is based on survival development for humans and organizations and we do not see any difference between an individual and an organization from this point of view. The only difference is that humans know they are sick, and knowing it, they go to the doctor. When organizations are sick, in contrast, they keep their pathologies. Learning needs, indeed, to be renewed over time, just like we need a regular check up with our doctor.

Conference Participant: Is the training done in Spanish, or only in French?

Vincent Cristallini: Training sessions are done in Spanish in Mexico, Lyon and in Spain.

We can do either a formal or informal evaluation. However, if you want an effective process, you must evaluate it step by step, not *a posteriori*. Evaluating is another interaction and we do this with the client.

When you ask the client if he is satisfied, you are doing an evaluation. We capture many signals to be sure that everything is satisfactory.

Conference Participant: You are implementing SEAM in the United States with many partners, but are you in the process of such transfer in other countries? Are you experiencing the same issues when teaching SEAM? Vincent Cristallini said that language was not a great barrier, but to do this type of intervention in Mexico raises a challenge—did you work hard to speak Spanish? And why didn't you encounter the same problem as in English?

Henri Savall: We recently led a knowledge transfer program in Mexico, and it was a great experience. However, our two franchises had difficulties. We even dismissed one because control quality was missing. There are barriers created by language problems—for example, I can't speak English very well but I'm fluent in Spanish.

Amandine Savall: For the French, it's easier to speak Spanish. However, in France we have a team learning English and a team very fluent in Spanish.

PART II

WORLDWIDE EXPERIMENTATION WITH SEAM

CHAPTER 5

THE SOCIO-ECONOMIC APPROACH TO MANAGEMENT WITHIN AMERICAN COMPANIES

John Conbere and Tom Oestreich

CONFERENCE REMARKS:
Chapter Prologue

John Conbere

We spent a lot of time to understand the implementation subtleties of the SEAM approach. Thus, a case study on a transportation center will describe our intervention and serve as introduction to how we used the Socio-Economic Approach to Management. The focus of this case study is the first part of the SEAM approach. It concerns the process of change within the organization, a matter of facts, and the expert opinion that we built as interveners-researchers.

INTRODUCTION

In our efforts to understand the implementation subtleties of the SEAM approach, this chapter presents a case study of a transportation center describing the intervention through a focus on the first part of the SEAM approach. The discussion examines the process of change within the organization, and the expert opinion that we built as interveners-researchers. The SEAM approach and intervention process, as this volume illustrates, also involves the search for hidden costs, which will be examined in a follow-up chapter by Alla Heorhiadi and Barbara Milon.

The chapter and case are presented as an exchange between the client and consultant, drawing out the ramifications for this type of intervention.

THE TRANSPORTATION CENTER CASE STUDY

The Transportation Center is a public school transportation organization that was successful at its beginning, 13 years ago. Progressively, the school district had to face many issues and financial loss. The system currently operates with 110 schools buses that transport 10,300 regular education students and 520 special education students. Over 7,000 students are transported daily, twice a day. The transportation system also operates a travel service for athletics and field trips at a profit. Five mechanics keep the fleet operational, which also includes 125 trucks, skid steers, movers, and additional equipment services. The Center serves 19 public schools.

John Conbere

The SEAM process started with the horizontal stage: contracting, presentation of the mirror effect and the expert opinion, and, finally, the project stage. Then, it is extended to vertical stage. The intervention on the Transportation Center is currently at the horizontal project stage, just about to start the vertical stage.

When contracting in June and July, we noted the effectiveness of the Transportation Center, which maybe one of the few profitable transportation departments in the state. Most of these centers either run at a loss or contract out the services. Although the Bloomington Transportation Center was very entrepreneurial and worked quite effectively, the Human Resources Director in the Bloomington public school system thought that the transportation department could be even more effective. During the contracting phase of the intervention, we offered them a choice between a classic action-research intervention and the SEAM approach. They chose a SEAM intervention because they were attracted to its holistic approach, which included the education of managers and the coaching that is a core part of the SEAM paradigm.

Tom Oestreich

I had requested education materials for the managers in the system because I believe that team spirit on the actions that we operate would help us deal with many troubles and face the growing complexities in our overall processes. Without additional training, there would be the threat of a disconnection, as if head and body were not completely communicating, when dealing with many different people—it felt like my head was responsible for a lot of levels but my body could barely move. Our consultants, John Conbere and Alla Heorhiadi, contacted us at the beginning of the school year and awakened my interest about this holistic approach, and its approach to managing people and developing a new approach to the operation, somewhat similar to the idea of growing a tree. This interest was underpinned by concerns about the new school year, which is always the busiest time in transportation activity. Having read some of the articles that Conbere and Heorhiadi had written about SEAM, I approached them, confident and enthusiast about our participation in this process because SEAM touched the core of my beliefs.

THE SEAM PROCESS OF CHANGE

John Conbere

There are three different but related movements that support the SEAM intervention process. The first is the cyclical process of problem solving, implemented through a diagnosis that involves a mirror effect and expert opinion, and the implementation and evaluation of projects. The second movement consists of teaching and applying a series of management tools: time management, the competency grid, internal–external strategic planning, priority action plans, periodical negotiable activity contract, and the strategic piloting logbook. The third movement, SEAM involves the periodical political and strategic decisions that arise as the intervention progresses, such as agreeing on the new "rules of the game," redeploying resources, and decisions about the management system. Together these three movements are described by SEAM as the three axes of the socio-economic intervention, or the "trihedron."

An element that is not explicitly mentioned in the trihedron is coaching. In this intervention, I provided managers a minimum of one hour of one-to-one coaching each month for 6 months. This component is a very important step in the process of change.

In typical interventions, the process starts with top management, the organization's leadership, but in our intervention, we began our work with the steering committee, led by the superintendent of the schools and his close collaborators.

As illustrated in Figure 5.1, the steering committee, which oversaw the whole process, was composed of the superintendent, the director of finance, the director of human resources, the director of transportation, and the union representatives of the drivers and the office workers. A difficulty in the Transportation Center was that, in a system of about 130 people, 120 persons directly reported to the director of transportation. This situation raised questions early on as to whether the usual SEAM process, with its emphasis on starting at the very top, might be problematic. The process usually involves managers in the horizontal action including those on the top of vertical sections, as a way of ensuring that the process will cascade throughout the organization.

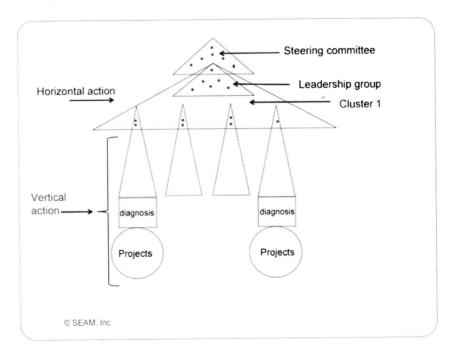

Figure 5.1 Intervention architecture.

In the Transportation Center intervention, a horizontal cluster was created that included seven representatives from across all categories of employees as a way of ensuring that the change process would be communicated to everyone in the organization. Moreover, since people did not trust the process of change, fearing it would have a negative impact on them, it was clear that a vibrant communication channel was necessary. As a result, the horizontal group included roles not typically involved in large-scale systems changes, in this instance, for example, the representative of the driver union (see Figure 5.2).

During the first month of the intervention, we undertook the first training on time management and the initial in-depth exposure to SEAM. We interviewed everyone in the clusters in the horizontal group and analyzed the collected data, using the SEAM software that categorizes the various dysfunctions into clusters. Dysfunction analysis is essential in the SEAM approach, a process that is similar to the classic action-research data collection feedback but more stylized. Classification into dysfunctions adds a critical element of analysis that is different across organizations. One month after the interviews, the dysfunctions were presented to the horizontal group in a mirror effect, accompanied by training on the SEAM competency grid. Expert opinion was presented a month later, followed by training on Internal/external Strategic Actions Plans and two projects:

The horizontal cluster

* Formed Horizontal cluster: managers and others

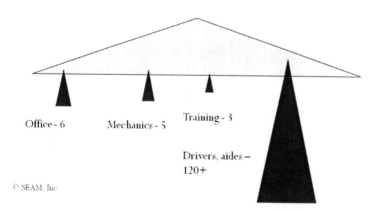

© SEAM, Inc.

Figure 5.2   Socio-economic intervention architecture.

- Improve the communication systems at the Transportation Center.
- Improve the way in which the Transportation Center is led—make sure everyone feels safe and heard, develop managers' abilities, improve time management and prioritizing of each manager's tasks.

The timeline of the process is captured in Figure 5.3.

UNDERSTANDING AND ADDRESSING DYSFUNCTIONS

Many intervention processes focus on structures and behaviors as a way of managing change. The SEAM approach sets its sight on dysfunctions that have been identified through 38 years of intervention-research. Six main categories of dysfunctions are typical in every organization. Thus, we looked for these core dysfunctions in the Transportation Center—as illustrated in Figure 5.4—which, according to SEAM theory are a pathway toward hidden costs.

Such dysfunctions have financial consequences on which real and possible change can bring profitability to the organizations. In the mirror effect undertaken in this intervention, we had 119 quotes—61 from managers, 58 from others—that were presented to the horizontal cluster.

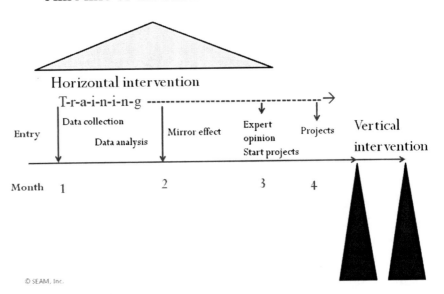

© SEAM, Inc.

Figure 5.3 Time line of the SEAM Intervention.

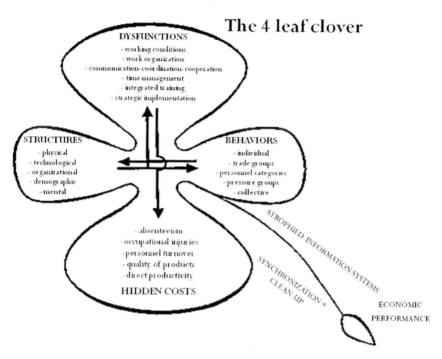

The 4 leaf clover

DYSFUNCTIONS
- working conditions
- work organization
- communication-coordination-cooperation
- time management
- integrated training
- strategic implementation

STRUCTURES
- physical
- technological
- organizational
- demographic
- mental

BEHAVIORS
- individual
- trade groups
- personnel categories
- pressure groups
- collective

- absenteeism
- occupational injuries
- personnel turnover
- quality of products
- direct productivity

HIDDEN COSTS

ATROPHIED INFORMATION SYSTEMS

SYNCHRONIZATION + CLEAN-UP

ECONOMIC
PERFORMANCE

Figure 5.4 The SEAM "4-leaf clover."

Tom Oestreich

In a way, from an organizational vantage point, the word "dysfunction" created some fear—and the challenge of building on negative realities to get to positive outcomes. In reality, however, the mirror effect was very enlightening. It was a great process that spelled out the issues, literally laying them on the table, that needed to be addressed. It was necessary to work on those problems openly, with governance composed of several unions and many different factions that must be dealt with in our large organization. The consultants were very helpful collecting the data and analyzing them. As we learned, they followed the SEAM process diligently and spoke those concepts and dysfunctions in an effective way, so that we had the chance to digest and share them with our colleagues.

John Conbere

We presented the expert opinion a month later. There is a logic that shapes the expert opinion. It begins with key points from the mirror effect and is completed by elements that were observed and analyzed, combining the elements that the interveners heard with those that remained unexpressed, which we "read between the lines." Thus, we looked at the root causes of dysfunctions, at the themes connecting the dysfunctions, that needed to be dealt with, first within project baskets and finally with project groups. The logic of this process carries everyone into a change dynamic that really makes sense.

As illustration, here are different examples of key points from the mirror effect:

- Not everyone feels safe. Some employees fear managers will retaliate.
- Some see management and the drivers' union in on-going conflict.
- Different people blame managers, union, drivers, office workers, mechanics, and the district. Everybody gets a share of the blame, a dynamic that shaped work conditions, morale and feelings in the organization.
- Managers' workloads are overwhelming at times. As a result, some tasks are not done, and holding managers and employees accountable is difficult. It is very clear problem for doing good management.
- Another key point is that there is no clear district strategy for the Transportation Center. The superintendent only said "Keep everyone safe, make money, and be on time." These concerns were linked to the lack of time, and the fact that there was no strategy for the Transportation Center for the future.

As part of our analysis, we also brought to light nine root dysfunctions causes:

- Communication systems didn't work. The context is that many people among the 130 employees of the Transportation Center have a working day from 5:00 in the morning to 7:00 at night, with a few hours of driving to pick up 7,000 students twice a day in a city of 100,000 people. Many of the drivers are retired, and some are incredibly skilled, including former engineers or former vice presidents of finance. Although retired from their previous roles, they clearly did not want to stop being active, but the communication structure made it difficult to get messages across the system.
- Many Transportation staff did not feel sufficiently valued.
- There were ongoing unresolved conflicts that prejudiced the organization. Some of these conflicts were between departments, while others were between people and with union managers.
- Lack of professionalism was a problem and gave power to gossip and rumors.

- There was not enough cohesion among the employees. Loyalty was low to nonexistent.
- Managers were overloaded.
- Expectations were not always clear. Too often, they appeared as a lack of accountability, which undermined trust.
- The Transportation Center did not have its own strategic plan.
- There was no clear sense of shared values among Transportation Center staff.

Every organization, of course, has dysfunctions, but the difference between organizations is the willingness to look at those elements and to work on them rather than pretending they are not there. The Transportation Center was a healthy organization that looked for solutions to their problems. Corrective work efforts have been started through teams, focusing on the root causes of the dysfunctions—communication, low levels of trust and morale, poor working conditions, and a lack of clear expectations, accountability and strategy.

Tom Oestreich

Communication was an important theme to address due to the diversity of the groups and people involved in the Center. Probing that issue raised questions about how to enhance cohesion throughout the system, getting people talk with each other, sharing and accepting the organization's values. It was a great challenge that could not be achieved by only one person, which is the main reason I was interested in the process. I was very surprised, and excited, by the healing that began at the very beginning of the process. You could feel a healing process among the people that were participating. They almost immediately got involved into the process—the SEAM dynamic was a collective process, an inside-out process of healing, which is the best way to heal. It worked for our organization.

LOOKING BACK AND LOOKING FORWARD

John Conbere

The focus groups began right after the dysfunctions analysis. The steering committee was informed and very supportive of this next stage of the process. The district managers and finance director joined the project groups as it was realized that the issues that were being raised were larger than the Transportation Center itself, concerning the interactions with other organizations in the district. Involving these individuals also seems to enhance the probability that the project will be successful. As an example, one illustration of improvement was the recognition that in the interaction with every organization, within the district, every school, special education, and so forth, there was no coherent and on-going communication. Instantly, the project group planned to figure out the interfaces and the district helped gather people together to develop new systems to ensure that communication improves.

Tom Oestreich

I also believe the energy that I put in the project came partially from my own excitement. When we laid the dysfunctions out, tears were shed in the groups of the school district's special education. We did fear that we could not "dry things up" in the organization and that we could only work our way down. But such fear has no place in the SEAM process. The involvement and the excitement of the human resources department and other departments in laying out dysfunctions contributed to their effective participation in linking the communication pieces of the organization. This process became a cornerstone of this "growing tree." My sense is that it is truly going to affect the organization in a positive way.

APPENDIX:
Conference Dialogue

Conference Participant: Is the Transportation Center a private company in the service of a school district or a unit of the Bloomington public school?

Tom Oestreich: John Conbere referred to the "entrepreneurial" aspect of the Transportation Center, but it is definitely part of the public school system for the past thirteen years.

Conference Participant: We were cooperating with the Transportation Center because they were isolated, while their union had a significant voice. The workers from the Center refused to work alone, but the communication system did not work well enough to address the issue. It was really important to us to reverse that idea.

Tom Oestreich: We knew the issues of transportation and wanted to make changes. However, a change led by only people from the Transportation Center was difficult because we feared a lack of methodological support to uncover dysfunctions and improve the situation. John Conbere and Alla Heorhiadi showed us the process, and the outside intervention really helped.

Conference Participant: A point was made that the transportation department was a profit center for the district. I wonder how it was able to achieve that result, making a profit. Does SEAM support profitability—does it make it grow or does the process sustain profitability?

Tom Oestreich: We are a nonprofit organization. We have to work with unfunded mandates, but with equipment our bottom line is an important cost factor. We try to work at a profit, through additional business that enables us to grow additional profits.

SEAM has made a huge difference. For instance, an excellent truck driver was with the Center for many years. Now, the cost of his vehicle is next to nothing. If we study the situation and know that we can share his approach and, as a team, we could get everybody to accept the challenge of driving more effectively, an outcome that will be less costly on our vehicles. We could stop adding additional costs. As an example, a driver runs an average of 40–50 hours of idle time alone in a year in one vehicle. Further study showed us that many things can be reduced when driving effectively, like reducing the need for fuel. These elements are money that we really can save.

CHAPTER 6

A CASE STUDY
OF A NONPROFIT
COMMUNITY CENTER

Alla Heorhiadi, John Conbere, and Barbara Milon

CONFERENCE REMARKS:
Chapter Prologue

Barbara Milon

The *Phyllis Wheatley Community Center* (PWCC) was established in 1924. It originated as one of the first settlement houses to primarily serve the African American community in North Minneapolis, Minnesota. The Center was a "safe port" in the midst of a racially segregated city, intended to respond to discriminatory practices. PWCC has a legacy of serving youth, families, and children. The environment of the 1920s, when PWCC was established, was rooted in fear, paternalism, racism, and prejudice, thus creating a settlement house for Blacks in Minneapolis was a good idea. In fact, the Mary T. Welcome Child Development Center, which is part of PWCC, is the oldest continuously operating early child development center in the state of Minnesota, and it was accredited in 2009. We have been able to document that over the past five years that 98% of the children who

---

Facilitating the Socioeconomic Approach to Management, pages 61–74
Copyright © 2014 by Information Age Publishing
All rights of reproduction in any form reserved.

graduated from the Mary T. Welcome Child Development Center have met kindergarten standards. We also have other youth services programs such as the academic achievement program focused on kids meeting grade levels standards. Family Services supports families to acquire skills that are necessary for self-sufficiency, decision making and to abate violence. Today, we have served 200,000 families.

As the Executive Director, I came on board about ten years ago. One of the things I had to face was the financial strategic plan. The organization had a huge amount of liabilities, and we were forced to do a lot of difficult restructuring.

I have been studying SEAM (Socio-Economic Approach to Management) for the past couple of years and I was attracted to SEAM because of its capability to focus on human potential. As a consequence, I was thrilled that PWCC had the opportunity to be selected as a pilot program for SEAM implementation. The SEAM experience has been good for a pioneer organization like PWCC and the challenges we face.

INTRODUCTION

The focus of the intervention is a community center located in Minneapolis, Minnesota, founded in 1924 as a settlement house for the Afro-American community. Today the Center's mission is to provide comprehensive quality programs in life-long learning, child development and family support for the diverse Greater Minneapolis community. According to the Center's mission, its "programs address the needs of children, youth, families, and elders by providing tailored education and skill building opportunities to help individuals and families discover their strengths, develop their personal networks of support and take control of their futures."

The center's staff includes an executive director and directors of development and marketing, family services, and youth services. The largest single program is a child care center, with 9 staff and a program director. The budget is approximately $1 million, most of which comes from gifts and grants, and is spent on personnel. Funders include the State of Minnesota, Hennepin County, the United Way, and more than 16 foundations and companies. Some of the funding comes from tuition in the child care program and fees for services in other programs.

THE INTERVENTION

In recent years funding for the Center diminished, a situation not uncommon for nonprofit organizations in the current economic climate. The decline led to layoffs for some of the staff, combined with an attempt to maintain the same level of services. The remaining staff struggled to juggle the Center's many tasks. Due to these challenges, the executive director of the Center, who learned about SEAM during her doctoral program, subsequently she requested a SEAM intervention.

Contracting

The contract spelled out who would be involved in the horizontal intervention, who the consultants would be, and timeline for the work for a 10-month period. The leaders in the horizontal intervention were the executive director, the directors of marketing and development, family services and youth services, the assistant director of youth services who was responsible for the operation of the early child development program, and two youth services coordinators. This configuration was somewhat different from the usual SEAM approach in that the only other employees in the organization were 14 early child development staff, 2 part-time administrative assistants and one other youth program coordinator. As a result, we decided to include a hidden cost analysis in the horizontal intervention, and later to do only one vertical intervention with the school.

The Horizontal Intervention

Month 1: The intervention began with a meeting of the steering committee, composed of the executive director and two members of the Board of Directors, followed by an initial session with the horizontal group. The latter meeting included an overview of SEAM and the application of the ISEOR approach modified for an American audience. The concept of six dysfunctions that lead to hidden costs was introduced (see Savall & Zardet, 2008; Figure 6.1). Also the ISEOR time management grid was introduced, with the request that the horizontal team try using the grid for 3 to 5 days. Following the presentation, interviews were held with each of the horizontal team members. Most interviews were about an hour in length, and they were focused on the perception of each person on the extent to which each of the 6 dysfunctions was present in the organization. The offer of personal assistance was made to all the horizontal team members for anytime within the following month. Three of the staff requested the assistance.

Over the next two weeks, after reviewing the transcripts, possible hidden costs were identified, and interviews with two of the leaders were undertaken to discern an estimate of the hidden costs.

6 dysfunctions lead to 5 indicators of hidden costs and 6 financial consequences

6 dysfunctions	5 indicators of hidden costs	6 financial consequences of dysfunctions
• Working conditions	• Absenteeism	• Excess salary
• Work organization	• Occupational	• Overtime
• Communication-	injuries &	• Overconsumption
coordination-	diseases	• Non production
cooperation	• Staff turnover	• Noncreation of potential
• Time management	• Nonquality	• Risks
• Integrated training	• Direct	
• Strategic	productivity gap	
implementation		

© SEAM, INC.

Figure 6.1 Dysfunctions and hidden costs.

Month 2: The mirror effect is the feedback to the group on what they said to the interviewers—in essence, the "organization talking to the organization." The presentation was created by transcribing all of the pertinent interview comments, and entering these into the ISEOR software for analysis. The result was 56 separate dysfunctions, each accompanied by a quote that brought it to life. These were incorporated into the PowerPoint presentation.

The slides were shown to the group, but by the group's choice the slides were not read aloud. At the end of each dysfunction, the presentation was stopped for comments from the group. At this point in the process, the intervener-researchers did not offer any comments. The presentation took about 90 minutes. The overall effect was shock, but most people agreed that the overall findings were on target. The shock may have been the result of seeing for the first time all of the dysfunctions spelled out and supported by a staff quotation.

Following the mirror effect, the discussion turned to an assessment of the Center's Hidden Costs. This analysis was composed of three calculations:

- Nonproductivity: The value of the hours wasted, plus the margin (the fixed cost per hour per person of the organization (i.e., what it costs to stay open).
- Shift in function: The cost per hour when an employee does work that a lower costing employee could do.
- Risk and lost opportunity: The real losses in the future, but not given a dollar figure.

Fifteen areas of hidden costs were identified. Although this level of specificity is typically not identified until later stage vertical interventions, due to the makeup of the Center they were included at this point:

- Coming late to management meeting
- Missing or leaving early from management meetings
- Attending meeting at which one was not needed
- Problems with temperature—heating and cooling
- Being locked out of the building
- Distractions in the workplace
- Scheduling problems
- Difficulties communicating with school staff
- Shift in function (people doing work of their subordinates)
- Problems logging into the computer
- Accounting software slowness
- Construction in the summer
- Turnover
- A director doing unneeded work
- The loss due to juggling too many tasks

The value of the hidden costs was determined to be $77,700 per year, and this was only for the work of the horizontal group. The group members said that they thought the figure was certainly fair, and probably underestimated. We do need to stress that these hidden costs are absolutely normal in organizations—they are not a reflection on the Phyllis Wheatley Community Center. They are a reflection of every organization that will have equal, and usually greater, hidden costs.

Month 3: A month after the mirror effect, the consultants presented the expert opinion. The heart of this exchange is the response of the intervener-researchers to the organizational dysfunctions. The key here is to address the dysfunctions in a manner that is supportive, nonblaming, direct, and hopeful. We think of these as the SEAM *koans*, referring to the thought provoking statements of Zen monks to their students as reflected in the following two examples:

- You all have a passion for your mission, but you do not agree on what the mission is. Then when a potential client is not served, different employees feel pain. Sometimes this pain turns to anger and/or blaming others because the mission was not met. Agreeing on the mission and how to carry the mission out together could help you become a cohesive team.
- Conflict lurks behind the dysfunctions that exist in the organization. People get hurt, even though no one intends this to happen. Each

person has a role to play in developing real peace in the workplace, and to succeed, people need wisdom and personal courage.

Following the Expert Opinion is the suggestion of "baskets"—clusters of problems that can then be turned into projects. We suggested 5 possible project baskets: Communications, Space, Use of time, Cohesion, and Strategy. Each basket had subthemes. For instance, under Communications the following themes were listed:

- Meetings: There needs to be a balance between learning about the rest of the organization and not feeling like you are wasting time because information does not pertain to you;
- Meeting behavior: Being on time and present, drawing out skills for productive meetings;
- Interacting with the Board of Directors: Giving them honest feedback and hearing about their direction;
- Communicating with the community: Determining what needs to be communicated, listening to communication and how it might get carried out; and
- Interacting with other agencies: Assessing how to go to what is essential, getting the right person(s) engaged.

The staff discussed the baskets, recognizing the fact that they were already busy and pressed for time. They chose to invest some of their time in projects. Eventually they settled on two projects, developing expectations about managing differences respectfully, and maximizing the use of existing resources, with half the staff working on one project, and half on the other.

Months 4–7: The next phase of the intervention focused on the projects. As with any intervention, a critical point is difference the intervention made. Measuring outcomes in a case study can be difficult, because there is no comparison group that allows one to make sound causal claims. With SEAM, there is the potential to measure changes in hidden costs, which can form the basis for such comparisons.

REFLECTIONS

This section draws out some of the key reflections from the client and one of the consultants, focusing on the Center itself, the SEAM approach and its underlying processes (see also Conbere & Heorhiadi, 2011), and outcomes from the intervention .

The Center

The Community Center began as in 1924 as one of the first settlement houses to primarily serve the African American community in North Minneapolis, Minnesota. It was a "safe port" in the midst of a racially segregated city and it responded to discriminatory practices with a legacy of serving youth, families, and children. When the Center was established, the environment has been described as "highly charged," rooted in fear, paternalism, racism, and prejudice. Since its founding, the Center has served more than 200,000 families.

Barbara Milon

As the Center's Executive Director, I came on board about ten years ago. One of the things I had to face was the financial strategic plan. The organization had a huge amount of liabilities and we were forced to do a lot of difficult restructuring. I had been studying SEAM for a couple of years and was attracted to this approach because of its capability to focus on human potential. As a consequence, I was thrilled that the Center would serve as a pilot program for SEAM implementation in the United States.

The SEAM experience has been good for a pioneer organization like the Center, especially because of its ongoing challenges. Today fewer than 50 percent of Kindergartners in North Minneapolis are on track to read well by 3rd Grade, North Minneapolis has higher incidents of domestic violence than most other communities, and the achievement gap between white students and students of color in North Minneapolis has the greatest gap than anywhere in the State. I strongly felt that SEAM was going to be good for our organization as a way of truly engaging staff members across departments—a challenge I was not able to undertake due to other organizational pressures and needs. SEAM provided a methodology for inter-departmental staff engagement.

Alla Heorhiadi

The discussion in the chapter captures the timeline of the SEAM intervention in the Center over a 10-month period. In the United States, the tendency is to focus on a short-term intervention. One argument about resistance to change in American companies is probably the fact that they look for "quick fix" solutions. Going through the SEAM process, however, makes it clear why such interventions can take up to a year of rigorous data collection, and analysis, and information exchange, constantly interacting with the company, diagnosing, coaching, and supporting its actors.

Implementing the SEAM Horizontal Diagnosis

The horizontal intervention includes the mirror effect and hidden costs analysis.

Alla Heorhiadi

Because the Center was a small organization of 28 employees, we calculated hidden costs while being on horizontal level. Given this experience, I now more fully understand now why SEAM is referred to as a rigorous, but flexible approach because hidden costs are usually calculated in the vertical intervention. In this particular situation, given its unique characteristics, during the horizontal intervention we interviewed Center staff and undertook a mirror-effect analysis and exchange.

Barbara Milon

Looking back on the process, all our staff members were interviewed at the beginning. Then, during the mirror effect and reflecting on what they had said, I felt a sense of failure as the director of the organization. I wondered what we had been doing and whether our time was used well. At the same time, as Jim Collins noted in his book *Good to Great,* when one is looking under a rock and sees "yucky stuff," one wants to slam the rock down. I was faced with looking at what was underneath the rock by hearing what my staff was saying, and I wanted to model to my staff the importance of respectful and careful listening. It was a learning experience for me and I have been doing this type of deep listening ever since. A key learning was that even though I knew about the SEAM process, I didn't realize exactly how those steps could be fearful.

We had to allow the process to move forward. Moreover, I wanted to be consistent with my belief and values: honesty and candor are important in the organization. I hoped that by using SEAM, our staff would be able to see that we can all come together. In my opinion, the willingness of the staff to speak honestly is important, so rather than thinking of the mirror effect as something that ripped us apart, I knew we could look in the mirror and move forward.

Alla Heorhiadi

It was a very interesting experience for the leader to look in the mirror, truly hearing what the staff had to say. In the SEAM mirror effect, participants were with their comments, not in terms of typical OD patterns, but as clusters of generic dysfunctions. As examples, in the "working conditions" theme, the team members noted the "difficult layout of workspace" as a sub-theme, and more importantly concerns about the "loss of confidentiality due to their workplace layout." Presenting the mirror effect in this way takes away from putting the blame on people. This process is aimed to put the spotlight on the organization's dysfunctions, but it takes real courage for the leader to face this reality.

We were also advised that consultants do not usually talk during the mirror effect, because this is the time when the organization speaks for and to itself. This silent role, however, was very difficult to carry out, especially when people started to express their emotions and stating their disagreement with particular comments. But by not playing a guiding, expert role, the consultants give people the space to say everything that is on their mind—in essence, encouraging them to look in the mirror and see themselves.

The next part of the intervention was to calculate the hidden costs from the interviews with the managers. We took every dysfunction and looked for the details, the possible reasons, and the possible financial impacts for this dysfunction. For instance, we calculated the hidden cost of "going to meetings that are not needed" as $6,994. Another example was the problem with the temperature because the heating system was very ineffective, so on 30 days each year the building was much too hot or cold. Every time one manager spent 15 minutes trying to fix the system, for a total of 7.5 hours per year. The staff decided that their efficiency was reduced by an average of 15 minutes each per day, as they tried to find ways to stay warm when it was too cold, or struggled with sleepiness in the heat. Ten staff times 15 minutes times 30 days totals 75 hours per year. So the total amount of wasted time was 82.5 hours per year, which multiplied by the cost per person per year equals a hidden cost of $3,499.

Our favorite was the dysfunction "people juggle tasks," especially referring to times when people interrupt others who are already focused on something else. This hidden cost was calculated by four managers to reach over $28,000 per year. When starting working by numbers, it is impressive to see people asking how they might create an antivirus, because it means that they realized they are losing money. At the horizontal level, the estimated hidden costs reached $77,000 per year.

Barbara Milon

The Center's total annual budget was about 1.4 million dollars—so $77,000 in hidden costs was significant for a small organization. It became clear that it was important to understand the ways in which these dysfunctions contributed to our inability to be productive and focus on our mission. As an organization serving the Twin Cities, we are proud and responsible for focusing our programs and services on area children and families. If we can improve what we are doing, then we are adding value back into the organization. As a nonprofit organization, our bottom-line is not to seek and earn profit but to be able to control the costs while enhancing our services.

The Expert Opinion

During the expert opinion phase, the consultants explicitly share their thoughts and insights about the data, providing their interpretation of the company's diagnosis. Within the SEAM process, however, there are rules that shape way in which this expert opinion is delivered. First, the consultants share the summary of key dysfunctions, followed by their own observations of unvoiced concerns, what the French call the "*non dit.*" Then the root causes of dysfunctions are identified and based on this, themes for corrective action. Finally projects for corrective work are suggested. If the order of these steps is followed, then the logic of change work is very obvious to the organization.

Alla Heorhiadi

Although the expert opinion might seem to consist of bullet points that have almost a chronic nature, it is an important step in the process of helping the organization to understand its current state. An initial concern we had was that in the United States people might not understand this kind of subtle message—we were thinking that they needed more direct guidance. Overall, the entire experience was very positive, and it was clear that people did understand the message. They might have been overwhelmed at first, but the message did appear to make them think.

Barbara Milon

Faced with this expert opinion, there was initial skepticism. For instance, one staff member was holding back and wanted to wait and see, but her distrust is now changing. I knew SEAM was making a difference when she stated that she was glad we were engaged in the SEAM process.

As the executive director, I wonder how we will sustain SEAM so it does not become one of those things that we begin but never finish. Thinking about the various tools that are part of SEAM, for example, a conscious effort is needed to enable leaders to truly move forward. SEAM has to be something that is consistent and systematic, something that becomes part of the system.

As we took more steps through the SEAM process, the engagement became institutionalized. I like that part because when I was first hired part of my mission in the Community was to change the business culture. Since then, the Center successfully restructured, paid its debts and received some forgiveness of debt, achieved a breakeven point, and stabilized its operation. Looking back, it was a lot of hard work—shedding some tears and facing fears along the way, but working with very good people and always being supported by our Board of Directors. It has been a challenge—trying to see beyond roughly $200,000 in liabilities that have to be shrunk down and getting to a breakeven point. As we realized, if the Center's staff members did not integrate our mission, we would not be able to do anything effectively. SEAM is not just a theory—it is a process that provides something very special in the organization.

IMPROVING THROUGH THE SEAM PROCESS

Barbara Milon

The SEAM process taught us how to solicit from donors and contributors to support our mission. Through a participatory method in the horizontal intervention project stage, the staff has been able to come together with ideas to improve the organization's functioning. An important step forward was that the staff began to see their role in solving this problem.

There were two SEAM groups led by two team leaders, who were not managers but had the ability to lead these groups. This type of involvement further helps the organization to groom leadership by engaging other members with leadership skills. The SEAM tools help support the organization's development and leadership, and these two emerging leaders have been assuming increasing responsibility and each group has continued to come up with different ideas.

The first SEAM management tool is the competency grid. During the follow-up meetings with our team leaders, this tool was handed out and we discussed what competencies are needed for our group to be effective. Another tool is the SEAM Four Leaf Clover. SEAM leaders now better understand when we talk about structures and behaviors. For instance, we took an entire day to reorganize staff offices, getting rid of 75 cubic foot containers of "stuff." The SEAM Four Leaf Clover helped us to more fully understand the relationships of structures, behaviors, dysfunctions, and hidden costs.

We also manage our time by using technology as an enhancement to support scheduling the facility. The idea is by using Microsoft Outlook any member of the organization will be able to see what opportunities are available for scheduling and space utilization.

Although the Center does not experience significant conflict, the project group recommended that we create a conflict management handbook. One of the members, who is a doctoral student, helped us facilitate this process. The conflict management handbook was introduced and presented to all our staff and is accessible on the Shared Use computer folder. Personally, I consider conflict management from a positive perspective, and it can be a useful tool supporting a productive work environment. The conflict handbook provided a process that helps our staff to give voice to those areas are contentious, to know where there may be disagreement, and to know how they can handle disagreement in a learning and constructive way.

As mentioned before, after the intervention we have more engaging conversations during our meetings. Individual members have also become much more aware about their time and accountability within this group. The questions they ask and their expectations have changed as well. One of the ISEOR intervener-researchers visited the Center and met our SEAM team. When asked if SEAM was making a difference, one of the team members reinforced that that it was really helping. Given their comments and exchange, I am confident that we are moving forward together.

Being an executive director involves many different external and internal responsibilities. However, through the SEAM engagement and the development of human potential, we are better able to conceptualize the reality that we face. In the Center, we can feel that there is a lot of collected energy, not always visible, but we realize that we are not stagnating.

Alla Heorhiadi

Reflecting on the comments above, the person who responded to the ISEOR intervener-researcher was the most resistant team member at the beginning of the intervention. During her interview, she said that she experienced many consultants and did not trust them at all anymore. Three months later with SEAM, she became a leader of the project with a new approach to conflict management. Such turnarounds create hope for organizations.

We assume that the Center will keep moving. At this point, the major portion of the intervention has been completed and the client seems to be pleased with the SEAM process and our consultant role. Going forward, our role is only to assist them in the moving process, because the Center now has SEAM champions that illustrate how the process can sustain itself. It is definitely different from a short-term intervention coming into a company, doing something quick, and potentially going back. With SEAM, you teach the organization to fish.

REFERENCES

Collins, J. (2001). *Good to great: Why some companies make the lead . . . and others don't.* New York, NY: Harper Business.

Conbere, J. P., & Heorhiadi, A. (2011). Socio-economic approach to management: A successful systemic approach to organizational change. *Organization Development Practitioner, 43*(1), 6–10.

Savall, H., & Zardet, V. (2008). *Mastering hidden costs and socio-economic performance.* Charlotte, NC: Information Age Publishing.

APPENDIX:
Conference Dialogue

Conference Participant who had been part of the PWCC Intervention: In a meeting I attended last week, it was remarkable how the staff was fixing things even as we were going through the mirror effect. This quick action is one of the dynamics I think SEAM provides.

CHAPTER 7

SOCIO-ECONOMIC APPROACH TO MANAGEMENT WITHIN MEXICAN PUBLIC ORGANIZATIONS

Raúl Arceo Alonzo, Martha Margarita Fernández Ruvalcaba, and Véronique Zardet

CONFERENCE REMARKS:
Chapter Prologue

Raúl Arceo Alonzo

This section concerns my experience with the socio-economic model and its implementation in the unit of Human Resource Policies of the Federal Government of Mexico Ministries. Before implementing the SEAM model in Mexico, I had worked with ISEOR in the Yucatán State government and Ministry of Administration. That first implementation resulted into SEAM certification by ISEOR. As I later went to work with the Federal government, I saw an opportunity to implement the model to improve efficacy.

Facilitating the Socioeconomic Approach to Management, pages 75–93
Copyright © 2014 by Information Age Publishing
All rights of reproduction in any form reserved.

SEAM AS A PROCESS OF CHANGE
IN MEXICAN ORGANIZATIONS

The Unit of Human Resources Policy is a department of the Federal Government Ministry of Public Administration. It sets up and implements public policies on human resources for 282 institutions counting more than one million public employees. The unit is composed of a director of general offices and five general directors. In 2010, the unit suffered a severe downsizing, with a decrease in the number of employees from 128 to 88. Moreover, the remaining public servants were kept far from their duties, assigned to other areas of the ministry. This change had a widespread, negative impact, causing a lack of integration of the entire administrative and operational staff. It also resulted in a decrease in its attraction to the general public, resulting in a poor external image of the unit.

The socio-economic intervention began in February 2011 through a horizontal and vertical diagnosis. Two top managers and ten middle managers were interviewed in the horizontal diagnosis. The vertical diagnosis consisted of interviews with eleven groups. A consulting team helped the external consultants in their intervention. While the external consultants were from ISEOR and the Autonomous Metropolitan University of Mexico, the internal consultants were directors. The work was organized through five clusters (see Figure 7.1).

The diagnosis revealed that hidden costs represented 10% of the budget. These hidden costs resulted mainly from excess time, non-production and non-creation of potential. The diagnosis phases were extremely complicated because the public servants did not want to change the way they worked. To reduce the dysfunctions, we organized groups that worked on proposals that reached 75 actions, focused on:

- improving the quality of the labor environment and working conditions;
- reducing excessive of interruptions;
- improving the flow of supplies on basic equipment;
- clarifying the communicated attributions of roles of the Unit and its staff;
- improving the quality of service provided to internal and external users;
- developing concerted delegation between hierarchical levels, accompanied by integrated training on the roles and the use of tools of strategy implementation;
- determining internal devices of communication, coordination and cooperation;
- developing stimulated management practices (e.g., by holding weekly meetings with team members); and

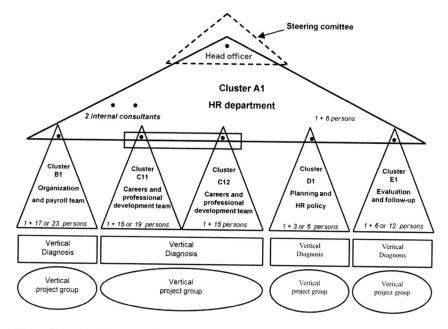

Figure 7.1 Architecture of the intervention in the Unit of Human Resources of the Ministry of Administration—Government of Mexico.

- defining a strategy on the information system concerning the internal and external actions of the unit, involving the entire staff for the strategy implementation.

The intervention was followed by personalized assistance on socio-economic tools. In 2012, ISEOR conducted a socio-economic evaluation of the Unit, including: an Internal and External Strategic Action Plan (IESAP), 22 Priority Action Plans (PAP), 22 Periodically Negotiable Activity Contracts (PNAC), 11 Strategy Piloting Logbooks, and 21 Competency Grids.

Gains in Efficiency and Serenity

Since the beginning of the process, the interviews indicated that organizational members observed more support facilities, improvements in the supply of equipment for servants, a better working environment, a process of work simplification, a better sense of autonomy and accountability, and a general improvement in efficiency and rigor in the implementation of projects. We also improved communication through the application of different tools, including bulletin reports for general meetings and a more united work team through better services to our customers and better planning of actions.

In November 2012, the Unit was SEAM certified by ISEOR for two years. In order to maintain and improve the implementation of the model in the Unit, the intervener-researchers stressed the need to improve cross-functional and cross-departmental communication, implement competency grids in all areas, develop further discussion on 30 more Competency Grids, improve the pursuit of efficiency and effectiveness, and finally improve collective time management. This event will be "carved in stone" to remind the following government and its future president that these reforms modified the public administration through the application of SEAM. This action is set because the Ministry of Public Administration will be erased and the Unit is to be transferred to the Ministry of Finance. Our hope is that the model will be kept despite the disruption—but this might be difficult to accomplish.

INTRODUCTION: THE EXTERNAL CONSULTANT'S REMARKS

The following section provides a description of the application of SEAM inside a Mexican Governmental organization from the vantage point of the external consultant.[1] These notes, in addition to the ones provided by the head of the organization where SEAM was applied (the Conference Remarks section of the chapter) provide a more complete overview of the process and its results.

The intervention took place from February 2011 to May 2012 in the Human Resources Policy Making Unit (UPHR) of the Public Service Subsecretary of the Federal Government Agency for Public Service (Secretaría de la Función Publica—SFP).[2] The engagement involved a complete cycle of SEAM implementation in both dimensions, horizontal and vertical, and included every phase of the SEAM process: diagnosis, project design, implementation, and evaluation. It also included training in SEAM concepts, techniques, and tools.

Background

SFP's main goal is to improve the performance of all agencies constituting the executive branch of the federal government. Its services were organized into four units corresponding to priority factors: (a) human resources, (b) information and communication technologies, (c) planning processes for implementation, and (d) improving established practices and embracing a culture of self-evaluation. An internal policy was also implemented requiring an assessment at the conclusion of each process. The SFP (deputy ministry of public function) was organized into four units, but the Ministry of Public function included more departments.

UPHR was been given the major task of making sure that every agency at the federal government level would have the talent required in order to best fulfil their functions. For this goal, UPHR established a professional human resources function (see Table 7.1).

Table 7.2 describes the objectives of the three other units at the Subsecretary. It is quite important to point out that cross-departmental cooperation is required to better accomplish the objectives of each government agency and, of course, within this units of SFP. So in order to set an example, the SFP would have to implement SEAM itself.

Public Service Career is a key reference for UPHR; it was first established in the Federal executive branch in April 2003, by means of law. The act established the Public Service Career as a mechanism that promotes and warrants equal opportunity in access to jobs in public service, based purely on merit. It also seeks to develop public service administration to benefit society (Article 2 of the Service Career Act). Intending to decentralize the Federal Government administration, new statutory rules were passed in 2007, the Public Service Career mechanism was to be decentralized into a more flexible scheme of implementation, with the intent of easing the flux of information to be analyzed and assessed.

To more fully understand the context in which the external consultants were hired, in 2010, after the publication of the SFP internal regulations,

---

TABLE 7.1   Services Offered by the Human Resources Policy Making Unit

Services

- Consultation regarding the Government bureaucracy career and human resources at the Federal Government
- Public Servants Unified Register management
- Managing human resources data bases and information systems
- Registry of Organizational and occupational structures in the Federal public Government
- Registry of wage or salary scales at the Federal Government.
- Validating of posts valuations at the Federal Government
- Registry of contracts within dependent professionals by Federal Agencies
- Consultation regarding organizational and occupational structures, post valuation, compensation, independent services, risk premium, the national prize for Federal public service and organizational climate

Source: http://www.funcionpublica.gob.mx/index.php/ua.html (accessed September 20, 2013)

TABLE 7.2 Objectives of the Three Other Units at the Sub-Secretary for Public Service

	Services	
e-Government Unit	Public Administration Improvement Policy Unit	Management and Organizational Performance Policy Unit
Fostering and promoting the use of Information and Communication Technologies in all processes within the Federal Government in order to strengthen governance and improve the delivering of services	Maximizing the quality of processes and services provided by the Federal Government to the fulfillment of citizens expectations. All of this through the improvement and certification of processes, the adoption of better practices, disregarding excessive standards or over regulation, providing tools for increasing effectiveness and cut down operation costs.	Designing and developing tools and methodologies for a comprehensive assessment of management and government performance in the Federal bureaucracy, including the issuance of guidelines, criteria, standards, systemic and permanent mechanisms of coordination, in the search of instilling a culture of self-evaluation.

Source: http://www.funcionpublica.gob.mx/index.php/ua.html (accessed September 20, 2013)

the staff of UPHR was decreased by roughly 30% (it went from 128 to only 88 persons). The remaining staff was highly dissatisfied with the new working conditions—they felt that the new offices were far too small, they lacked privacy, and diminished their access to employee-related amenities. The UPRH downsizing took place in 2009 and early 2010, before the publication of the new internal regulations.

The Actors and the Process

Implementation of the SEAM engagement involved a series of interrelated phases:

1. Collaborative training and personal assistance on the use of the SEAM model and its different tools. Emphasis was placed on improvement of time management (tool: self-assessment of time); communication–coordination–cooperation (tools: agenda and resolution charts), individuals' competences in relation to their posts (tool: competency grid), and strategic planning (tools: internal and external strategic actions plan, priority actions plan, piloting logbook, periodically negotiable activity contract).
2. A horizontal diagnosis covering typical dysfunctions at the executive level.

3. A vertical diagnosis covering typical dysfunctions in the operational level of the 4 analyzed departments and an illustration of the amount of hidden costs related to their regulation (e.g., the lack of a unified and clear policy over days off[3]). Table 7.3 presents a summary of hidden costs found.
4. A project to reduce dysfunctions revealed through the horizontal diagnosis. Six baskets of action were set (See Table 7.4).
5. A vertical diagnosis in the 4 departments: group interviews were conducted among operational staff; hidden costs caused by regulation were estimated.
6. Vertical projects: focus groups came to the conclusion that action baskets set for the horizontal project could define concrete activities in the 4 departments.
7. Implementation of the improvement project and its evaluation. In some cases implementation was immediately accomplished. As an example, recurrent use of the resolution chart (UPHR used a similar tool, which was not effectively used): following the agenda, keeping schedules and deadlines, writing down resolutions and agreements, consulting and reading them to every participant, and so forth.

Gradual changes were also observed. For example, efforts to improve time management resulted in reductions to the time allocated to the regulation of dysfunctions and tasks not properly assigned. The implementation plan was not met in other cases, for example, the periodically negotiable activity contract; evaluation was done through interviewing directors and staff, who had to provide evidence to back their opinions.

The consulting group was composed of 4 external consultants (EC) and 8 internal consultants (IC). Two of the ECs were based in the same city where the organization object of the analyses was located and two were in France. In consideration of budget restrictions, time schedules, and services that were deemed necessary, 8 internal consultants were appointed.

The intervention architecture (see Figure 7.1) sets the members of the UPHR in clusters to participate in the required activities to implement SEAM model. This intervention architecture was organized into one steering committee, one core group, one wider task force, and six focus groups. The steering committee included the Head of UPHR, the General Director of Human Development and Public Service Career, and four external consultants (EC). One core group included the members of the steering committee and the other three general directors: Organization and Wages, Evaluation and Continuity, and Human Resources Policy. Their role was to authorize proposals made by each of the focus groups in the six strategic baskets. One wider project group, which included the members of the core group and 21 directors as well as eight internal consultants (IC),

TABLE 7.3 Hidden Cost Analysis Overview

Hidden Costs Abstract

	Over Wages	Overtime	Over Intakes	Nonproduction	Nonpotential Development	Risks	TOTAL
Absenteeism	N.E.	N.E.	N.E.	$1,656, 576	N.E.	N.E.	$1,656,576
Work accidents	N.E.	N.E.	N.E.	N.E.	N.E.	N.E.	$0
Personnel turnover	N.E.	N.E.	N.E.	N.E.	N.E.	N.E.	$0
Product quality	N.E.	$1,212,800	N.E.	N.E.	N.E.	N.E.	$1,212,800
Direct productivity variance	N.E.	$6,456,278	N.E.	$3,190,872	$1,724,251	N.E.	$11,371,401
Total	$ 0	$7,669,078	$0	$4,847,448	$724, 251	$ 0	$14,240,777

Note: Full time personnel = 85; that is 167,539 Mexican pesos per person annually; N.E.=Not estimated, due to short time for intervention

TABLE 7.4   Illustrative Dysfunctions in Basket 1

Dysfunctions Related to Working Environment	Dysfunctions Related to Time Management	Dysfunctions Related to Strategy Implementation
Basket 1: Improvement of working environment and working conditions; reduction of interruptions and last minute tasks, improving office supplies and basic equipment		
• Settings and everyday cleaning of the offices brings discomfort and reduces concentration at work. Lack of privacy in working spaces as well as not enough meeting rooms has a negative effect in the quality of services delivered personally or by phone. • Among other factors perceived by the staff as obstructing their performance are the bad conditions of hardware, software, access to internet, office supplies, lack of useful appliances as answering machines or no breaks.	Due to the common practice to change both priorities and the agenda set, the staff has to put up with extra responsibilities. Any change in the agenda at higher levels could generate a wipe effect that increases in lower levels, causing delays and diminishing quality in final results.	Distrust towards the information systems generates uncertainty (for example, a number of certified public servers in the HRnet could drastically change in 2 hours)

was directed to detect possible inconsistencies among the different cluster's proposals and to propose alternatives.

Six different task forces were created during the horizontal project phase. A member of the wider group led each of the working groups playing a proactive role toward the wider task force and the core group in charge of conciliating decisions affecting their spheres of responsibility. A brief description of actors and their programmed activities is shown in the following planning scheme (Table 7.5).

One plenary group, which was comprised of all of the members of UPHR, was informed three times about advancements that were attained in each phase of the project. All plenary group requests, such as making more practical suggestions, were complied with.

Another part of the process involved training the IC and keeping the schedule. There were four primary objectives ruling the contract of services between ISEOR and UPHR: (a) introducing a common and shared model of management; (b) aligning UPHR in the Federal public administration in order to achieve socio-economic performance objectives; (c) standardizing tools and processes in socio-economic management; and (d) developing training programs for the staff. To facilitate the ability to reach these goals, the consultants' know how, methods, and actions were clearly defined. A

TABLE 7.5 Intervention Planning: Synchronization of Horizontal and Vertical Actions

ACTIONS / MONTHS	Feb. 2011	March 2011	April 2011	May 2011	Jun 2011	July 2011	August 2011	Sept. 2011	October 2011	Nov. 2011	Dec. 2011
1. Steering group (8 sessions)	1			2			3			4	
2. Collaborative training . Board of Directors A1 (6 sessions)	1		2	3		4	5	6			
3. Collective collaborative training . Clusters B1, C11, C12, D1, E1 (6 sessions)	1		2		3	4	5	6			
4. Personal assistance . Head Officer. (4 sessions) individual 1p.	2			3			1			4	
5. Personalized assistance . Board of Directors individual (5 sessions)		1		2		3	4	5		6	
6. Personalized assistance collective (5 sessions)			1		2	3	4		5		6
7. Horizontal Diagnostic *											
8. Focus group . Board of Directors and management (4 sessions)						1	2	3		4	
9. Fourth in depth vertical Diagnostic *											
10. Fourth vertical focus group (4 sessions)								1	2	3	4
11. Monitoring and technical coaching assistance of the internal consulting team	x	x	x	x	x	x	x	x	x	x	x
12. Synchronization and integrated training of the internal consulting team	1		2	3		4	5		6	7	

Legend: ▨ Services taken in charge by Dr Henri SAVALL and Dra Véronique ZARDET with the collaboration of the external consultants
⊛ Services taken in charge by the external consultants   *: Services taken in charge by the external and internal consultants
● Services taken in charge by the internal consultants

ISEOR 2011

scheme was created that indicated the details for each service, participants, and persons in charge of their operation (see Table 7.6 for an example).

Created as a consultancy-research method, SEAM goes beyond analyses of technical operations and provides expertise in conducting processes that improve the overall performance of organizations. People in executive positions are considered to have the most powerful leverage in order to fully engage operational-level employees with the organization's objectives. Therefore collaborative training and personal assistance of the personnel are two key services that are implemented. The client, in this case the head of UPHR, has decision-making power with respect to contract specifications (e.g., costs, objectives, time frame) and is the main interlocutor for the consultants.

Training a large group of internal consultants was meant to reduce intervention costs to a limit that was reachable by UPHR. ISEOR has a general purpose in its interventions to provide the assessed entity with the skills and capacities to independently handle the tools and processes of socio-economic management. The eight internal consultants (IC) accepted this role, even when it meant an extra work load. They also accepted the challenge of completing tasks they did not master and showed a positive attitude towards the extended implementation of the new model among their colleagues. They played a very important role in getting the ICs involved, accepting all risks implied. An assessment meeting was programmed monthly, during which the ICs and ECs could expose and discuss their impressions and agree over them, for as long as the process took place.

Particularities of the Process

While SEAM has developed a general theory of organizational performance, it also admits that each entity has particular aspects that influence the different modalities in which the process to conduct actions of improvement is manifested. Having conducted a successful experience applying SEAM as well as having been in a position of power with adequate resources, there were very high expectations about SEAM's application. Implementation in UPHR, however, diverged from the process originally designed by ISEOR due to changing circumstances.

First, there was limited decision power. A new set of norms made it very difficult to contract the consultancy. This obstacle was overcome by redefining the terms of the contract, giving priority to training on the use of the model and its tools, and using the diagnosis, project draft, implementation, and assessment phases as means of verifying the appropriation of the tools.

Second, the appointment of the project leader to the UPRH was made in the last two years of the Administration period (an appointment that lasts 6 years). The team was already set up and since there had been a recent

TABLE 7.6 Objectives, Methods, and Services Related to SEAM Implementation in the Unit of Human Resources Policy

Products-Objectives	Products-Methods	Products-Services
No. 2 1. To set a common shared management method 2. Alignment of different visions and practices inside the UHRP to achieve socio-economic performance objectives. 3. To standardize socio-economic management process and tools. 4. To develop potential capabilities	**Collaborative Training Action and Personal Assistance for the Board Directors About the Socio-Economic Management Tools** • Mastering concrete and easy management tools • Transposing and implementaion of shared common work methods • Couching to customize and implement the strategic project	**Integration of 1 Board Director's Collaborative Training Cluster:** • Cluster A1 (Unit of Human Resources policy): 1 + 3 persons + Internal Consultant • Three collaborative training sessions, 2.5 hours each one, taken in charge by the ISEOR consultants with the participation of external and internal consultants; operating frequency around one time by month. • Three sessions carry-out without the ISEOR presence

Source: ISEOR 2011

process of downsizing, there was negative environment with high levels of mistrust and a permanent threat of firing.

Third, the budget was limited, making it impossible to hire more time for the external consultant. To respond to this challenge, a senior researcher from a public university who was fully conversant with the SEAM methodology was brought in as an external consultant. To complement and support the activities of the senior consultant, a junior consultant was hired.

Fourth, there was slow adoption of the new mission. Originally, being part of the Contraloria General de la Federacion (General Controller), the UPHR was conceived as a controlling unit, focused on accountability. As it became part of the Secretaria de Contraloría y Desarrollo Administrativo, its controlling functions were reduced by accepting that control functions were related to development and the processes of learning gained importance. This new perspective was adopted in 2003, when the UPHR was presented as a planning and consulting unit strongly focused in the Public Service Career. However, events such as the downsizing and change in working conditions were perceived by the members of the Unit as a clear sign that their objectives were just a facade.

Fifth, a number of challenges remained, including the need to synchronize the activities of the 12 consultants and reach homogeneous quality and methodology alignment among the services provided by the internal consultants. Initially some of the ICs tried to show they had previous consulting experience with a different, and in their opinion, superior methodology. This behavior slowly turned different as training sessions, individual personal assistance, and meetings with the CEO of the Unit and the external consultants took place, as expectations were set and steps to achieve them were planned.

Finally, a number of issues were never mentioned. The external consultants observed some particularities that were not expressed by the staff during the diagnosis phase. The formal organizational structure did not correspond to the one observed in practice. Norms ruling structure modifications inhibited any formalization of the changes that were implemented, even when most of the norms were created by the UPHR.

The organizational structure also responded to political power. Some staff members identified issues or dysfunctions that were not included in the baskets of possible solutions since there was a general acceptance of their role as power symbols. An evidence of this culture was seen in the appointment of personnel in the units as the organization was unbalanced in the size of its units (some having figures as low as 6 members compared to 40, the largest had) and there was no real option or will to modify the structure. There was also a lack of disciplinary actions for staff members with little or no interest or involvement in improving the Unit's performance. Overall, political dynamics created a poor environment and promoted negative behavior patterns.

The criteria for decision making were also highly ambiguous. There was no clarity in the rules and guidelines for assigning resources, tasks, even permissions or reasons to decide to put an end to the working relationship. There were also signs that there was significant opposition to long-rooted habits. In Mexico, it is generally expected that the government bureaucracy, especially at high levels, surreptitiously changes priorities without encountering any resistance. This also observed during the first months of the intervention, but different from a conforming attitude shown in most personnel. Once the comprehensive improvement plan was adopted, the staff was able to stand up and argue in favor of the priorities formerly established. The planning document provided the staff with arguments and solid criteria (actions, timing, persons in charge, resources) to preserve previous priorities.

RESULTS AND LEARNED LESSONS

Drawing the estimated hidden costs turned out to be a very important exercise, it triggered everyone's energy into the project, promoting due engagement (see Table 7.3). As a result of the horizontal diagnosis, 6 baskets of solutions were drawn, which were found suitable to overcome the dysfunctions identified in the vertical diagnosis. There was also a relation between the 6 baskets and their associated dysfunctions. As an example, Table 7.4 illustrates one of the baskets and its related dysfunctions. Each cluster or focus group was assigned one basket, under the direction of a manager, and they had to propose concrete actions to overcome the dysfunctions. At the end of each descriptive sentence for each basket, the number of members constituting the group is mentioned. Table 7.7 presents a sample of concrete actions associated with Basket 6.

1. To improve working environment and working conditions, reduction of interruptions and last minute tasks, and improving office supplies and basic equipment (3 members).
2. To clearly set and communicate attributions and roles in each of the 4 departments in order to improve the quality of services delivered to in-house and external users (e.g., other government offices and citizens) (6 members) .
3. To negotiate delegation of responsibilities among hierarchical positions with clear rules, using tools for strategy implementation and follow up (4 members).
4. To identify means of internal communication–coordination–cooperation needed individually or collectively, and define their correspondent functions horizontally and vertically (4 members).
5. To develop demanding and stimulating human resources management practices (4 members).
6. To design a strategy on information systems that includes internal and external actions and involves all the staff in its implementation (4 members).

These baskets allowed for the identification of 75 concrete actions to improve the performance of the UPHR (see Table 7.7).

Executive evaluation was made by ISEOR consultants using the "Grid for Certification of Executives" (see Table 7.8) that covers two core components: competencies and behavior. Achievement levels were noted as follow: (a) regular and efficient practice–mastered; b) occasional practices or not entirely mastered; c) knowledge of principles without practice; d) no knowledge nor practice; and e) to be built. The level of achievement was supported with evidence presented by the directors.

The following quotes were captured during evaluation sessions and indicate part of the advancement gained by applying SEAM:

- "SEAM is a change management model that requires many changes in habits. That should be strengthened. The original idea was to ap-

TABLE 7.7 Sample of Concrete Actions in Basket 6 in the Project

General Dysfunction/ Aimed Objective	Specific Dysfunction	Suggested Solutions	Execution/Viability Phase	Priority
Basket 6: To design a strategy on information systems that includes internal and external actions and involves all the staff in its implementation				
Inconsistent Data Bases/Need for more reliable data bases	Authorization of each data modification originated in not automatized flows of information (i.e., Correcting dates) (e.g., Art 25 RLSPC Cambios de puestos eventuales a puestos del SPC)	To document processes with occasional data modifications	Processes and services/viable in the short time	2.2
		To Define documents, formats and standards to be used to document processes with occasional data modifications	Processes and services/viable in the short time	3.2
		Automatized modules to update data delayed due to operational delays; allowing for a record of modifications.	Implementation improvement systems/hardly viable in the short time	19.0

TABLE 7.8 Matrix of Preparation for Certification: Directors

Competences / Positions	Management	Technical Competences						Behavioral or Soft Competences				Comments	Certification Proposal
		Use of Logbook Tool	Use of Priority Action Plans Tool	Use of Competency Grid Tool	Use of Periodically Negotiable Activity Contract Tool	Conduction of Innovative Socio-Economic Actions	Conduction of Socio-Economic Management (SEAM)	Commitment	Change Energy	Rigor	Professional Loyalty		
Director URHP			■										
Direction A													
Direction B													
Direction C													
Direction D													

Legend: ■ = Regular and efficient practice–mastered; □ = Knowledge of principles without practice; ▨ = Occasional practices or not entirely mastered; .... = No knowledge nor practice—to be built

ply it as a pilot program in the Unit and then have it applied in the
rest of the Administration."

- "There was no management model, management worked only if the
leader was good. The intention was to certify management processes. This affected the Human Resources handbook; the competency
grid is valued as a tool for other organizations to detect their needs.
Before the competence grid was applied, any one could do it their
own way."

- "When we were working on this year's Organizational Culture and
Environment Poll, we considered the concept and estimation of hidden costs. This poll included 5 or 6 contributions from the SEAM
model."

- "The competency grid was also considered in the Human Resources
handbook . . . the program for public service career, in the section
concerning evaluation of performance. If there were no more significant incidences it is because it is hard to achieve cultural changes. People did what they should."

- "The Subsecretary has mentioned that he observes a better organized functioning of the Unit. Outsiders' perception of the Unit is
better now."

- "Opinions reflect that it is better to have something organized than
nothing at all. That is what attributing sense and organizing means
and that is precisely what all the administration needs. At the end,
the Secretary recognized we were right. We were perceived as the
worst of all the Units, but at the end he recognized we were in the
best position. What the Subsecretary saw was an organized Unit,
with clear objectives. The Subsecretary said publicly in various occasions: the most important and transcending result were those of the
UPHR. It was evident we were following a model; we had tools other
units did not have. Even as regards punctuality, statistics show this
unit was the most punctual."

Added to the results, there was an opportune observance of activities stated in the original planning, even against adverse modifications in the environment due to the imminent change of the political party in power. During
the consultation, many unplanned issues intervened that altered the internal
consultants' participation—including ceasing to work in the unit before entering the project phase, medical leave, and overload with unexpected superior requests not considered in the planning. However, commitment and
cooperation overcame these obstacles. This experience reveals that when
people experience conditions where collaboration pays off it is possible to
go forward. It is clearly worth trying, even in the presence of the extreme
adverse circumstances as were present in this case in most of the entities of

the Federal Government Administration. The most valuable lesson learned was that gaining the conviction that, no matter what, it is always possible to conceive a plan, to follow it, and to reach the expected results.

NOTES

1. Martha Margarita Fernández Ruvalcaba thanks the intervener-researchers who participated in this pilot intervention: Henri Savall and Véronique Zardet and the junior external consultant Julio Julián Hernández Fernández.
2. This federal government agency has worked under different denominations; it is undergoing a restructuring process to a public constitutional organization, which will be endowed with anticorruption powers.
3. Federal government employees have the right to take up 10 days off provided they have the authorization of their direct supervisor. The directives withhold a discretionary power to provide the mentioned authorization.

APPENDIX:
Conference Dialogue

Conference Participant: Why would 30 or more competency grids be audited? Where will those be found?

Raúl Arceo Alonzo: The Unit is composed of four general directors and 20 directors of different areas. Each general director has a specific competency grid for his or her area. This structure is the reason why we need more specific competencies to be analyzed and improved.

Conference Participant: A comment was made about the critical situation of this entity of the Mexican Government. It is a pity that the Unit is to be eliminated because it was in charge of overseeing the performance of public services—more than two million people depend on the mission supported by that public service. The work that the Unit has done with SEAM is outstanding because of the specificity of this area.

John Conbere: You mentioned the Unit was a very disobedient team. We would like to know if they remained disobedient at the end of the process. If not, what may have caused the change?

Raúl Arceo Alonzo: At the end, we had a group with integrated people. The stimulation of training, the partition of missions, and the fact that they were now speaking the same "language"—which were all brought by the SEAM intervention—played a major role in the change.

CHAPTER 8

USING SEAM AS THE PHILOSOPHICAL BASIS FOR A GRADUATE CONSULTING PROGRAM

Employing Diverse Consulting Tools and Approaches

Lawrence Lepisto and Randall Hayes

In 2000 a faculty team was charged with building a Management Consulting concentration in our MBA program. We found few models for such programs until we built a relationship with ISEOR and its SEAM framework. We subsequently participated in numerous training programs in SEAM and the approach became the foundation of the new concentration. The Institute for Management Consulting (IMC) initiated its program in the fall of 2003 and ran through 2011, when the university administration decided to discontinue funding for niche programs such as the IMC.

Facilitating the Socioeconomic Approach to Management, pages 95–100
Copyright © 2014 by Information Age Publishing
All rights of reproduction in any form reserved.

THE ACADEMIC PROGRAM
IN MANAGEMENT CONSULTING

The program enrolled a cohort of students for two contiguous semesters, with MBA students and doctoral students from the Industrial/Organizational Psychology program constituting most of the enrollment. Each year, there were three or four consulting engagements that were integrated into the program. These were paid engagements, and depending on the extent of the services the fee ranged from $5,000 to $8,000. The fee provided assurance that the client would treat the engagement seriously, students would feel sufficient pressure to perform, and it would generate funds to help sustain the program.

Clients and Engagements

Clients ranged from large corporations such as Dow Chemical, Dow Corning, and Domino's Pizza to mid-sized companies and start-ups. The nature of the engagements was wide ranging, including SEAM interventions and a variety of other engagements including marketing research studies, pricing studies, and process improvement projects. The program incorporated a practicum model in class where the consulting teams presented the progress of their engagements to the class, referred to as Engagement Updates, on what had transpired in their engagements every other week. This exchange allowed the entire class to follow and learn from the challenges encountered in the respective engagements.

Incorporating Additional Consulting Tools

It became evident to the faculty that other consulting tools would be needed as the variety of engagements widened. We also felt that graduates of the program should be exposed to the variety of management consulting tools and protocols currently used in the U.S. consulting community.

An advisory board of current and retired consultants met annually with the faculty to evaluate the curriculum and practices of the IMC. They made several important suggestions to make the program more consistent with their experience in the consulting industry. As an example, the board believed that students needed more explicit exposure to project planning and related planning tools such as Microsoft Project and critical path analysis. Another suggestion was to include a "hypothesis-testing" approach as used by many U.S. consulting firms. This approach minimized consultant intrusion into the client's activities by the early identification of probable organizational or procedural problems through initial interviews and review of available data. From that assessment, the consultant forms initial hypotheses, and then collects data to test those hypotheses.

A third suggestion from the board focused on the adoption of a corporate culture measure, such as the Denison Organization Culture Survey, incorporating it into the program and, when appropriate, applying it in selected engagements. The board and faculty also believed that Six Sigma—the "language" of industrial engineers—was important for process improvement projects and it became our frame of reference for process improvement projects in the manufacturing area. Finally, both the board and the faculty came to realize that we needed to provide additional coverage of management tools and perspectives meant to encourage and implement innovations. It was frequently a challenge to guide our clients to develop a future-oriented perspective instead of day-to-day crisis management. Too often, their focus was on their existing operations and products, while paying little attention to the possibility of exploring new opportunities or operating more entrepreneurially.

Because clients used the IMC program as a "helping hands" option, we tended to develop consulting engagements that had a well-defined scope and specific deliverables. In addition, we had a defined timeline since students met their clients for the first time in early October and the engagements had to be completed by late April.

FORMAL APPLICATIONS OF SEAM IN THE PROGRAM

SEAM was incorporated into the program by teaching its tools, presenting the approach's underlying philosophy, and by demonstrating its direct application in various engagements.

SEAM Tools

All students learned numerous SEAM techniques by emphasizing certain techniques of the SEAM protocol. These included transformation of demand (termed it "shaping the engagement" because that phrase was clearer to students), the mirror effect, hidden costs, priority action plans, strategic piloting indicators, HoriVert analysis, strategic assessment, and team/project management tools. We also taught the need for well-crafted expert opinions. Finally, we emphasized the need to keep the application of SEAM tools synchronized between the process improvement dimension, the strategic assessment dimension, and the management development dimension.

The SEAM Philosophy

While we covered a range of tools and approaches, the SEAM philosophy was interwoven throughout the entire program. A guiding theme was that the root of all issues in an organization was people: their perceptions, concerns, and behaviors. Policies and strategies, in the end, must be interpreted and applied by organizational members. We also encouraged students to accept the philosophy that they are working with the client, rather than for the client. We emphasized that it was important to have the client work through the engagement with the consultants so they would trust the process and the results of the engagement. We also emphasized that it would enhance the clients' understanding of their own organizations and the nature of necessary organizational changes.

Unlike some American consulting firms who promise to "get in and get out," SEAM understands the need for the client to become part of the engagement and also become engaged in the engagement. We incorporated the SEAM orientation that changing the client's organization over the long term is as important as the more narrow focus of the engagement. And the client's organization is really the people who work and manage in the organization.

SEAM Engagements

The IMC had a number of engagements that were solely focused on applying the SEAM protocol. Often, the decision to adopt SEAM came from early meetings, held months before the engagements started, that revealed that the client didn't adequately understand the origin or depth of their organizational problems. On these occasions, we were often able to convince the client that the first engagement should follow the SEAM approach. This would help them understand the critical issues in their organization and provide guidance to address them. After the initial SEAM engagement was completed, we could undertake further engagements that would target specific process improvements or personnel training issues. These follow-up engagements would use the findings of the SEAM engagement to establish the appropriate deliverables and project scope. In this effort, the hidden cost analysis and Priority Action Plans developed in the initial engagement were particularly useful.

An example of this sequence was a manufacturing firm who wanted us to "fix" a production process and make it "employee-proof" so that the process would be structured so that anyone could be plugged in to run the machines. Early data collection found that the organizational environment surrounding the process was deeply flawed. Communication was problematic, supervisors lacked direction, workers lacked training and felt unappreciated, work assignments were unsystematic, and the working conditions were arduous. We were able to persuade the client that a SEAM engagement would be more appropriate to allow everyone to understand the organizational climate because no lasting change could be implemented without changing that climate.

APPLICATIONS OF SEAM IN NON-SEAM ENGAGEMENTS

We normally had at least one SEAM engagement every year which allowed us to teach the basic SEAM approach to the non-SEAM engagement teams. The SEAM engagements, in essence, became a teaching opportunity for the entire class. In particular, we taught that all engagement teams had to focus on discovering the root causes of the dysfunctions they encountered, and they had to work with the client in this discovery effort. In addition, almost all engagements involved a stakeholder analysis, a strategy assessment, a hidden cost analysis, an assessment of personnel training and capabilities, and some form of a Priority Action Plan for key managers. In effect, we modified the hypothesis testing approach and Six Sigma approaches to include these SEAM techniques. We showed students the parallels between SEAM and these techniques to show that hypothesis testing and Six Sigma, while different in orientation, actually are quite similar to many of the tools used in SEAM.

We also used the SEAM engagements to discuss the client's early (mis) perceptions of their problems and why it is often necessary to transform of nature of these perceptions. We emphasized that this is true no matter what the nature of the initial consulting request was from the client. In addition, the SEAM engagements developed a mirror-effect document and we emphasized how this approach could be useful in future market research studies and process improvement projects. Finally, we demonstrated that the HoriVert approach of SEAM is a necessary step in any Six Sigma or hypothesis testing project that involved a process that crossed a number of organizational boundaries. For example, improving a production process that was impacted by supply chain issues, inventory control, and worker training required an organizational understanding of the interrelationships of these functional areas of the firm.

The Engagement Updates were another vehicle for opportunities to apply the SEAM philosophy, whether the engagement was a marketing research intervention, a manufacturing issue, or a pricing study. The Updates gave faculty an opportunity to use the SEAM philosophy to broaden the students' perspectives of the goals of their specific engagement as related to the root causes behind their engagement or the organizational dysfunctions that related to their engagement. In non-SEAM engagements, student teams often heard comments from client employees that suggested that there were other issues lurking within the firm. A formal SEAM engagement would have probed these issues more directly, but this indicated to students that seldom are there simple issues that can be "fixed" within an organization without addressing the overall organizational dysfunctions.

CONCLUSION

SEAM has proved to be an extremely useful tool in a graduate management consulting program. It provided the philosophical underpinning for the consulting approaches taught by the faculty as they used the approach to formally guide consulting engagements or to augment engagements that had different objectives and deliverables. We believe a management consulting program that teaches multiple consulting tools and strategies will find that SEAM provides an excellent foundation for such a program.

Teaching management consulting is not just teaching a tool bag of skills and tools but necessitates a deeper understanding or the organizational climate, its people, and their relationships within the client's firm. Consulting is not a sterile profession of just employing analytical techniques and leaving for another consulting engagement, but it is an opportunity to understand and appreciate the people within the firm, what they experience and what they feel. SEAM provides that deeper human perspective to management consulting that, in turn, enriches students' learning and appreciation of the consulting profession.

CHAPTER 9

SEAM IMPLEMENTATION IN MERGERS AND ACQUISITIONS

Jean Caghassi

CONFERENCE REMARKS:
Chapter Prologue

Alla Heorhiadi

Jean Caghassi is a business practitioner from France. He has had significant experience with SEAM as he has implemented it for over 12 years in
the companies he managed.

Jean Caghassi

We came to SEAM in the context of a company takeover. I had managed
the absorbing company for six years and as one of our competitors had
gone bankrupt, we made the decision to take over the company.

The parent company had $15,000,000 in revenue and an average of 5%
profitability. It had 75 employees on its payroll. Historically, the company

Facilitating the Socioeconomic Approach to Management, pages 101–110
Copyright © 2014 by Information Age Publishing
All rights of reproduction in any form reserved.

was a spin-off from a larger industrial concern. We had a traditional organization culture with well-established departments, organization, and functions. The target company was a slightly larger firm, least in appearance. They had $20,000,000 revenue and 5 years of cumulated losses, up to $3,500,000. It had 120 employees on its payroll. Historically, this company originated from a small workshop with a "handcraft" approach to organization. It was a family-owned business with autocratic management system.

So there were significant differences between both organizational cultures. However, both companies operated in the same field of activity—the car industry—transforming utility vehicles into ambulances and sanitary vehicles.

The target company's owners and I had a respectful relationship. The confidence between the two companies had been created through two types of previous collaboration: (a) a joint-subsidiary established 5 years earlier to manage the marketing of second-hand vehicles; and (b) on-going cooperation for new products' development in order to reduce the inherent development costs.

INTRODUCTION

Just before the take-over, I was planning to implement a pay-rewarding system based on objectives. I had heard about ISEOR and discovered the SEAM method. In fact, it was more than what I had initially envisioned— SEAM was a *fully integrated management system.*

The decision-making process of implementing SEAM was long ending and full of hesitation. Henri Savall teased and provoked me about me not having enough time to strategize my company. He convinced me and I ended up signing the contract without hesitation.

Our SEAM process was immediately launched. The construction of the project took three months. Our objectives were first that both companies learn a *new common management language.* Having the image of one winning company with best practices, and one losing one, would have been a problem for the merger success. As soon as the merger took place, we started from scratch learning this new language. This commitment enabled managers to really drive a global change of management practices. Another objective of the SEAM project was to *improve productivity* and the economic return on the organization's activities. This economic objective was important, due to the company's capitalistic structure: the parent company was two thirds owned by a venture capitalist and one third owned by me, and it was agreed that the merger decision should also be an opportunity to improve our financial assets.

In March 2001, we launched the horizontal diagnosis, then the vertical diagnostic in May. In September 2001, ISEOR presented the qualitative and quantitative diagnoses. In January 2002, we launched two vertical projects—one per industrial site. In parallel, the acquisition of tools through collaborative training and personal assistance was important. Fifteen top and middle managers and supervisors went to Lyon to be intensively trained. Four main strategic tools were built: the internal and external strategic plan, the priority action plan, the remuneration chart, and the definition of the social policy. The remuneration chart was one the most important factors of success, as one of the most important cornerstones of the SEAM method. The partial redistribution of the benefits to all the company's stakeholders allows the method to thrive.

EVALUATION OF SEAM IMPACTS

As part of our evaluation of the SEAM intervention, we undertook both quantitative and qualitative analyses.

Quantitative/Financial Results

During late 2003, an evaluation of the SEAM implementation took place. Up to $4,200,000 was calculated as hidden costs at the launch of the initiative, i.e., $28,600 per person per year. After three years of utilizing the SEAM method, we achieved a $2,300,000 global reduction—$17,550 per person per year. There was also significant improvement in economic efficiency as measured through the *hourly contribution to value-added on variable costs* (HC-VAVC). This indicator is the same parameter used to calculate hidden costs.

It should also be noted that these $4,200,000 hidden costs were not localized where everybody thought they would. The parent company personnel thought that the hidden costs would be much higher in the target company. In the same way, the target firm was concerned about the hidden cost disclosure. At the end, the amount of hidden costs was almost strictly equal across the two companies. This revelation sent a shock throughout both organizations, particularly in the parent company where people thought they were better because they seemed to be more efficient and making money.

Sales of the three production units (including the joint venture created prior to the take-over) had increased from $35,000,000 in 2000 to $50,000,000 in 2003–04. We achieved a 5% net profit across the whole organization. Since early 2003, the incentive scheme had distributed an average 6% of the wages. For some collaborators, it represented almost one additional salary per year. This pay-rewarding system did not cost anything, as it has been totally financed by the conversion of hidden costs into value-added.

Qualitative Results

The qualitative results showed that the management scheme and activity control had been consolidated. Moreover, we succeeded in entrenching SEAM management tools and the new operational system into the organization. Everybody was working with the same tools.

As Executive Director, I was finally able to share the strategic objectives with all operational levels. This was a relief because I was unable to do it before without the strategic tools we now had it place. SEAM also helped in developing the employees' trust toward the company's objectives.

SEAM improved the decision-making process by developing a higher level of responsibility: every employee was able to adapt the decision-making process to the level of responsibility he or she had. In short, the more the method was integrated in the organization, the less work I was faced with because organizational members were better able to make decisions.

To sum up, this evaluation showed in both companies: a better response capacity to market evolution and its environment; a renewed social climate; and enhanced confidence in the potential development of the company. These outcomes reflect what is meant by economic performance accompanied with social performance. The link between social and economic welfare is mutual—one feeds the other.

TETRANORMALIZATION PHENOMENON AND ITS IMPACTS

While experiencing SEAM implementation, we had to deal with the impact of an ever-changing business and political environment. This dynamic refers to another SEAM concept named "tetranormalization" and the impact it can have on organizational performance (see Savall & Zardet, 2012).

Tetranormalization: Proliferation of Norms and Standards

Tetranormalization reveals the various issues that managers face when making decisions in an ever-changing environment. There are four different sets of pressures on the organization (see Figure 9.1): (a) financial and accounting norms, (b) social norms, (c) international trade norms, and (d) quality, security and environment norms.

Examples of each set of pressures (see Figure 9.2) can be:

- Evolution of IFRS accounting norms and awkward financial practices in some countries;

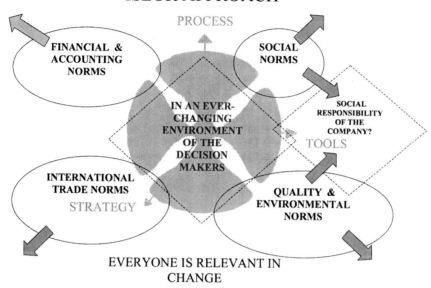

Figure 9.1 SEAM and tetranormalization.

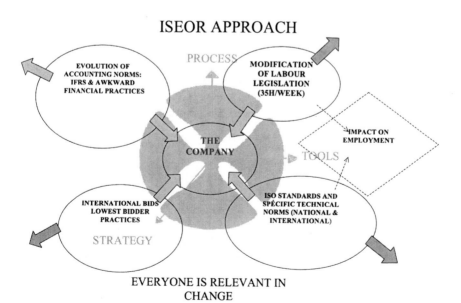

Figure 9.2 SEAM and tetranormalization: Case application.

- Regulation of international bids, with lowest bidder practices revealing the issue of the existing pressure on costs;
- Modification of labor legislation. As an example, the French Socialist Government has imposed a legislation restricting weekly working hours to no more than 35 hours per week, when, in the European open market, competitors from Germany, Spain, and Italy, had weekly working hours of 42 or 45 hours a week; and
- Evolution of standards, such as ISO standards.

Accounting norms are also not uniformly applied, and depend on the company's size, as well as different interpretations in foreign countries. Taxation systems are also not uniform.

- Regarding the financial norms, there are differences in banking regulation, credit policies, risk analysis, and interest rates. In fact, this has led to the situation in which Spain, Italy, and France found themselves the past two or three years.
- Also, differences in social legislation raised costs without any compensation to the end-user, which induced competitive advantages for non-national competitors. The competitiveness gap has become automatically larger.
- Quality and environmental norms reinforced requirements for end-users, the environment, such as the CO_2 reduction and compulsory external audits, which add costs to company operations. This new legislation had to be anticipated and required additional investment to adapt production systems and products to regulation of national markets.
- In trade regulation, market liberalization opened competition to suppliers that were not subject to the same social and financial regulations. "Low-bidder" practices, especially in public tenders, had become the main evaluation and decision criteria.

Corporate Social Responsibility

Regarding the social responsibility of the company, I was truly concerned about rejecting local practices to protect direct employment and indirect employment, and to maintain the company's potential as well as that of its local suppliers. Our purchasing policy was based on establishing true partnerships with our suppliers to make sure that they would be able to accompany our development qualitatively and quantitatively as well. However, if it was not possible to do so, we would go abroad, but it was not acceptable for us to buy cheap products in China or in Eastern Europe based only on low-cost criteria.

Tetranormalization Impacts on Organizational Performance

The tetranormalization impact on the company was mostly financial: higher production costs, higher normalization costs, and more low-cost competitors. Our strategic answer to tetranormalization was SEAM, with an additional focus on *socio-economic management control*. The objective was to differentiate costs and precisely identify sources of value creation. At that time, no one knew how to implement such a system, but we were able to do it thanks to our 6-year experience in implementing SEAM, and a strong conviction of the management.

We complemented the managers' organization by elaborating a full mapping out of the activities at all managerial levels. From this, we established time budgets for each activity. We improved the competence grids at all levels, especially within each department. For instance, we integrated management indicators to the competence grids, aimed at introducing new management practices or complementing them by promoting the individual capacities of each manager. Managers were able to revitalize their self-analyzed situations, improving their decision-making autonomy and adapting it to the more pertinent level.

This in-depth strategic breakdown had brought decision-making process closer to the problems we faced, and freed upper management levels from decisions and responsibilities that could be made at lower levels. Another key factor was to integrate qualitative and quantitative analysis in each assessment level, determining precisely the importance of all individuals and their capacities to meet their responsibilities. The objective was to better assess the individual priorities to find their adequacy with the company's priority action plan.

The implementation of the SEAM management control system led to the establishment of enterprise resource planning (ERP) for almost everyone in the company, whether they were directly or indirectly involved in the production process, being a manager or not. Everybody was able to budget the time needed to achieve the required work, decide if the time was enough to cope with the mapped activities, and decide what needed to be done to improve performance, from receiving additional training, acquiring new management tools, suggesting organizational changes, and so forth.

REFERENCES

Savall, H., & Zardet, V. (2012). *The dynamics and challenges of Tetranormalization.* Charlotte, NC: Information Ag Publishing.

APPENDIX:
Conference Dialogue

Conference Participant: Is ISEOR still involved with evaluation or is the job finished?

Jean Caghassi: Yes of course ISEOR is still involved. The evaluation is an ongoing process and continues as long as the top management wants it to continue.

Conference Participant: As you were going through the acquisition, did the mirror effect consist of only feedback the existing company or did it include views and observations from both companies?

Jean Caghassi: The diagnosis was made for both companies at the same time, but the results were localized for each company. So the mirror effect was not the same for the two companies, and the expert opinion was differentiated as well, even if some recommendations were common to both sites.

Conference Participant: What did the new people coming to the company think when they might have had experience with SEAM in another situation?

Jean Caghassi: SEAM is a method that allows the integration of all individuals as well as building their collective skills, whether existent or nonexistent in the company.

The company was sold two years ago. The buying company had 1,000 people on its payroll, and was 5 times bigger than ours. Despite this, they were totally astonished about the level of knowledge of each manager. The quantity of indicators had them lost at the beginning—they did not understand that the indicators were shared among everybody in the company. Instead of being only necessary for specific people, they found that such transparency enabled them to find immediate answers to their questions precisely because of the quality of the indicators they discovered. In fact, the introduction of their management practices was definitely eased because we had SEAM. They did not find one single discrepancy between the reality of the company and the due diligence report, which has accompanied the takeover operation.

Conference Participant: Did you get your performance pay-rewarding system?

Jean Caghassi: Yes, and I can confirm that the performance pay-rewarding system is the cornerstone of the SEAM management practice. It took us 2 years to build a battery of management performance indicators, which are essential for feedback in the system. These indicators had to be objective and not dependant on anything else than a measure of guaranteed performance. They should never be based on personal opinion or the feeling of a supervisor or manager towards the individual performance of the individuals in question.

The pay performance system was based on a philosophy that redistribution of the value added should be shared at one third with the employees, one third to be kept in the company, and one third to the shareholders. As mentioned in my remarks, the one third to the employees represented an annual amount equivalent to an average 6% of the pay roll.

Conference Participant: You had engaged ISEOR prior to the takeover but the new owners already had a management system reference. They could have seen ISEOR as a cost-cutting method. They had no idea of what would have happened if these costs were held back and removed.

Jean Caghassi: The company had its own management system, in which the owners believed in. So either they had to change their beliefs or at least had to accept that their beliefs had to go through an evolution. It was a family-owned business with an autocratic CEO, so it will take time to change this. SEAM can only work if the top management is convinced that the person at the top has to abandon his or her decision power and allow core teams to become more responsible for their performance. To express this differently, it means that a company should move from "power management" to "socio-economic management." To my knowledge, SEAM is the only integrated management system which allows, in an organized manner, the transfer of power and responsibilities at all levels of an organization.

Conference Participant: Before you implemented SEAM, did the company have formal leadership development performance management?

Jean Caghassi: No, we did not have a system in place.

Conference Participant: How did SEAM create it?

Jean Caghassi: I have been educated as an engineer, without any training at all in management. My approach was hands-on management based on my cumulated professional experiences. SEAM has allowed me to organize my skills as well as the skills of all my collaborators into a comprehensive and integrated management system that has enhanced our collective performance.

Conference Participant: Even new managers who came into the organization had not been trained in management?

Jean Caghassi: Yes. Training in SEAM was essential and the first step of the integration of newcomers to the organization. The week following his arrival, the manager attended the ISEOR training seminar in Lyon to make sure that he understood the model.

Conference Participant: About the aforementioned companies that were not ready for SEAM, I noticed that the two clients here both seemed opened and ready to approve and willing to listen and hear things they may not want to. I think that what has to change is really important, because we have clients who have gone through some of process, but they went through it only half way... and it did not have much impact. I think the people in your organization were ready for it.

CHAPTER 10

A FRENCH MULTINATIONAL FAMILY FIRM CASE STUDY

Amandine Savall

CONFERENCE REMARKS:
Chapter Prologue

Amandine Savall

This case study is an analysis of a family firm that ISEOR has been working with for almost thirty years. I use SEAM both as a methodology and a theory in my doctoral research. I also use SEAM as an intervention consulting method in ISEOR activities.

My comments will present a case study of a family firm, which was one of ISEOR's first clients. Through this research, I wanted to explore the internationalization process of family firms and the way they implemented SEAM, not only France but also in the rest of their overseas subsidiaries. As a way of presenting this research, it seemed relevant to present the firm's international strategy and the way socio-economic intervention helped them to improve the quality of their internationalization.

The main SEAM concept that the company implemented was synchronized decentralization. This implementation means that all organizational functions are decentralized into the subsidiaries and all employees are

Facilitating the Socioeconomic Approach to Management, pages 111–127
Copyright © 2014 by Information Age Publishing

involved at each and every level. To be effective, we need to synchronize this decentralization process in order to make it coherent and relevant for the company as a whole. This is also the meaning of the Horivert concept—horizontal and vertical foci. If you want to be efficient on the vertical line, you also have to be efficient on the horizontal level as well to synchronize the whole system.

The management approach used in this family business was socio-economic intervention- research. All the SEAM trihedral axes have been implemented in the company, which represent the change process. This study was not at the early stage of SEAM implementation, since the intervention had started thirty years ago with the diagnosis, project and evaluation. We are currently carrying out a more in-depth intervention-research in this company.

THE CONTEXT

The French food industrial company founded in 1974 had four business units. Three of them were traditional pastry producing units and the fourth was an international business unit, which oversaw the entire international strategy. The company has twenty subsidiaries, half of them are in France and the other ten are in the rest of Europe and the world. The company has 4,000 employees on its payroll, and its 2010 overall revenues amounted to €550 million, 16% of which came from outside France. This company is very healthy, fully held by the family, and has been experiencing SEAM for the past thirty years.

The traditional structure of each subsidiary is human sized, which means that each one employs a maximum of 300 persons. This was a deliberate choice, a major bet the company made in 1986. The bet was that economies of scale would have been a mistake because of the hidden costs that increased with internal growth. Each subsidiary is fully autonomous regarding its industrial and sales activities. In the sense that, each unit makes products that are sold in a specific geographical area.

At every organizational level, there is a dual management principle: one industrial and one sales manager who manage together the business unit, the subsidiary, the department, and so on. They also develop the employees' responsibility, awareness and skillfulness. This strategy is the opposite of Taylorism: each worker does not make only one task but all workers achieve a comprehensive mission so that they are fully empowered in their jobs. There is also a high level of skillfulness in the production line, and between two lines of products. So when absenteeism is observed, management can easily and internally replace the workers. There is also a balance between operations and support functions. This means that marketing, R&D, and finance are linked: each subsidiary has all the necessary support functions to perform its activities, whereas the headquarters is limited to a minimal size. This is the "TFW antivirus" ingredients they implemented, so the recipe can operate.

Referring to the internationalization strategy, the main target countries were formerly the Latin countries, but there were a lot of disappointments. In response, the firm made the decision to focus on the British and American markets. As a consequence, they acquired a company in California in early 2012. They made the choice of international settlement of the subsidiary: they did not have exportation activities, and they did not create a subsidiary limited to sales and distribution. Each subsidiary is fully independent from the headquarters or from the other subsidiaries. The finance strategy of the internationalization effort is self-financing, except for the acquisitions that were funded through bank loans, though the company remains 100% family owned. The rhythm of the internationalization process is totally under control. As the CEO said (six months ago): "*I don't have any internationalization schedule; one or two years more or less won't make the difference.*" He wants to thrive and develop the business internationally but he does not take too many risks, which seems to be a family businesses' characteristic. The three other key points are: organizational adaptation, intangible investment, and strategic vigilance of the internationalization strategy. These concepts were covered in the presentation by Jean Caghassi (see Chapter 8).

THE PROJECT

I am about to present a preview of the intervention project for 2013. This endeavor is going to be a collective project for the ISEOR intervention team, but I will also draw on it for my doctoral research. The main purpose of this project is to improve the strategic management methods of the company in order to succeed in the internationalization strategy in various countries, including Spain, the UK, and the United States.

Breaking down this main objective consists of identifying key factors that influence decision-making in the internationalization strategy and improving the strategic management methods of the company to determine the strategic levers for success. The third objective is to measure the socio-economic performance of the internationalization strategy in order to better steer it.

In the intervention architecture we designed, on the horizontal action, we will meet the pilot of this intervention, i.e., the CEO, and the four directors of the business units. On the vertical action, we will conduct interviews at the three main foreign subsidiaries and the international business unit teams, which are located at company headquarters (see Figure 10.1).

To provide more details on our research in those subsidiaries, the Spanish subsidiary is managed by another unit, the Toast subsidiary, as

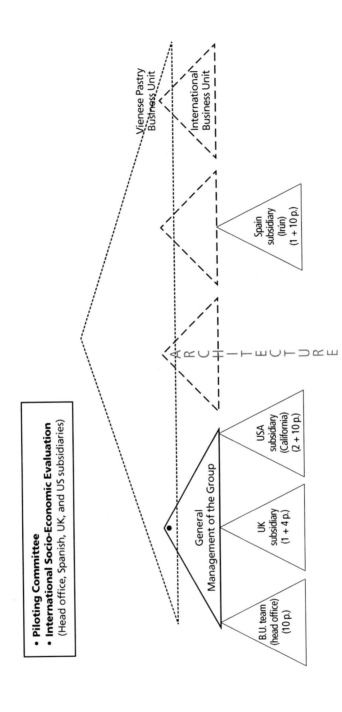

Figure 10.1 Intervention architecture.

opposed to being managed by the international business unit. This isolated case operates because it was the first foreign subsidiary, and at that moment the international business unit had not been created yet.

The Intervention Plan

On the work plan (see Figure 10.2), we can observe that these are six services that we are going to provide:

- The Piloting Committee composed of the CEO, the International business unit director and the ISEOR senior intervener-researcher
- A qualitative evaluation in the headquarters with the executive management (CEO, business units management and the international business unit team)
- Spanish unit: a qualitative evaluation is scheduled in February
- UK unit: assessment in March
- U.S. unit: evaluation in July.
- A mirror effect will take place in all the three cases
- Then, a quantitative evaluation: from April to August in the three subsidiaries

In October 2013, the expert opinion for both the qualitative and quantitative evaluations will enable the intervener-researchers to suggest piloting internationalization indicators.

CONCLUDING COMMENTS

This case should have given you an overview of an in-depth intervention in a company that has already implemented the basics of SEAM. In order to clarify the "evaluation" concept, this means that it is not only about observing the dysfunctions but also looking at the positive aspects. In the quantitative evaluation, we will not only measure hidden costs, but also hidden performance so that they can create economic balance for the company's international projects, such as a takeover of a new subsidiary.

INTRODUCTION

This chapter is based on a family firm case analysis. Socio-economic intervention-research has been carried out in this company for several decades, which enabled me to access many field materials. I decided to name this

MONTH / ACTIONS	July 2012	Aug. 2012	Sept. 2012	Oct. 2012	Nov. 2012	Dec. 2012	Jan. 2013	Feb. 2013	Mar. 2013	April 2013	May 2013	June 2013	July 2013	Aug. 2013	Sept. 2013	Oct. 2013	Nov. 2013	Dec. 2013
PILOTING COMMITTEE	1						2					3			4			5
QUALITATIVE EVALUATION Executive Management, B.U. Management, International B.U. team	X						X			← ME →						← EO →		
QUALITATIVE EVALUATION Spain subsidiary								X										
QUALITATIVE EVALUATION UK subsidiary									X									
QUALITATIVE EVALUATION US subsidiary													X		ME			
QUANTITATIVE EVALUATION Costs & Performance of internationalization															ME			
INDICATORS FOR PILOTING INTERNATIONALIZATION STRATEGY										↕						1		2

Figure 10.2 Intervention plan.

company PR as to ensure business confidentiality, which is essential for success in our collaborations. This longitudinal study also enables an in-depth analysis of family firm internationalization challenges.

The Socio-Economic Approach to Management at PR Company

The Socio-Economic Approach to Management (SEAM) was created by Henri Savall in 1974. The postulate of this research stream is that organizations rest on a "fabulous treasure": hidden costs and performance caused by social and economic dysfunctions. These hidden costs can be—sometimes, easily—converted into added value by the firm. Savall, Zardet, and Bonnet (2000, 2008) emphasize the importance of the human potential concept, underlying hidden cost-performance origins as well as the strategic lever to enhance change, both at the organizational (macro view) and company actor level (micro view).

Some SEAM concepts seem to be particularly interesting in order to analyze the strategic success of organizations (Savall & Zardet, 1987, 1995) as well as the internationalization strategic success of family firms. Within the framework of an international settlement, for instance, the synchronized decentralization concept is considered as a key success factor. The genealogic firm concept (Savall & Zardet, 2011) also points out why intangible investment, seen as an intangible asset reservoir, is so important to family businesses. The genealogical firm is not only about family firms but it is a company with a significant intangible capital; thus, its strategy is long-term oriented. This capital is almost crucial for its survival and development. The strategy suggested to these companies would be to hand down this intangible capital to the next generation, both governance and staff.

Socio-Economic Intervention-Research

The ISEOR research center, created by Henri Savall in the 1970's, has experimented with intervention-research methods for 37 years, working with more than 1200 companies and organizations in eliciting hidden costs, implementing a set of management tools to initiate micro- and macro-changes, and developing their socio-economic performance. In my conference remarks, I also referred to socio-economic intervention-research, which is a transformative longitudinal research carried out in PR Company, in an attempt at implementing a change process. Intervention-research is an exploratory and confirmation research technology that consists of in-depth analysis in a company, as a process conduction actor (Buono & Savall, 2007;

Voyant, 2010). Indeed, this research methodology is based on organizational immersion and cooperation between scholars and company actors, in order to get reliable experimental materials and lead to organizational improvement.

The practical methodology used to capture empirical data was "IDO": interviews, documents, and direct observation (Savall & Zardet, 2011). I collected and analyzed official and nonofficial documents from the company, e.g., PR's Executive Committee report from 2005 to 2011, individual interviews with PR's former and current CEOs from 2005 to 2011, and so on. Finally, I conducted expert interviews with two intervener-researchers who were in charge of carrying out these actions.

Research Context

Globalization is not only an economic phenomenon. It is an anthropological and essential transformation that must be addressed (Abeles, 2008) at both levels in the world: microeconomic and macroeconomic (countries, organizations and people). As a matter of fact, today most companies are forced to go international by the environment.

Family firms have become a new trend in research due to the fact that a significant body of research in Europe and North America showed that many of these companies experience better economic performance than traditional firms (Allouche & Amann, 1998; Daumas, 2012). Family firms are also the world's main economic driving force. They account for 60% to 93% of the European economy, 93% of North-American companies, 75% of Australia and more than 65% in Latin America.[1]

Emerging from growing organizational globalization and family firm economic weight, the chapter attempts to capture the internationalization strategy of one family business. The analysis is based on a socio-economic intervention-research case running from almost three decades, which is one of the most complete applications of the SEAM model. The chapter describes and analyzes the extent to which this company's internationalization strategy and implementation draws on the major concepts with the SEAM framework.

The PR Case

PR is a French food-industry company, which was founded in 1974 by five brothers. They were five shareholders with equal stakes in the company, with each one owning 20% of the firm's capital. Three brothers were top managers and had the following positions: the elder was a commercial and marketing genius, the second was the CEO who quickly took over for his elder brother, and his 10-year younger brother who entered the company with small responsibilities and moved up through the hierarchy, from site manager to CEO in 2010. Today, PR has 4,000 people on its payroll and is the French leader in its market. Its revenue is roughly 550 million euros in 2011, 16% of which was from international operations. Despite this exponential growth, the same family still owns 100% of the company. Moreover, PR has no financial problems: cash flow, profit, and growth are up to the marks, and PR is financially self-sustained. Indeed, the family decided to withdraw from the stock exchange in 2004, because they felt that the financial analysts' comments did not match the company's real performance. Three main business units can be identified: Viennese pastry and bakery, traditional pastry, and continental toasts. The fourth business unit is 10-year-old and overarches all the international activities.

ISEOR and PR have been working hand-in-hand for 28 years, through socio-economic intervention-research, making the company the best example of a near-complete implementation of the SEAM model. Some of the most outstanding results of this work reflect the framework's main socio-economic organizational rudiments, including employee skillfulness, cross team working, synchronized decentralization of management (i.e., subsidiaries overarching all the different organizational functions), every organizational actor's involvement, industrial and sales balance, and cooperation between operations and support functions (see Savall & Zardet, 1995, 2005).

Subsidiaries Overarching All the Different Organizational Functions

The twenty national and international subsidiaries are completely decentralized. This functioning mode underscores the industrial and sales autonomy of every subsidiary. In 1985, the growing company made the decision not to increase its historical factory, since it did not respect the company's product strategy. Then, in 1986, PR opened a new factory in Eastern France. From then on, this decision established the "human-sized subsidiary" principle, with no more than 300 employees per subsidiary.

Employee Responsibility Awareness and Skillfulness

"*Make responsible those who make the actions*" is one of the main internal slogans in this company. In order to accomplish this goal, PR chose to implement an organization and an industrial strategy by product lines. This approach enabled organizational members to know when a problem occurs, and which production part is involved. Intra-line and inter-line skillfulness is also high: workers are responsible for their tasks, but also for technical arrangements, quality norm fulfillment (self-control) and work station cleaning-up.

Operations and Support Functions Balance

This skillfulness policy is also in force regarding support functions (e.g., marketing, research & development, human resource management). They are not located, as usual, in the headquarters but directly on site, in the subsidiaries.

Industrial and Sales Balance

PR's second slogan is "production is sales; and sales are production." This slogan reflects why it is so important that every function of the company is physically located in the same place, so that each one can promote cross team-working. This organizational balance enables the company to make the most of its sales under PR's own brand name. This tactic constitutes a huge competitive advantage regarding international food-industry competitors, and makes PR part of genealogic firms.

PR's Internationalization Strategy

PR's internationalization strategy began in 1998 and has accelerated since 2007. During the 1990s, the brothers decided to go international, and they decided to start by exporting their products from 1998 to 2002.

Target Countries

The first countries where they decided to go were Belgium and Latin culture countries such as Italy and Spain. This decision was made so they could use the existing French subsidiaries and fulfill their strategy which claims that "*every product directly leaves from each site.*" Products for Italy consequently left from Eastern France, for Spain from Southern France, and for Belgium from Northern France. The company also held a significant asset: its French customers were already present in the aforementioned countries. Indeed, at that moment, French large retailers were moving all around Europe. Nevertheless, PR realized from the very beginning that its sales force should be locally present in order to immerse into the other cultures and their consumption habits. So the managers asked employees to go there. In contrast, their competitors did not implement the same strategy since their sales forces were highly centralized.

In the early 2000's, the company decided to enter the United Kingdom. They rolled out the same strategy as in previous occasions, except that it was more challenging—large French retailers were not present there yet. They really started from scratch. However, the company used the same human resource strategy—transferring people to the UK.

In 2001, the internationalization process continued with the acquisition of a Spanish manufacturer and an Italian company. The objective of these two operations was to gain additional industrial entities and work with local people, not only with French expatriates.

The results of these first experiments were quite controversial. Italy was a failure: the company soon resold the factory it had acquired. The acquired Spanish subsidiary is still working, but is not a huge success either. Indeed, the Viennese pastry and bakery business unit in Spain has not succeeded in making more than six or eight million euros. Exportation towards Belgium keeps growing at its own pace. However, the United Kingdom business is a total success. The company reached twenty-five million euros of revenue within a decade. As a consequence, the CEO decided to build a factory there because of the exponential UK market growth.

PR recently bought a company in California at the beginning of 2013. Why did it go to the United States? In 2006–2007, the company acquired two small- and medium-sized enterprises (SMEs) in France, which were already exporting to North America. The company decided to take advantage of this previous experience and capitalized knowledge. Moreover, the U.S. target was set due to the success in Britain. Indeed, the managers consider that the UK and the United States have cultural proximity, such as having a large retailing sector, food-shop atmosphere (packaging, marketing, and so on), cosmopolitanism in big cities, and so forth. The acquired U.S. subsidiary is comprised of 160 people from 26 different nations. This was a great opening signal. PR top managers organized meetings between the United States and the UK managers, so they could share their own experience, taking into account the cultural convergences and specificities.

Modes of International Establishment

After a few years of exportation and internationalization, success and failure, the CEO and the international business unit director wrote a new business plan: "*producing local*," "*developing strategic alliances*," and "*spreading the management system*" (e.g., sales and industrial balance, PNAC,[2] business plan) but respecting national and organizational cultural differences. Another rule is also to erase the word "exportation" in favor of "international," since exportation means that people and products go to and come back from foreign countries, but they are still located in France. "International," in contrast, was seen as the company, rather than the product, is moving to and then staying in the target countries. It becomes an establishment exclusively set up in the foreign country. Being local with sufficient infrastructure, a sales force, and production, enables the firm to avoid import restrictions, find missing resources, use intermediary experts in international business, and cut down production costs among others (see Avenel, 2008). PR's organizational structure was the same abroad as in France: subsidiaries/sites overarching all the different functions and synchronized decentralization of industry, sales and support functions.

The company holds twenty subsidiaries mixing external growth by acquiring existing companies and internal growth by constructing new sites. It seems that the company does not have any preference regarding this. Indeed, PR's international development is a great example of hybrid growth. However, as a genealogic firm, the company wants to thrive so it does not take too many risks by acquiring companies all the time. So PR's top managers want to integrate and merge the two companies humanly speaking. Family firms tend to establish strategic alliances with other family firms abroad (De Farias, Natarrajan, & Piros, 2008). Indeed, the probability of a strategic alliance to be successful is higher between two companies that share the same values and objectives (Swinth & Vinton, 1993). As a matter of fact, PR creates its alliances by developing relationships with local partners. This strategy makes it possible to have efficient partnerships regarding technical, IT, sales, and so forth. This alliance process was implemented with the U.S. company:

> We have met them four or five times a year since 2008. We created trustful relationships until we eventually crossed the capitalistic stage. It wasn't only phone calls, but a strong partnership: travels, promotional events, and so on (Personal Communication, PR CEO, July 2012).

Finance and the Rhythm of Internationalization

Regarding finance issues, the entire international development is self-financed. However, for acquisition projects, PR takes out bank loans. Nevertheless, the company started from scratch in the UK and did not need any bank loan for its development. Indeed, the CEO noted that:

Borrowing money is really a brake for us, especially in this economic crisis context. For instance, I think that the project in China would have succeeded had we been in better macroeconomic conditions. Besides, our main business is in France, so we're not going to put all our money and resources abroad. (Personal Communication, PR CEO, July 2012).

Indeed, going international means cultural adaptation on a large scale and takes time and money. As reflected in the quote above, the CEO does not want to take too many human and financial risks. Family firms want to thrive so as to be able to hand it over to next generations, whereas larger corporations often do not think in the same way. This orientation is one of the reasons why PR's CEO does not seem hurried, and prefers to slowly develop his company abroad, noting "*I don't have any internationalization schedule. One or two years more or less won't make the difference!*"

Organizational Adaptation: Headquarters and International Subsidiaries

Regarding PR's internal organization for internationalization, the key system is referred to as "file," which is comprised of permanent strategic project groups. Each one of these groups consists of a transverse team (industrial, sales, and support function people from different subsidiaries) and managed by a pilot who is usually one of the subsidiary directors. This team is allocated a permanent topic, such as a given product or function, and aimed at thinking about and establishing the long-term strategy of that topic area.

In early 2000, these project groups were still carried out by French subsidiaries because the former CEO did not want specific people dedicated to exportation. In 2004, a new organization was suggested: three product line business units, not segmented through geographic criteria anymore, and one international business unit. The plan concerned adapting the headquarter organization to the growing size of the company and new international business.

This new business unit holds a monthly committee meeting, made up of the International Director's closest colleagues. This top manager is responsible for all the managers and teams located abroad. The business unit revenue is about 45 million euros, and is expected to reach 90–100 million euros within the coming years.

Managing the foreign subsidiaries and activities is based on integrating them to the group, and transferring skills and information to them. Unlike the situation in many companies, the organizational and management system is broken down into all the subsidiaries and sites. However, the company does not want to make it compulsory. As explained by the CEO, "*We don't tell them to do this or that, but to think about how they're going to do it to make it successful."* Thanks to the company's approach to strategic alliances, PR and the U.S. manufacture managers are working in the U.S. organization, respecting national and organizational cultures.

Intangible Investment and Strategic Breakdown

Implementing internationalization strategy is a new challenge for family firms. They have to manage both intangible capital and human potential. According to a 40 company sample, Savall and Zardet (2008, 2011) showed that the profitability of intangible investment regarding human potential qualitative development (IIHMQD) is between 200 and 4,000%. The need for IIHMQD rests on a differential factor, which is created within the organization, thanks to an intergenerational transfer of capitalized know-how and skills. Intangible investments, such as training, create noncopyable resources and value (Charreaux, 1998). One of PR Eastern subsidiary's directors explains that his human resource strategy is based on 800 hours of in-house training per month for 300 people, which means that every employee, whether that person is a manager or a worker, spends 3 hours each month in training.

In SEAM, managers play an essential role in organizational performance. Every business unit or subsidiary is led by a management duo: an executive manager and his or her assistant. The first one is responsible for methods and tools implementation, and that individual's main specialty is sales or industry. Depending on this specialization, the second manager is complementary. They share and talk about their issues and make operational and strategic decisions about the business unit or the subsidiary they are in charge of. This management scheme is applied throughout the organization, including the international business unit.

Due to geographic and psychological distance between people, the implementation of SEAM tools plays a specific role in the strategic breakdown of internationalization. However, any management tool needs understanding and support by managers, so they can explain them and encourage human energy.

PR has a commitment to the implementation of SEAM management tools, including the: external and internal strategic action plan or EISAP (called "business plan" in PR), priority action plan (PAP), and periodically negotiable activity contract (PNAC) (see Savall, Zardet, & Bonnet, 2000, 2008). EISAP and PAP are respectively long-term and short-term strategic tools, designed to break down the collective objectives and teams' actions, from the top management team (TMT) to employees. These tools drive the TMT to think about and formalize the company's long, middle and short-term strategy. At the same time, these tools help staff better understand what their work is for, and motivate them.

The PNAC, for example, is a management tool that formally states the priority objectives and the means made available for attaining them, involving every employee in the enterprise (including workers and office employees), based on a biannual personal dialogue with the employee's direct hierarchical superior (see Buono & Savall, 2007). The purpose is to link the company's strategy to individual objectives. This motivating and piloting tool is applied throughout the company—from the CEO to workers. The TMT calls it "a permanent lever of improvement and planning for the company," and is a highly useful tool for managerial authority maintenance.

Implementation of Strategic Vigilance

In the PR company, strategic decisions rest on advanced and decentralized practices of strategic vigilance with regard to the internal and external environment. This strategic watchfulness is structured through the aforementioned permanent strategic groups ("files"). There are roughly around 20 of these groups, whose composition was described earlier. The objective of each *file* is to watch the field they are in charge of and to elaborate strategic suggestions for PR's Executive Committee. As an example, the strategic groups in charge of given products analyze food consumption habit evolution, and also new regulations which will have a long or short-term influence on recipes.

CONCLUSION

As this case has attempted to detail, PR has implemented all the socio-economic organization principles as part of its internationalization strategy. This approach is aimed at fighting against TFW virus (see Chapters 1 and 2). The main advantage of this company rests on its management system, which is the reason why the CEO and his team plan to transfer this system to all the international subsidiaries, whether they are an acquisition or a creation of a new site.

NOTES

1. These statistics were taken from http://www.fbnet.be/fr/statistics.aspx.
2. PNAC refers to the Periodically Negotiable Activity Contract, which is discussed more fully later in the chapter" (see page 11 for definition and more explanation).

REFERENCES

Abeles, M. (2008). *Anthropologie de la globalisation [Anthropology of Globalization]*. Paris, France: Payot.

Allouche, J., & Amann, B. (1998). La confiance, une explication aux performances des entreprises familiales *[Trust, an explanation of the family businesses performance]. Économie et société, série Gestion [Economy and Society, Management Series]* (Special Issue).

Avenel, J.-D. (2008). *L'essentiel de la Stratégie des Organisations [Core aspect of Organizations Strategy]*. (G. Editeur, Éd.) France. [Paris: Gualino Eds]

Buono, A., & Savall, H. (Eds.) (2007). *Socio-economic intervention in organizations: The Intervener-Researcher and the Seam Approach to Organizational Analysis*. Charlotte, NC: Information Age Publishing.

Charreaux, G. (1998). La Gouvernance des PME : Actes du colloque Professionnalisme des consultants *[SME's Governance : Consultant Professionalism Conference proceedings]*. In ISEOR, *PME-PMI: Le métier de dirigeant et son rôle de changement [SME, SMI : the leader profession and role]*. Paris, France: Economica.

Daumas, J.-C. (2012). Les dirigeants des entreprises familiales en France, 1970–2010. Recrutement, gouvernance, gestion et performances *[The family businesses leaders in France, 1970–2010. Recruitment, governance, management and performances]*. (P. d. Po, Éd.) *Vingtième Siècle. Revue d'histoire [Twentieth century, History Review]*, 2 (114), p. 296 pages.

De Farias, S., Natarrajan, R., & Piros, E. (2008). Global business partnering among family-owned enterprises. *Journal of Business Research, 62*, 667–672.

Savall, H., & Zardet, V. (1995, 2005). *Ingénierie stratégique du roseau [The reed strategic engineering]*, Préface de Serge Pasquier. Paris, France: Economica.

Savall, H., & Zardet, V. (2011). L'Entreprise Généalogique: Esquisse conceptuelle et recherche en perspective *[The geneological enterprise : concept sketching and research perspectives], Cahier de recherche de l'ISEOR. [ISEOR research notebook]*. Lyon: Iseor.

Savall, H., & Zardet, V. (1987). *Maîtriser les coûts et les performances cachés [Mastering hidden costs and performance]*. Economica. 5th édition (2010). *Mastering Hidden Costs and Performance*. Charlotte, NC: Information Age Publishing.

Savall, H., & Zardet, V. (2011). *Qualimetrics approach: Observing the complex object*. Charlotte, NC: Information Age Publishing.

Savall, H., & Zardet, V. (2008). Le concept de coût-valeur des activités. Contribution de la théorie socio-économique des organisations. *[The concept of cost-value of activities, contribution of the socio-economic theory of organizations] Revue Sciences de Gestion-Management Sciences-Ciencias de Gestión, 65*.

Savall, H., Zardet, V., & Bonnet, M. (2000,2008). *Releasing the untapped potential of enterprises through Socio-economic Management*. Geneva, Switzerland: International Labour Office for Employers' Activities (ILO); ISEOR.

Swinth, R., & Vinton, K. (1993). Do family-owned businesses have a strategic advantage in international joint ventures? *Family Business Review, 4*, 19–30.

Voyant, O. (2010). *Contribution à l'identification d'une cartographie de l'environnement externe: cas de PME familiale Belge* [Contribution to identify external environment cartography: A Belgian family SME case]. Congrès de l'AIMS. France.

APPENDIX :
Conference Dialogue

Eric Sanders: You said that the recent growth this family group experienced last year through acquisition of a bakery operation so they can remain independent. If they remain independent, what sort of control do they have on the SEAM process? And, will SEAM be used for changing this independent bakery they acquired?

Amandine Savall: It is a good question because it is actually one of the main concerns of the CEO. This is one of the international strategy's main goals of the business unit. He says that the strategy they adopted has to be based on strategic alliances, which is why he is willing to implement such a management model. My assumption is that SEAM intervention-research will help him in that way.

    They do not want to impose compliance of the SEAM model itself, since they prefer to respect the acquired company's history and share some fundamental values such as strategic breakdown, human potential, and the respect for the sustainable managing principle, which represents the philosophy of SEAM. When growing externally, however, they implement the whole SEAM system.

CHAPTER 11

AN APPROACH TO SOCIO-ECONOMIC MANAGEMENT CONSULTING IN CHINA

Mark Hillon and Yue C. Hillon

CONFERENCE REMARKS:
Chapter Prologue

Mark Hillon

We would like to welcome our friends from ISEOR to the United States. Marc Bonnet asked us to make this video podcast because we could not be at the conference in person to meet everyone.

We are going to present a few observations based on our experience with socio-economic management. The most recent event is a conference that Yue attended and presented a paper last summer in Beijing, China. The other couple of issues that we'll present focus on teaching SEAM to American students and some points extracted from my doctoral dissertation.

Facilitating the Socioeconomic Approach to Management, pages 129–143
Copyright © 2014 by Information Age Publishing
All rights of reproduction in any form reserved.

Yue Cai-Hillon

During this past summer, I went back to Beijing to visit my family and also to attend a conference with scholars from all over the world. I was hoping to talk about SEAM at the conference and to see if any businesses or educators were interested in exploring the concept.

Mark and I researched SEAM potential in China. Through that, we found that most Chinese management is based on Chinese philosophy. Further we realized that SEAM reflects Lao Tzu's philosophy of complexity and problem solving, interconnectivity, respecting human potential, and also investing in education and in people for the organization's self-renewal. Through this understanding we realized that there probably is a potential for SEAM application in Chinese management.

I want to introduce the key points for the potential of this method in China, as well as the challenges we face. SEAM delivers systematic and methodological management process that can be easily understood. The process itself is clearly designed and has no ambiguity or uncertainty—the way many Chinese learn. Investigative and critical thinking skills help diagnose and correct problems, a process that helps to decrease frictions and also increase harmony within the Chinese business among employees and managers. Lastly, SEAM delivers a long-term, self-renewal approach to management, which is a focus of many Chinese businesses. This orientation really reflects the Chinese culture of long-term planning and thinking.

We also found that there are challenges to implementing SEAM in Chinese companies. The first is that Taylor's scientific management is considered a good practice in China because it offers a specific set of guidelines. However, while scientific management's rules are clearly spelled out, it lacks SEAM's humanistic approach.

The second challenge is that the Chinese learning model is primarily a banking model of feeding students and expecting them to recite and remember, rather than creating. Therefore, introducing problem solving, self-investigative, reflective, and critical thinking and learning might be a challenge for the Chinese educational system.

Lastly, SEAM does not investigate the "right" answer, as Chinese students expect from their professors. Instead, SEAM searches for the most appropriate answer. Chinese employees are also dependent on authority for decision making, therefore, a style of independent problem solving might not easily be absorbed and accepted by Chinese management.

Mark Hillon

The cultural fit with SEAM in China mirrors the same issues we have in the United States. For all the talk of creativity in America, students still reflect that same desire for certainty that we see in China. Thus, we saw a French management consulting system as a potential bridge between cultures. In terms of the experience of American students, Yue has been teaching her MBA course with SEAM for three years. We do a semester-long SEAM program, which is just enough time to conduct a diagnostic with mirror effect to the client.

The mirror effect offers evidence for the cultural similarity with China in that clients usually react in a personal manner to the data. This is because work is tied directly to their identity in both America and China—it is part of their status and who they are. It is very difficult to point out problems or frictions in the work environment and not have those things tied directly back to a person. This reason is why it often takes multiple attempts, especially in America, to get business owners or upper-level managers to accept that there might be a problem that they could fix.

This semester we had a very interesting client with a post-industrial culture, open to new ideas. Given this type of facilitative culture, the results might be more welcome to them and it might be easier to get these ideas across.

Yue Cai-Hillon

Throughout the past three years, we have worked with small businesses in the areas of aviation, manufacturing, professional services, and education. It has been very interesting to see the differences across industries and it has been a wonderful experience for the students. This is a brand new way of learning and each semester, students have been extremely engaged. This is very different from their reflections of participation and engagement in other classes. We have twenty to twenty-five students per class and they work as one team, collaborating, discussing, and learning around the intervention. So far, we are getting very good feedback. Figure 11.1 provides an example of key ideas about dysfunctions from one of our projects.

Mark Hillon

It is a very different role for a professor who runs against the traditional academic MBA culture. The professor has to be the lead consultant and is doing as much work as the students on reporting and helping them analyze the data. The students are learning the method at the same time they

EXAMPLE

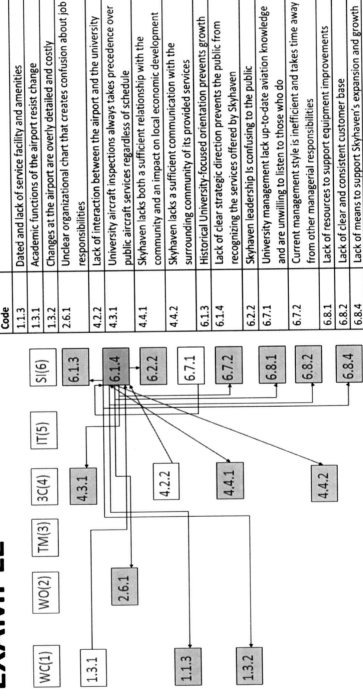

Dysfunction Code	Dysfunction Key Idea
1.1.3	Dated and lack of service facility and amenities
1.3.1	Academic functions of the airport resist change
1.3.2	Changes at the airport are overly detailed and costly
2.6.1	Unclear organizational chart that creates confusion about job responsibilities
4.2.2	Lack of interaction between the airport and the university
4.3.1	University aircraft inspections always takes precedence over public aircraft services regardless of schedule
4.4.1	Skyhaven lacks both a sufficient relationship with the community and an impact on local economic development
4.4.2	Skyhaven lacks a sufficient communication with the surrounding community of its provided services
6.1.3	Historical University-focused orientation prevents growth
6.1.4	Lack of clear strategic direction prevents the public from recognizing the services offered by Skyhaven
6.2.2	Skyhaven leadership Is confusing to the public
6.7.1	University management lack up-to-date aviation knowledge and are unwilling to listen to those who do
6.7.2	Current management style is inefficient and takes time away from other managerial responsibilities
6.8.1	Lack of resources to support equipment improvements
6.8.2	Lack of clear and consistent customer base
6.8.4	Lack of means to support Skyhaven's expansion and growth

Figure 11.1 Illustrative dysfunctions in a course project.

are doing a real diagnostic. The professor really has a role of coach in that process.

Using the English version of Savall and Zardet's (2008) book on hidden costs, the students were required to read the volume for the first part of semester. As they were learning the method, they had a lot of questions about the approach. But, as they start working on the project, interviewing the people in the company, the method tends to make more sense and that draws them in. The students have a real and participative engagement in their learning because they realize that they are doing something valuable—they are diagnosing real problems, and, through the mirror effect, the company is going to listen to them.

Yue Cai-Hillon

Many students hope someday to meet the ISEOR team. Several of our students are extremely interested in the method and want to be further trained to become SEAM consultants in the United States. It has been a rewarding experience.

I want to read a couple of quotes. One is from a student and the other is from a company that we worked with, focusing on their reflections of practicing and being a part of the SEAM process.

From the student:

Although Americans have a more individual outlook on life and SEAM ultimately analyses the organization as a whole, it records stories from every individual in the company. I thought this was one of the main reasons for its success. The whole method is based on discovering the nature of the organization through the lenses of individuals.

From the company:

I guess we ought to listen and consider what is presented carefully because these are our own words and experiences. This method takes time like a slow cooker, but it is very structured and reward is incremental.

This last quote came from a client who was very frustrated at the final presentation because one of the root causes discovered was in the leadership of the organization. However, over time, he reflected on the process and results and realized that there were some rewarding results.

Mark Hillon

That same client implemented some of the recommendations to solve some of their problems and we have heard that they are doing much better. It takes time to see the results and usually the students have graduated and moved on from the university. But, I suppose that we can follow up someday and let them know that their work with SEAM really made an impact.

My research focuses on socio-technical methods—what they do, how they work, their theoretical basis, and the practical translation of theory into something that actually works for change in organizations. One of the defining features of the socio-economic approach from the methods I studied is that it actually does quantify the costs of dysfunctions. The root causes that we discover actually have financial implications.

With the projects we have done thus far, one thing the clients haven't disputed are the values we have calculated for dysfunctions. In many cases, they have noted that the costs are probably more than what we've estimated. They have issues with the personal angle of the diagnostic, however, fearing that they might not be effective managers.

Yue Cai-Hillon

To conclude, I want to talk about the many wonderful contributions that SEAM has brought to student learning in terms of American management and business practices. Over the years teaching SEAM and learning along the way, we've realized that there were some remaining challenges as well.

The first challenge is that the textbook, the terminology, and processes in SEAM are very different from traditional management textbooks, so it takes some time for students to adjust and to begin to understand.

Second, companies in the United States are focused on short-term performance and measuring metrics for resource allocation and productivity. Therefore, companies are hesitant to consider a long-term method that doesn't focus on familiar metrics.

Third, students in the United States are more open and direct in their expression. Therefore, in interviews, they often can't keep from asking leading questions based on their own perceptions. Most U.S. business students do not have prior research skills or experiences, therefore, it takes time for them to learn how to interview, observe, take notes, transcribe, and practice reflective thinking.

Lastly, American businesses often view consultants as very expensive investments. Therefore, they expect quick returns. We all understand that SEAM is a long-term incremental method that pays returns over time, but companies are often hesitant when introduced to SEAM. We hope that by introducing this method to students in America, the knowledge will slowly disseminate and they'll have the tools to take a longer-term view on problems that don't have short-term solutions. The new emphasis on sustainability in the United States may also lead to a more long-term outlook and provide an opening for SEAM.

INTRODUCTION:
MANAGEMENT CONSULTING IN CHINA

Management has been called the most important development of the 20th century (Drucker, 2001). However, the more we learn about creating healthy and productive work environments, the more we realize how much human potential was wasted by a century of poor management practice. Traditional management in an American context lacks accountability, two-way communication with stakeholders, and a psychological understanding of the motivations of employees, customers, and managers themselves (Ries, 2011). Americans have always been mobile and somewhat adolescent in their outlook on life (Rapaille, 2006). That is to say, they don't like to be told what to do and, rather than suffer under a poor manager, they will choose to move on to another job. Management may have been a major innovation of the 20th century, but we have yet to settle down to the real task of learning to manage well.

Reflections on American Managerial Perspectives

The purpose of this chapter is to propose an approach to management consulting in China that is neither American nor Chinese, but that has the capacity to span the gap between the two cultures. The French socio-economic approach to management addresses two main shortcomings of American management and, from a cultural perspective, may be adaptable to the Chinese context. The first deficiency in American management consulting is the lack of humanism. Drucker (2001) spoke of management as a discipline, management as the executive function, and management as the results-oriented workforce that defines the identity of an organization. Perhaps the lack of a single focus is responsible for the failure to address management of ordinary people, projects, and resources that actually result in customer value creation.

A century of Taylor, Fayol, and Weber firmly cast management consulting and practice in a technical-economic industrial mold. The socio-psychological level has been neglected in management practice. Sustainable value creation comes from the fundamental humanistic values of: (a) recognizing employees as human beings with complex sets of needs, rather than production resources; (b) realizing that opportunity lies within the organization as well as its vested individual members; and (c) meeting human needs for excitement and challenges to fulfill work and life goals (Margulies, 1972). Socio-economic management is based on the fact that the only sustainable source of long-term value creation is human potential (Savall, 1981).

The second major deficiency in American management is the lack of an open systems perspective. The public corporation, which became the default mode of industrial organization during Drucker's century, has recently gained a number of serious competitors. State-owned enterprises, public-limited companies, limited-liability companies, private-equity companies, and a variety of new partnership structures offer advantages over the traditional public corporation. Traditional management's lack of accountability has led to more attempts to regulate corporations, while the vocal interests of short-term investors work against long-term sustainability. Rather than lament the demise of an iconic management structure, it may be more insightful to view the entire "ecosystem of innovation and job creation" that has evolved new organizational forms to fit changes in the business environment ("The big engine that couldn't," 2012, p. 30). However, this lack of an open systems perspective was conditioned by a century of Taylor, Fayol, and Weber's "one best way" approach that managed a business more like a mechanical clock than a living organization in an ecological niche. The lack of a long-term vision is a result of viewing a business as a closed system.

Reflections on Management Consulting in China

From a cultural perspective, American management consulting is an inappropriate choice for the Chinese context. Management consultants working in China have found more clients among foreign companies needing assistance in navigating the complexities of the market than among Chinese firms. Backman & Butler (2004) note that Asian firms generally do not trust and are not willing to pay outside consultants to restructure their organizations for greater productivity and transparency. Further, these Western goals may not even be desirable and entrepreneurs tend to be skeptical of consultants who lack long-term experience in local markets.

"Asia's entrepreneurs also tend to operate very closely to their markets. Many personally know their customers and sellers. They observe keenly and gather in all the information they need from their observations; they do not rely on outsiders to tell them what is going on. Their knowledge base is both highly detailed and built up over many years. Thus, when a management consultant comes along offering a management model that can be introduced to the firm in a matter of months, Asia's entrepreneurs might well react with skepticism. Each feels that their own market is unique and complex, and major changes cannot be sensibly proposed unless the same intimate market knowledge is first acquired. Consultants, especially management consultants who work with theories and models that are broadly applicable to whole classes of firms, simply lack legitimacy in the eyes of many Asian entrepreneurs" (Backman & Butler, 2004, p. 190).

China is a high context culture, meaning that language and communication cannot be separated from the context in which they occur and America, as a low context culture, is just the opposite (Hill, 1977). A culture has a grammar or a structural pattern of meaning that enables an onlooker to understand this context (Rapaille, 2006). If we acknowledge that Chinese and American cultures structure meaning quite differently, then it seems logical to explore management consulting practices from a third culture that effectively spans the gap. French culture is a mix of high and low context, including the legal system, business practices, and "the tyranny of bureaucrats.... The French as a rule are much more involved with their employees and with their customers and clients as well. They do not feel they can serve them adequately unless they know them well" (Hill, 1977, p. 199). While these high context aspects of French culture fit well with understanding the network of relationships and philosophical history essential to Chinese business, the French also value the mental cultivation of reasoning and ideas (Rapaille, 2006). These attributes fit well with an American low context business culture that expects communication to be explicit.

A common cultural attribute to both China and America is the delicate nature of receiving constructive criticism about one's work. Americans derive their identities from the work that they do. Loss of a job or a suggestion that their work performance is deficient devalues their self-image (Rapaille, 2006). Likewise, it would be disrespectful to a Chinese manager to suggest that he or his employees were underperforming, however, for a very different reason. Chinese people derive their identities from the organization in which they are employed or from the social status of their positions (Backman & Butler, 2004). In both cultural cases, there is a barrier to diagnosing and correcting problems, a process that would decrease frictions and increase harmony in the workings of the organization. Americans err on the side of direct action without considering social consequences, while in China, "Individuality, minor dissent, and clashes of personality are handled by pretending that they do not exist. If one acknowledges the things that happened, then one must take action, and action is very, very serious" (Hill, 1977, p. 161).

Kluger and DeNisi (1996) observed that task-oriented behavior feedback can lead to behavior change, while person-oriented feedback leads individuals to question their confidence, thereby undermining desired performance improvements. However, we must realize that behind every task, there is a person that cannot be objectively detached from the task itself. A common theme running through Taoist, Indian, Greek, scientific, and many other philosophies recognizes that everything and everyone is interconnected. People are psychologically complex and when you try to force them to separate or compartmentalize their lives into arbitrary parts (e.g., work, family, education, health, well-being), people become ill because it is against the natural patterns of the human mind. Savall (1981) calls the resulting unhealthy, yet common condition, *the split man.*

SEAM AS A CROSS-CULTURAL BRIDGE

From a detached academic perspective, one can easily see that taken together, the American and Chinese perspectives on work and management cannot form a coherent whole. Authentic performance improvements depend on the understanding of the organizational and individual psychological contexts that are breeding dysfunctional patterns and prohibiting organizational advancement (Peron & Peron, 2003). Mindless celebration of the positive, ignorance of the harmful, and omission of the seemingly threatening are detrimental to organizational advancement and long-term profitability. Savall and Zardet's (2008) socio-economic approach to management has been proven effective across a variety of cultures because it involves a comprehensive and long-term study of all relevant stakeholders, contexts, and interests.

The value of socio-economic management consulting is in its long-term investments and sustainable returns. Collective learning involves the organization and all participants in working toward the common goal of understanding and releasing hidden human potential, as well as taking actions necessary to reduce preventable costs. A socio-economic management consulting task force is composed of trained internal and/or external intervention researchers and the organization's horizontal and vertical representatives from top management and supervisors, to technicians, workers, and staff. Through in-depth interviews, observations, dialogue, and critical thinking, the task force conducts a diagnostic to collect and mirror a meta-narrative, anti-narrative, and hidden narrative embedded within the organization (Boje, 2001; Stephens & McCullum, 1998).

The role of the intervener-researchers is to facilitate the organization's understanding of its problems, discover the less visible but fundamental causes, and develop strategies to reduce them. Although difficult, an intervener-researcher must learn to capture every shared story because all stories reveal an inner truth and have a purpose. Dialogical stories in direct quotes from members of the organization are the basis for mapping complex vertical and horizontal relationships within an organization. After stories are collected, recorded, and transcribed, they are mirrored back to the organization for reflection. This is a crucial step because during this phase the organization has the opportunity to clarify their stories to prevent contextual distortion. The complex relationships expose underlying dysfunctions that may be masked by other problems and a key contribution of socio-economic management is transforming qualitative information into quantifiable financial data. Accepting the root dysfunction is often another challenge in itself, as most often, the root cause is psychological in nature.

The consulting process is not linear with a clear beginning and end, but rather, the process itself is a living story evolving with the organization and the environment. The interaction between organizational structure and behavior endlessly narrates a life-story of the organization, of both glories and failures. Helping the voices living inside the organization to understand the qualitative and quantitative implications of their interactions would lead to the comprehension of actions to improve harmony and profitability. To this effect, socio-economic management facilitates the creation of internal consulting groups to strengthen the organization's own long-term outlook. The socio-economic approach to management is a life-long commitment to organizational development.

Fast economic growth in China has resulted in an increasing shortage of qualified managers to meet the demands of the 21st century competitive landscape (Branine, 2005). China, like many societies utilizes the education system to integrate younger generations into societal systems, a reality of conformity and social control (Liu, 2006). Chinese managers view learning as a passive activity in which teachers deposit knowledge in students, like a bank (Branine, 2005). Students constantly seek a "right answer" from their teachers, not from their peers. In contrast, Western education is problem-based to encourage mutual participative learning between the teacher and student. Mutual participation requires dialogue, yet fragmented and incoherent thinking and action can lead to defensive human interactions that prevent listening (Liu, 2006). Introducing problem-posing learning models into Chinese education is a challenge due to the ingrained banking model. A further challenge is the difficulty in applying new learning models at work. Taylor's scientific management is considered good practice and contemporary Chinese managers perceive management as "a set of guidelines and techniques" (Branine, 2005, p. 462). Even when students' curiosity and interest increase in the classroom, their dependency as employees on higher authorities for decision-making will prevent the practice of problem-solving at work (Liu, 2006). In reflection, the socio-economic approach delivers a systematic and methodological management process that can be easily understood and absorbed by Chinese managers and students.

As human resource management research in China moves from the surface of a phenomenon to investigating hidden experiences (Kong & Zhang,

2011), Chinese management scholars and practitioners are able to better conceptualize socio-economic management. The presence of a problem often signifies a deeper cause. Socio-economic management consulting investigates organizational hidden and wasted human potential from six aspects: working conditions, work organization, time management, training, strategic implementation, and communication/coordination/collaboration (Savall & Zardet, 2008). The investigation process is systematic, in-depth, and results in a strategic action plan with measurable metrics.

Socio-economic management is also in harmony with Chinese ancient management philosophies. The philosophies of Confucius, Lao Zi, Sun Tzu, Xunzi, Guanzi, and others reveal that people are socially dependent with a strong need for connections (Kong & Zhang, 2011). Li & Madsen (2010) found that Chinese managers' generally perceived work attitudes and values in state-owned enterprises could be synthesized into four influential behaviors: work is the center of life, social life is tied to work life, the boss holds absolute power, and hope is in the hands of the boss. Yet, people must be valued and respected. When a person with great virtue is ranked and valued low on a company ladder, it is usually a sign of dysfunctional management practices. Confucius' idea of working together harmoniously is believed to lead to business success (Kong & Zhang, 2011) and illustrates the human need for communication/coordination/ collaboration.

The source of a manager's power and capabilities comes from his or her people/subordinates. Recognizing and nurturing employee hidden potential empowers managers and strengthens organizational capabilities. This philosophy is central to socio-economic management and philosophers such as Confucius and Guanzi recognized that education shapes behavior, and therefore, should be a long-term strategy of an organization (Kong & Zhang, 2011). Investing in people rewards an organization with self-renewal capacity, as "learning is a never ending process" (Kong & Zhang, 2011, p. 375) and a much more sustainable return than any other type of investment.

Investments for state-owned enterprises (SOEs) are funded through domestic bank loans and the state budget in China. These funds have decreased from 30% of total investments in 1980 to roughly 5% today (Hersh, 2012). Changes in SOEs have led to emerging changes in Chinese management and human resource practices. Chinese employees have become gradually more mobile and flexible with the lessening of social and economic limitations. With more choices of state-owned or privately-owned opportunities, Chinese employees at privately-owned enterprises were found to be more intrinsically satisfied with their jobs and had increased levels of affective and normative commitments, while employees of SOEs showed higher levels of continuance commitment (Wang, 2008). Together, capitalism, communism, and Chinese ancient management philosophies interactively shape the 21st century Chinese management trends.

Without appropriate training, collaboration, and other healthy organizational mechanisms, companies tumble into disharmony, thereby encouraging preventable dysfunctions to germinate. Socio-economic management systematically diagnoses, analyzes, and reflects on an embedded organizational work/life community to uncover valuable hidden human potential and the costly hidden dysfunctions prohibiting growth.

The management consulting industry in China has existed for over a decade, but demand has shown an increasing growth during the past five years (IBISWorld, 2012), which is a direct result of China's WTO accession since 2001. Primary services include strategy, operations, marketing, and human resource management. The majority of management consulting companies in China are the big global giants like McKinsey, Accenture, and BCG who primarily serve multinational corporations, the Chinese government, and state-owned enterprises. They do not have broad partnerships with local businesses, a market served primarily by local Chinese consulting firms. Although limited, these firms are also thriving by borrowing theories and practices from the global giants.

CONCLUSION

The future of Chinese management research lies in two directions, developing a theory of Chinese management or developing a Chinese theory of management, with both grounded in deductive reasoning (Barney & Zhang, 2009). A *theory of Chinese management* path amplifies Western theories through studies of uniquely Chinese phenomena. Whether Western theories are simply placed in a Chinese context or whether the apparent contradictions and underlying principles are simply hammered into submission, the new Chinese theory is often just a shadow of the Western theory. A *Chinese theory of management* path seeks to develop uniquely Chinese management theories without the references of Western theories. Chinese management scholars cite early U.S. management theories that were based on inductive and deductive studies of early 20th century U.S. managers and organizations. Therefore, these theories lack the relevant context of Chinese history and its implications on 21st century Chinese enterprises. Neither path is optimal, but academia thrives on creating and exploring false dichotomies.

No matter the route Chinese management scholars choose, the best way to understand practical and contextual implications of global economic phenomena and management practices is through global collaboration among management researchers. Instead of force fitting specific Western management consulting techniques into a uniquely different culture, or creating something so entirely exclusive that implications cannot expand into the global economy, we propose an alternative path. The socio-economic approach to management seems to have the capacity and flexibility to integrate a very contextual, collaborative, and learning-based management consulting approach into a Chinese economic and social setting. Its cultural roots, theoretical base, and practical application offer a mix of East and West, while remaining highly compatible with Chinese ancient management philosophies.

REFERENCES

Backman, M., & Butler, C. (2004). *Big in Asia.* London, UK: Palgrave Macmillan.

Barney, J. B., & Zhang, S. (2009). The future of Chinese management research: A theory of Chinese management versus a Chinese theory of management. *Management and Organization Review, 5*(1), 15–28.

Boje, D. (2001). *Narrative methods for organization and communication research.* London, UK: Sage.

Branine, M. (2005). Cross-cultural training of managers: An evaluation of a management development programme for Chinese managers. *Journal of Management Development, 24*(5), 459–472.

Drucker, P. F. (2001). *The essential Drucker.* New York, NY: Collins Business.

Hersh, A. S. (2012). Chinese state-owned and state-controlled enterprises. Testimony before the U.S.—China Economic and Security Review Commission. Washington, DC: Center for American Progress Action Fund, February 15.

Hill, E. T. (1977). *Beyond culture.* Garden City, New York: Anchor Books.

IBISWorld. (2012). Management consulting in China: Market research report, March. http://www.ibisworld.com/industry/china/management-consulting.html

Kluger, A. N., & DeNisi, A. (1996). The effects of feedback interventions on performance: A historical review, a meta-analysis and a preliminary feedback intervention theory. *Psychological Bulletin, 119*, 254–284.

Kong, D., & and Zhang, J. (2011). The research on Chinese ancient management philosophies' similarities with contemporary human resources management thoughts, *Chinese Management Studies, 5*(4), 368–379.

Li, J., & Madsen, J. (2010). Examining Chinese managers' work-related values and attitudes. *Chinese Management Studies, 4*(1), 57–76.

Liu, S. (2006). Developing China's future managers: Learning from the West? *Education and Training, 48*(1), 6–14.

Margulies, N. (1972). *Organizational development: Values, process, and Technology.* New York, NY: McGraw-Hill.

Peron, M., & Peron M. (2003). Postmodernism and the socio-economic approach to organizations. *Journal of Organizational Change Management, 15*(1), 49–55.

Rapaille, C. (2006). *The culture code.* New York, NY: Broadway Books.

Ries, E. (2011). *The lean startup.* New York, NY: Crown Business. The big engine that couldn't. (2012, May 19). *The Economist, 403* (8785), 27–30.

Savall, H. (1981). *Work and people: An economic evaluation of job-enrichment.* Oxford, UK: Clarendon Press.

Savall, H., & Zardet, V. (2008). *Mastering hidden costs and socio-economic performance.* Charlotte, NC: Information Age Publishing.

Stephens, J., & McCullum, R. (1998). *Retelling stories, framing culture: Traditional story and metanarratives in children's literature.* New York, NY: Routledge.

Wang, X. (2008). Analyzing work attitudes of Chinese employees: A comparison between state-owned and privately-owned enterprises in China. *Chinese Management Studies, 2*(3), 215–228.

PART III

BRIDGING SEAM WITH AMERICAN PERCEPTION

CHAPTER 12

THE ART AND SCIENCE OF REVEALING STRATEGIC VALUE THROUGH SEAM

Eric Sanders

CONFERENCE REMARKS:
Chapter Prologue

This presentation is about art, science, and metaphors around the SEAM methodology. The pieces of art that will be shown are all French Impressionist works from the Art Institute of Chicago. A connection will be made between impressionist art, in particular, and SEAM. The presentation will conclude by a trip to the farm. It also will be punctuated by mathematical references on behalf of the economic dimension of this research. Srivastava and Barrett (1988) wrote about metaphors as useful in group development. For groups to develop well, metaphors are useful as a way to develop shared reality. It can be done verbally and through many channels such as music and visual supports. Teaching and learning SEAM requires some visual metaphors.

The Art Institute of Chicago is an imposing building four blocks long and four blocks wide (See Figure 12.1). The first hall is dedicated to impressionism and many pieces of this important collection are shown there, including

Facilitating the Socioeconomic Approach to Management, pages 147–167
Copyright © 2014 by Information Age Publishing

Figure 12.1 The Art Institute of Chicago. (Photo by chapter author, with his mother (Louisa Thurber) in the foreground by the lion.)

works by Pissarro, Monet, and other renowned artists. One of the masterpieces of this collection is Georges Seurat's "A Sunday on La Grande Jatte" (see Figure 12.2), an imposing oil on canvas of 7' high by 10' across (207 cm x 308 cm).

To compose it, Seurat used pointillism. When getting closer to the canvas to analyze details, the various pieces of the painting are made of numerous little dots. Upon the giant canvas, those little dots come together to give the piece of art that is revealed at first sight. One cannot appreciate the technical artistry without that close perspective, and yet the dots cannot be understood without the big picture perspective. The metaphor relates to SEAM in that we also have to hold two different focuses when observing an organization. We have to see the big picture and also the dots. Those dots are the small details that are, typically in a firm, people looking at one to another. Most people do not see both the details and the big picture simultaneously. The job of consultants is to help people who are part of the organization to manage that duality.

In our job as consultants we strive to help reveal the hidden costs of the organization and to look for ways to change those hidden costs. There are two ways to increase net profit in a company: to grow revenue or to minimize costs. Growing revenue is what American people like to do; they are not fond of containing things. Growth is prior to minimizing costs, although the latter remains a solution. As an illustration, I had a client whose job was purchaser and he signed his email with "Speed, quality, and cost . . . choose

Figure 12.2   Georges Seurat, French, 1859–1891. *A Sunday on La Grande Jatte, 1884,* 1884–86. [Oil on canvas, 81 3/4 x 121 1/4 in. (207.5 x 308.1 cm). Helen Birch Bartlett Memorial Collection, 1926.224, The Art Institute of Chicago. Used with permission.

two." If you want to lower cost, then you have to either lower the speed or the quality. If you want to have higher quality, the product or service will cost more or take more time. If you want something to be done faster, you will have to either give up quality or pay at a higher price. If we can help our clients to minimize their cost, these are elements to think about.

IMPRESSIONISM'S CONTRIBUTION TO REVEALING HIDDEN COSTS

In any organization, there are hidden costs and visible costs. From an optimistic perspective, looking at hidden costs means revealing value out of the following buckets: costs incorporated into visible costs such as excess salary, overtime and overconsumption; and costs not included in visible costs. These are opportunity costs, such as missed production, noncreation of strategic potential and risks. Opportunity cost is what you give up to get something else. There are many elements that can be taken from the SEAM box and the model in Figure 12.3 is a useful way of looking at hidden costs.

When observing an impressionist piece of art, the master word is "Use your first impression." When working with your client, the first stage is

Components of hidden costs / Indicators	Overcharges (historical costs)			Nonproduct (opportunity costs)			Total
	Excess salary	Overtime	Over-consumption	Non-production	Non-creation of potential	Risks	
Absenteeism							
Occupational injuries and diseases							
Staff turnover							
Nonquality							
Direct productivity gaps							
Total							

Figure 12.3 General model for calculating hidden costs.

asking his or her impression of what is happening inside the firm when that individual observes the staff at work, because clients typically have an initial idea of what is going on. All first impressions might not be correct but trusting them can possibly guide us to the right way. Moreover, one's impressions are going to differ from others. People have different impressions and see different matters whenever they look at the same things, which is one of the reasons why many people need to be involved. It allows broadening the analysis and getting the most of people's impressions to confront them.

Measuring costs is usually done through three different steps and times of measurement. In the SEAM process, those times are very well defined. Overlaid on top of it, the first measurement concerns the estimation of what is to be invested in the firm for the process that is going to be undertaken. This investment might even be estimated in the contract and might be based on previous clients or case studies in which similar interventions have been carried out. Only then can the project be sold. With an internal-external action, you collect data on the organization to sell the idea of investing in SEAM for improvement.

The first measurement concerns the investment on the work to be undertaken. The second part of measurement concerns forecasting, which is undertaken during the pilot phase of the program in order to predict the value of the results of the program for the organization. There are interviews with managers, on the concern of what employees are doing, or the changes that have been noticed and on indicator numbers that are increasing or decreasing. This collected data is used to forecast and estimate forward changes. The goal here is to see what is working or not within the organization. The last part, when the program is over, consists of collecting data about the actors' achievements and the organization situation. The three measurements are important to make the work valuable.

In my experience, problems might occur during the post-program analysis. Once the intervention is over, people sometimes do not want to see interveners again. Even if a follow up measurement is set in the contract as part of the intervention for the three months after its end, people might say that they are "good" so there would be no need to "bother them." This part of the work may be hard to undertake. However it is very important to show to the client (and also for the consultant's self-assessment) the value that sprang out of the intervention in the organization. Thus, collecting data from different sources—interviews, focus groups, observation and financial reports—is important to qualify the intervener's assumptions. Lights are put on the elements to be held constant to ensure the organization change and to set the actors' perpetual sight on costs and benefits.

When interview data are collected, especially in an American environment, consultants have to gain more credibility by showing numbers. What I assume about the SEAM methodology is that when interviewed people often refer to various numbers that they know during the interview. At the reporting stage, however, those same people might say that what they said was not right. This change of position provides the consultant with a means to discount those numbers, using a couple of simple factors. Clients are asked to think about the factors that may contribute to the things they talked about during the interviews, which might include organization changes. To illustrate this point, I worked in retail electronics for about 20 years. In the retail sales environment, if there was a training program and then sales grew, people would have straightforwardly said that the enterprise earned the extra dollars of revenue because of the sales workers or because of the training program. That might be true, but there might have been other factors, for example an advertisement campaign or an increase of competitiveness of the business, that led to the improvement in sales. Thus, interviewing the manager in the process is critical in attempting to more fully understand what else might have contributed to the improvement. As an example, they might indicate that the training program was responsible for 50% of the improvement, while the ad campaign and competitiveness of the business line was responsible for the other 50%. This type of deeper analysis enables the consultant to increase credibility.

The next factor is the confidence level of the managers, asking them to estimate it by themselves. They could say that they are 90 % confident and this factor has an impact on hidden costs calculation. For example, if you start with $100,000 of value, you multiply that value by the contribution factor of the trainee program of 50%, so that hidden value is $50,000 dollars. By multiplying that amount by your 90% confidence estimate, you would get $45,000 of benefits, which is a good return from a one day training program. The calculation itself is correct, but it would be amazing that only this particular training program would have contributed for 50%. There are other elements that might have caused the improvement, and the role of the consultant is to reveal those relationships because even if hidden costs are a little bit discounted, a $100,000 of hidden costs remains a serious business on a $1.5 million budget.

Value is also revealed to clients when every employee is involved through the *horivert* process. The core of this process is about joining and involving those people so that they feel better about being part of the organization and better about their commitment. The first time that I heard the word *horivert* pronounced by Marc Bonnet at the Academy of Management in Boston, I misheard *"haricot vert,"* a "French green bean." I wondered what green beans had to do with SEAM, because it did not make sense.

However, I grew up on a farm and harvested green beans in the summertime. There is a last metaphor that I can share using that experience. Beans can be grown two ways. The first way is growing them in a small bush and picking some beans, which requires rummaging inside the bush. The other way to grow beans is called pole beans, on which beans lay on a trellis.

Figure 12.4 Haricot vert growing on a trellis.

To harvest, going across the path along the vines is enough to get all the beans. The lesson is that if you want to get all of the vegetables off the vine, you must take care to pick them thoroughly, both horizontally and vertically (see Figure 12.4). You do the same when you research a company, by going top to bottom in the hierarchy and side to side across all departments and functions. So that is my connection between *haricot vert* and *horivert*.

Looking at Figure 12.5, the two girls represented on this Renoir canvas are junior arts performers after a show who are thrown oranges by the spectators as a tribute. At the time this was painted, oranges were expensive and a valuable reward for the effort of the performers. When we document results to be shown to our clients, we have to show them tangible data to validate the work that they are doing. In a nonprofit that for example works on education for children, for example, documenting these results can be challenging. But it is rewarding to see the results and to see afterwards the fact that kids meet the criteria of a good education upon basic skills and health indicators, but also on program improvement. In my earlier research, I worked on a longitudinal study of early childhood education in a preschool program in Chicago. The study showed that giving health and access in basic education preschool facilitated the ability of the children to succeed in life. The key is that as consultants we must show the value that matters to the client.

To summarize, SEAM implies that we must look at the big picture and the details simultaneously, reveal value by unraveling and eliminating hidden

Figure 12.5 Pierre-Auguste Renoir, French, 1841–1919. *Acrobats at the Cirque Fernando* (Francisca and Angelina Wartenberg), 1879. [Oil on canvas, 131.2 × 99.2 cm (51-1/2 × 39-1/16 in.)] Potter Palmer Collection, 1922.440, The Art Institute of Chicago. Used with permission.

costs, involve everyone, from top to bottom, side to side, and last, but not least, document and publicize successes.

INTRODUCTION

The Art Institute of Chicago is a large, impressive building on Michigan Avenue. As you walk toward the museum, its famous lion statues greet you. Passing through the gold doors and the entryway, you can climb the main stairway from four different angles. The North and South stairs take you to architectural artifacts that were developed in Chicago. The West stairs take you to a white marble statue of Sampson wrestling a lion and beyond that the renaissance European collection. The East stairs lead to a wall of glass doors, and the Impressionist collection.

The main hall has a variety of works by Monet, Renoir, Degas, Caillebotte, and other well-known artists. Passing through this hall, in the next room you see Georges Seurat's master work, *A Sunday on La Grande Jatte*, a beautiful painting of people in Paris walking in the park along the Seine. It is a huge canvas, measuring over nearly 7' high by 10' across (207 cm x 308 cm). The most amazing thing about the painting is that as you approach it you realize that it is done entirely with little dots. There are green and blue and yellow and red dots all grouped and blended together to make the work that we enjoy. Seurat pioneered the use of pointillism, making the little dots come alive as you back up enough to give them the perspective they need. It was a great effort for him, as the duality that it required—seeing up close and at a distance simultaneously—was not accepted in the art world of his day. Now it is, and indeed the high-definition TV displays and the computer monitors we view use that same basic technology—lots of little dots (pixels). But it is no walk in the park to do so. It requires conscious thought in the design of the system, and proper perspective on the part of the viewers.

STRATEGIC ORGANIZATION DEVELOPMENT IS A WALK IN THE PARK

So it is with business strategy and strategic organization development (OD). With a little distance and the right perspective, we can see "the big picture." If we get too immersed in the tactical details, we get lost in them and just see the dots, rather than the entire painting. How do we get that perspective? To answer that question, we need to go back a few years, to the origins of our profession.

Our relatively young field of OD has a strong history of being an important component of the process of developing and implementing business strategy (Head, 2009). As OD has become more accepted and integrated into mainstream business practices, it is applied in more tactical situations, and thus is sometimes viewed as being less strategic. I argue that all OD must have a strategic component, or at least strategic alignment. Without that, it will be irrelevant at best, and a wasteful, unnecessary expense at worst.

Organization Development and Strategic OD

The OD Network (n. d.) offers three different definitions of the profession. They begin, as do many others, with Beckhard's (1969, p. 9) definition of OD:

> Organization Development is an effort (a) planned, (b) organization-wide, and (c) managed from the top to (d) increase organization effectiveness and health through (e) planned interventions in the organizations "processes," using behavioral-science knowledge.

This classic definition reflects the command and control nature of business organization that was prevalent at the time, and also shows the point of entry for Beckhard and the OD consultants who worked with him. They were brought in at the highest level of their client organizations, and implemented interventions that affected the entire organization through cascaded change.

Cummings and Worley (2009, pp. 1–2) integrate several definitions of OD (including Beckhard's) to describe our profession as follows:

> Organization development is a system wide application and transfer of behavioral science knowledge to the planned development, improvement, and reinforcement of the strategies, structures and processes that lead to organization effectiveness.

They go on to stress that the work of OD applies to the entire organization, or entire subsystems of an organization, such as a division, function or individual location. In other words, OD is a systemic approach that can be applied at any level of the organization. Here the point of entry is unclear, as is the level of work that is done.

Returning to the OD Network's website (n.d.), we can add another level of complexity, along with a partial listing of OD interventions in Minahan's definition of the field:

> Organization Development is a body of knowledge and practice that enhances organizational performance and individual development, viewing the organization as a complex system of systems that exist within a larger system, each of which has its own attributes and degrees of alignment. OD interventions in these systems are inclusive methodologies and approaches to strategic planning, organization design, leadership development, change management, performance management, coaching, diversity, and work/life balance.

Minahan gives a nod to inclusion, one of the core the humanistic values of our field, along with a broader systemic analysis that now may include the environment in which we work, as well as the varying systems within our client organization(s).

When looking at this evolution of the definition of OD, we can see how the emphasis on core business strategy has faded. Beckhard did not need to mention anything about strategy in his definition of the field, because he was at the highest level of strategy in what he did regularly. Even though his interventions may have included small-group processes and interpersonal relations, they were directly connected to organizational-level strategy. As we move to the Cummings and Worley definition of the field, we see a much broader application of OD, where systemic analysis is used to improve organization effectiveness in many ways at many levels. Then Minahan adds the additional breadth of analysis to include systems of systems, while also adding much smaller, more tactical interventions like coaching and leadership development. By expanding our work to include nearly all parties at all levels, the value of what we do and the target audience for whom we do it has been diluted greatly.

In the midst of this evolution, Jelinek and Litterer (1988) wrote their classic article "Why OD Must Become Strategic." They argued that with the changes in technology and globalization that businesses were facing at that time, the small interpersonal interventions that OD had become known for (such as T-groups) were increasingly irrelevant. OD had to change with the times or go the way of the dinosaur.

Twenty years later, Yaeger and Sorensen (2009) edited *Strategic Organization Development,* and in the introductory chapter, discuss the advances of strategic OD since the Jelinek and Litterer article, especially in terms of large-scale interventions like Appreciative Inquiry and the increasing collaboration between strategic OD and human resource management. They note that the current edition of the Cummings and Worley (2009) OD text includes nearly 100 pages on strategic change interventions, plus another 35 pages on global OD (which by implication is strategic to them), far more than in previous editions. They conclude by saying:

> There can be no question that OD has in fact become strategic. OD has a place at the table. It is a place that it has earned. If past is prologue to the future then there is little question that OD will sustain its place at the table, and of course, will continue to earn it. (p. 7)

What happened in the interim between the two articles? I think that the profession continued to do the good work that we do for our clients. The difference is that some of the OD practitioners (definitely not all, but some) did a better job of connecting their work with the larger business strategy they supported. I believe that if we define our profession only by the interventions we use, we are doomed to be tactical and eventually irrelevant. If we define our profession by the values and perspective we apply, and the outcomes that our clients achieve, then our interventions can adjust with the environment and we will stay both strategic and viable. Thus I propose that a working definition of OD that includes both regular and strategic OD interventions read something like this:

> Organization development is a systemic application of humanistic values, behavioral knowledge and the inter-relationship between people and technology; that is sponsored by senior leadership; and considers both internal and external environments and stakeholders; to improve strategies, structures and processes, and measurably improve organizational performance.

Using a broader definition of OD allows us to work at all levels of the organization, with the understanding that this work will be both sponsored and recognized by senior leadership as being relevant, because it will have a measurable impact on organizational performance. Without that sponsorship and the accountability of showing measurable impact that it implies, OD processes will either be irrelevant or be swallowed up by other professions (most likely Human Resource Management at this time).

Strategy—Specifically Business Strategy

The Oxford English Dictionary (2012) defines strategy as:

> In (theoretical) circumstances of competition or conflict, as in the theory of games, decision theory, business administration, etc., a plan for successful action based on the rationality and interdependence of the moves of the opposing participants.

This is a newer word, which according to the Merriam-Webster Dictionary (2012) had its first known use in 1810. Originally used in the context of military conflict, it has been adapted to business use. There are two key assumptions embedded in the Oxford definition: *rationality* of the parties in the situation, and *interdependence* between them. Does strategy still apply when people behave irrationally? Can you apply strategy when you are the only player in the market? I would argue yes on both counts, but as with any economic decision, it is useful to understand the assumptions that support your conclusion.

Military and business leaders alike study the work of one of the greatest strategists of all time—Sun Tzu, who lived approximately 500 B.C. In The *Art of War* (1910, pp. 8, 10), he said this about the use of strategy:

Thus we may know that there are five essentials for victory:

1. He will win who knows when to fight and when not to fight.
2. He will win who knows how to handle both superior and inferior forces.
3. He will win whose army is animated by the same spirit throughout all its ranks.
4. He will win who, prepared himself, waits to take the enemy unprepared.
5. He will win who has military capacity and is not interfered with by the sovereign.

Hence the skillful fighter puts himself into a position which makes defeat impossible, and does not miss the moment for defeating the enemy. Thus it is that in war the victorious strategist only seeks battle after the victory has been won, whereas he who is destined to defeat first fights and afterwards looks for victory.

Clearly, there is a lot of content built into those few sentences. Preparation and intelligence are both important. More important still is the motivation of the troops, and the wisdom of the leader to attack when conditions are in his or her favor. Last, but not least, the commander on the ground has to have the freedom from the sovereign (or the corporate board) to lead without interference.

Applying this in the business world, you find three core strategies that are generally accepted. A former client of mine put it very succinctly in his e-mail signature. It said: "Speed, quality or cost. Choose two." When you think about it, he is absolutely right. If you want to produce a high quality product and do so quickly, it will likely be expensive. If you want to have it fast and inexpensive, the quality will be sacrificed. If you want the product to be high quality and still be inexpensive, it will take time to develop. All firms have to be competent in all three areas, but need to excel in one to differentiate themselves from the rest of the market.

Now let us consider tactics, or the operational plans to put a larger strategy into action. Merriam-Webster (2012) defines tactics as: "the art or skill of employing available means to accomplish an end." Sun Tzu (500 B.C.) developed the concept of tactics as he discussed how to implement strategy according to the environmental conditions in which battles can be fought. That clear separation of strategy and tactics needs to be done more in the corporate world today as well. Strategy, as we noted above, is based on rationality and the interdependence of the players in the market. Tactics are based on the environmental conditions in which the strategy is executed. While it is useful and even necessary to conduct an environmental analysis in the development of business strategy, it is too easy for business leaders to get caught up on the minutia of tactical decisions and lose sight of the strategy that they support. As good OD consultants, we need to keep the concepts of strategy and tactics clear ourselves, so we can properly advise our clients.

OD Consultants and Strategy

As business leaders ourselves, OD consultants need to understand all these aspects of business strategy, and apply them in our work in order to be credible, and continue to earn our "seat at the table." The key is for us to balance the duality of strategy and tactics that I introduced with the initial metaphor of pointillism. We can do that by applying the definition of OD that I gave at the end of the first section of the paper. I'll develop that concept point by point.

Organization development is a systemic application of humanistic values, behavioral knowledge and the inter-relationship between people and technology. Jelenik and Litterer (1988) discuss the tendency for OD interventions to be small-group processes, and thus not be viewed as strategic. In and of themselves, the interventions may indeed be purely tactical. In practice as part of a system-wide change process, they may become strategic. Anderson (2009) puts it nicely as he presents different levels of interventions. Organization-level interventions are typically strategic. Group-level (think business unit) interventions may be strategic or tactical, and client-level interventions are tactical.

Sharkey (2009) takes the concept of the strategic value of OD in a related, but different direction, as she points out that many OD processes have become accepted as standard business practices. Thus, they are not viewed as worthy of special investment. Another way of looking at it is by whom OD processes are implemented. Frequently they are led Human Resource professionals or functional leaders trained in certain OD interventions. As part of the leader's "toolkit," there may not be an OD practitioner helping guide their use. That loss of systemic perspective may limit the interventions' strategic value to the organization.

Two not necessarily contradictory ways of gaining that systemic OD perspective for a client are Appreciative Inquiry (AI) and the Socio-Economic Approach to Management (SEAM). Sorensen, Yaeger, Savall, Zardet, Bonnet, and Peron (2010) discuss these two approaches to OD, stressing their common focus on strategic change, rather than highlighting their different approaches. AI stresses finding the best in the organization, and then developing processes to replicate that best work consistently. Much has been written about AI elsewhere, so I will not examine it in detail here. SEAM stresses qualitative research with leaders of client organizations to uncover *hidden costs* and then working with those same leaders to implement OD solutions to reduce or eliminate those costs, and thus uncover hidden profits.

Bonnet, Sorensen, Yaeger, and Beck (2012) went into greater detail on the SEAM methodology at the Academy of Management Annual Meeting in Boston. They showed that in the SEAM approach, the researcher/intervener first uses interviews with leaders to discover the hidden costs. Then working with the leaders they work to improve social performance (in such areas as working conditions, work organization, communication and training), which leads to changes in economic performance. Some of those economic gains are immediate, while others are investments in the creation of future potential. Again, we see the value of the skilled OD practitioner in using a systemic perspective to balance the duality of investment in present social performance for future economic performance. In our short-term focused corporate world, that can sometimes take a great deal of effort, and leads to another skill that OD practitioners can bring to the table.

Hidden costs, as uncovered and removed via SEAM, are real costs that are estimated by the functional business leaders. Another value that OD practitioners' systemic perspective might add would be explicit consideration of opportunity costs by our clients. In economic terms, an opportunity cost is defined as what you give up to get something else (Mankiw, 2012). Thus economic profit includes that opportunity cost, while accounting profit does not. For example, the return on investment for building a new plant might be forecast to be 7%. If the potential interest on a long-term bond is 4%, then while the accounting profit of the investment is 7%, the economic profit is only 3%. That still might justify the investment, but it makes it a more educated choice. If OD practitioners could help our clients consider the opportunity cost of say, investing only in facilities and not in human capital, then our clients could make better decisions, based on more complete data.

OD is sponsored by senior leadership. Anderson (2009) also stresses the perspective of the leaders who are engaging the OD consultants. Senior-level leaders have an outward focus, so they are most likely to appreciate the value of a well-executed OD intervention that helps the organization adapt to changes in the external environment. Front-line and mid-level leaders are more inward focused, so they are more likely to appreciate group-level or individual client-level interventions. Coughlan and Rashford (2006) add that as you get higher in the organization, the perspective for leaders and consultants changes to single-loop analysis (of actions), double-loop analysis (of goals) or triple-loop analysis (of purpose), and show how OD consultants can add value at all levels (see Table 12.1). Unfortunately, the middle and front-line leaders are not generally empowered to budget for those interventions, so unless their value is made clear to the senior leaders, as economic and competitive conditions restrict budgets, OD will be among the first "expenses" to be cut, instead of being the first strategic investment made.

OD considers both internal and external environments and stakeholders. In addition to having a systemic perspective and aligning humanistic values, behavioral knowledge and socio-technical systems, we do our work in the context of the internal and external environment in which our clients do

TABLE 12.1   How Organization Development Consultants Add Value at All Levels of Organizations

Organizational Level	Individual Tasks	Management Tasks	OD Consultant's Perspective	Outcomes
Individual	Membership & participation	Involvement	Matching needs	Matching needs
Team	Creating effective working relationships	Productive team functioning	Productive team functioning	Creating a functioning team
Interdepartmental Group	Coordinating joint efforts	Coordination of effective output	Coordination	Coordination
Organization	Adapting	Competitive advantage	Adaptation to changing environment	Adaptation

Source: Adapted from Coughlan & Rashford (2006, pp. 5–6).

their business. It is critical that we understand that environment, including the ever-expanding list of stakeholders to whom the firm has to show value. In business strategy, the typical environmental analysis technique is SWOT (Strengths, Weaknesses, Opportunities and Threats; the first two internal and the second two external). We need to understand the competitive market in which our clients work as well as they do, to provide them with useful assistance. In the AI methodology, it is argued that SWOT analysis tends to dwell on the negatives of internal weaknesses and external threats, rather than build on the positives of internal strengths and external opportunities. To compensate for that, the use of SOAR analysis substitutes positive *aspirations* (what we hope to achieve) and *results* (how we will measure our accomplishments) for the more negative external items.

While I have personally had success with both models of analysis, it seems best to me that we combine them to include the positive focus *and* competitive market considerations. Thus, the new methodology might be called SWAROT (not quite Seurat, but close). That again would balance dualities (or perhaps polarities in this case) of internal strengths and weaknesses, future-oriented aspirations and results, and competitive external opportunities and threats. In that manner, we could prepare for all contingencies that might come up in the environment.

Another environmental factor that is increasingly important is the stakeholders for whom results are generated and reported. In the classic free market model, Friedman (1970) argues convincingly that management's primary social responsibility is to create profits for the firms owners (the proprietors or shareholders). He goes on to argue that it is unethical for managers to spend company money on social causes, because it is not their money, but rather that of the shareholders. However, if there were good business reasons for social responsibility, such as marketing value and perhaps new markets to pursue, I'm sure he would favor it, so long as it ultimately led to higher profits. Freeman and others expand the list of key stakeholders of the modern firm include many other parties in addition to the shareholders, including customers, suppliers, employees, and the local community (Jennings, 2009). As business becomes increasingly global, environmental analysis and the variety of stakeholders becomes more important and more complicated. Thinking globally and acting locally (glocal) is a business norm that we as OD practitioners need to keep mindful of remain strategically relevant.

OD is focused on improving strategies, structures and processes, and measurably improving organizational performance. All of the good work we have discussed so far will be irrelevant if we do not show results that matter to the firm. So how can OD practitioners articulate the strategic value of our work? First, we must develop business leadership skills, in addition to OD and/or people development skills. In a related study, Huselid, Jackson and Schuler (1997) discuss the value of strategic and technical (what I would call tactical) HR processes and HR professionals. They found a positive correlation between firm financial performance and both strategic HR activities and technical HR activities. They went on to show that the HR professional's capability in Human Resource Management (HRM) was greater than their business skill, and that HRM skill was positively correlated with technical HR effectiveness. Thus, the HR professionals were good at tactical HR work, and it showed. Twenty years later, Sharkey (2009) argues that many HR professionals have become more strategic by incorporating OD capabilities and business acumen, and now automate or contract out the tactical work that used to be their mainstay. As I argued at the start of this chapter, OD practitioners started out as trusted business partners, and need to continue to cultivate business acumen and systemic perspective to be strategic, and even to be credible in tactical OD interventions.

One last factor related to business acumen that we need to show as OD consultants in order to be accepted as credible strategic business partners is an understanding of and demonstration of business results from our work in metrics that are both believable and matter to the client. If we can show that we have improved organizational culture by 15%, it is a fantastic accomplishment, and still will not matter to the firm's senior leaders. We have to show that we improved organizational culture by 15% *and* increased revenue (or some other strategic measure important to the firm) by a similar number for that result to have strategic value.[1]

Part of this demonstration of value relates to timing. Anderson (2003) presents a methodology that can help OD consultants see exactly what information they need, and when they need it. He recommends collecting and presenting data in three phases: Estimation, Forecasting, and

Post-Program. Estimation is done at the beginning of a project, during the initial discovery before any other OD work has been done (understanding that simply beginning discovery is an intervention that will have some impact on the firm), using data from previous similar or related projects that the can use to sell the value of the project to sponsors, and justify the investment in that development work. Forecasting is done during the intervention, especially in the pilot of an ongoing program such as leadership development, using data collected from the functional leaders of the firm to project what the eventual benefits of the intervention will be, in order to support ongoing investment. Post-program analysis is done using internal data from both the intervention itself ("soft" measures) and relevant business metrics ("hard" metrics) that the firm regularly collects (such as revenue, turnover, productivity levels, etc.) to confirm that you achieved the objectives that were established before the intervention began.

The SEAM approach to OD takes the methodology that Anderson (2003) presents for forecasting to much deeper levels when investigating hidden costs. Through interviews with functional leaders, they consider six types of dysfunctions commonly encountered in firms: working conditions, work organization, communication–coordination–cooperation, time management, integrated training, and strategic implementation. These dysfunctions lead to five categories of hidden costs: absenteeism, occupational injuries and diseases, staff turnover, no quality, and direct productivity gaps (Savall, Zardet, & Bonnet, 2008). The difference in the two methodologies is that in Anderson's forecasting, the value of the estimation is discounted by two factors: other possible contributing factors (such as improved technology or a marketing campaign) and the confidence level of the interviewee in the estimate (each expressed as a percentage). Thus an estimate of $1 million benefit from an organizational-level strategic intervention might be discounted by 50% because of other factors and by another 50% because of a lack of confidence in the estimate, leaving a net $250,000 benefit. In the SEAM methodology, the full $1,000,000 would be given, as the number the functional leader gives is taken at face value. Either way, the value of the human development work done in OD is presented in financial metrics that have value to the client organization. In that way, OD has credibility and strategic value to the primary stakeholders with whom we interact: the firm's leaders.

CONCLUSION

Strategic OD is a valuable process that we as practitioners can bring to our clients. Kanter (2009, p. 111) cites an adage that applies in this context: "When the climate is right, a thousand flowers can bloom." By being innovative in our approaches, and connecting our work to business strategy, we can create that climate. To do so, we first should expand our definition of OD to include what we do, how we do it, and the results we can generate. Next we need to understand business strategy thoroughly, so we will be effective business partners for our clients. Finally, we need to learn to balance the dualities of strategy and tactics, humanism and technology, soft results and hard finances. None of those tasks are easy, but all are possible. And like Seurat's pointillism, when it is done right the result can be a beautiful walk in the park.

NOTE

1. I entered the field of OD doing quantitative surveys of organizational culture, using Human Synergistics' Organizational Culture Inventory. With such an instrument, you can show measureable progress toward a cultural goal. I am increasingly conscious of the weakness of that methodology and the need to supplement it with good qualitative data. However, we also need credible quantitative measures to support our good "soft" work.

REFERENCES

Anderson, M. (2003). Bottom-line organization development: Implementing and evaluating strategic change for lasting value. New York, NY: Elsevier.

Anderson, P. (2009). Strategic organization development: An invitation to the table. In T. Yaeger & P. Sorensen (Eds.), *Strategic organization development: Managing change for success* (pp. 97–113). Charlotte, NC: Information Age Publishing.

Beckard, R. (1969). *Organization development: Strategies and models.* Reading, MA: Addison-Wesley.

Bonnet, M., Sorensen, P. F., Yaeger, T. F., & Beck, E. (2012, August).Transforming the informal economy existing within companies through SEAM and AI. Presentation at the Academy of Management Annual Meeting, Boston, MA.

Coughlan, D., & Rashford, N. (2006). Organization change and strategy: An Inter-level dynamics approach. London, UK: Routledge.

Cummings, T., & Worley, C. (2009). *Organization development & change*, 9th ed. Mason, OH: South-Western Cengage Learning.

Friedman, M. (1970, September 13). The social responsibility of business is to increase its profits. *New York Times Magazine*, pp. 32–33. Reprinted in M.M. Jennings (Ed.), (2009). *Business* ethics, 6th ed. (pp. 74–79). Mason, OH: South-Western, Cengage Learning.

Head, T. (2009). Strategic organization development: A failure of true organization development? Part two. In T. Yaeger & P. Sorensen (Eds.), *Strategic organization development: Managing change for success* (pp. 23–42). Charlotte, NC: Information Age Publishing.

Huselid, M. A., Jackson, S. E., & Schuler, R. S. (1997). Technical and strategic human resources management effectiveness as determinants of firm performance. *Academy Of Management Journal, 40* (1), 171–188.

Jelinek, M., & Litterer, J. (1988). Why OD must become Strategic. *Research in Organizational Change and Development,* 2, 135–162.

Jennings, M. M. (2009). *Business ethics,* 6th ed. Mason, OH: South-Western, Cengage Learning.

Kanter, R.M. (2009). *Supercorp.* New York, NY: Crown Business.

Mankiw, N. G. (2011). *Principles of economics,* 6th edition. Mason, Ohio: Thomson/South-Western.

Merriam-Webster Dictionary. (2012). Tactics. Retrieved from: http://www.merriam-webster.com/dictionary/tactics.

Organization Development Network (n.d.). What Is OD? Retrieved from: http://www.odnetwork.org/?page=WhatIsOD

Oxford English Dictionary.(2012). Strategy. Retrieved from: http://www.oed.com.libweb.ben.edu/view/Entry/191319?rskey=p2xWku&result=1#eid.

Savall, H., Zardet, V., & Bonnet, M. (2008). *Releasing the untapped potential of enterprises through socio-economic management.* Lyon, France: International Labour Organization and Socio Economic Institute of Firms and Organizations (ISEOR).

Sharkey, L. (2009). The future of organization development and its alignment to the business strategy. In T. Yaeger & P. Sorensen (Eds.), *Strategic organization development: Managing change for success* (pp. 9–22). Charlotte, NC: Information Age Publishing.

Sorensen, P. F., Yaeger, T. F., Savall, H., Zardet, V., Bonnet, M., & Peron, M. (2010). A review of two major global and international approaches to organizational change: SEAM and appreciative inquiry. *Organization Development Journal, 28* (4), 31–39.

Srivastva, S., & Barrett, F. J. (1988). The transforming nature of metaphors in group development: A study in group theory. *Human Relations, 41* (1), 31–64.

Sun Tzu. (1910). *The art of war.* Lionel Giles, Trans. London, UK: Luzac and Co. (Original work published circa 500 B.C.). Retrieved from: www.artofwarsuntzu.com.

Yaeger, T., & Sorensen, P. (2009). A brief look at the past, present, and future of strategic organization development. In T. Yaeger & P. Sorensen (Eds.), *Strategic organization development: Managing change for success* (pp. 3–7). Charlotte, NC: Information Age Publishing.

APPENDIX:
Conference Dialogue

Conference Participant: How do you get the contribution percentage?

Eric Sanders: The contribution percentage is given by the manager. When you're doing your intervention and the analysis, you have to ask to senior and middle-level managers the factors that contribute to the facts happening in the organization. Therefore, you have to ask them for the confidence they have about those overall factors.

Conference Participant: How do you justify the revealed value through the calculation of overall hidden costs when it comes to discussion about program performance and assume that it was successful or not? How can you be sure of your assumptions and insure that everybody agrees to those assumptions so that they will not become an issue at the end of the process?

Eric Sanders: Talking about assumptions requires above all explaining respectively the process and the time invested in the *horivert* analysis and then and only then the method to reveal the numbers. What I can say, from my experience, is that getting people to agree with the numbers assumptions is anchored in the fact that they are deeply involved in the process.

CHAPTER 13

ADVANCING RESEARCH THAT MAKES A DIFFERENCE

Peter F. Sorensen and Therese Yaeger

CONFERENCE REMARKS:
Chapter Prologue

Peter Sorensen

This paper addresses a number of issues related to what the faculty at the University of Southern California have referred to as "Doing Useful Research" (Mohrman & Lawler, 2011). This is a topic that includes a number of different approaches that share a number of common characteristics, which include doing research with, rather than doing research on, people. It is also research that is directed toward the improvement of performance, research that is action oriented, and research that is both situational specific and a contribution to more general scientific knowledge. Approaches sharing these characteristics include: Action Research, scholar-practitioner research, the socio-economic approach to management (SEAM), and Appreciative Inquiry. This chapter builds on earlier comparisons of Qualimetrics and SEAM beyond the comparison to Appreciative Inquiry and other forms of Action Research. The central organizing theme of the chapter deals primarily with a comparison of SEAM and Appreciative Inquiry to

Facilitating the Socioeconomic Approach to Management, pages 169–180
Copyright © 2014 by Information Age Publishing
All rights of reproduction in any form reserved.

other forms of Action Research, a continuation of a theme that was presented at the doctoral conference in Lyon, the National Academy of Management Conference, and an analysis by Sorensen, Yaeger, and colleagues (2010) in the *Organization Development Journal.*

INTRODUCTION

In the introduction to Savall and Zardet's (2011) most recent edition of *The Qualimetrics Approach,* David Boje (2011, p. xiv) relates the socio-economic approach to Robert Gephardt's (1988) ethnostatistics, Jacques Derrida's (1991) deconstruction, Norman Fairclough's (1992) neocapitalism, and Kenneth Burke's (1937–1957) excluded middle. Boje (2011, p. xviii) summarizes his introduction stating:

> ... my reading of Qualimetrics is that it changes the rules of the research game (the logic that embeds actors in the social and economic context). This is done through long-term intervention-research that keeps integrating financial with quantitative and qualitative traces of how information is produced and distributed, and how systems of reporting distort the processes they represent.

As with Boje's extension of SEAM to other similar approaches, this chapter extends the discussion of some of the characteristics of Qualimetrics and SEAM to other forms of Action Research (AR). It is quite clear that similarities and differences in these approaches exist. It is the differences that make SEAM and Qualimetrics such a valuable contribution to the family of AR methods.

This chapter represents our first attempt at expanding the comparison of Qualimetrics, SEAM and ISEOR's operations beyond earlier comparisons to Appreciative Inquiry (AI) and other forms of Action Research. As this is our initial attempt, there may be some unevenness in our coverage of the different approaches. Some of the comparisons may seem awkward, hopefully, just a little bit awkward, in particular the categories presented in Table 13.1. However, we feel that the issues raised in the chapter represent important considerations for the practice of AR and its contribution to both practice and knowledge. One thing is quite, uncompromisingly clear—that each of the approaches has made major and extensive documented contributions to *both* practice and knowledge.

Table 13.1 Comparison of Five Approaches to Action Research

	SEAM	Appreciative Inquiry	4 Systems	HCHP	USC–CEO
History	30+ years	20+ years	50+ years	40+ years	30 years
Origin	Management	Behavioral Sciences	Behavioral Sciences	Behavioral Sciences	Behavioral Sciences
Origin	ISEOR, University of Jean Moulin–Lyon 3	Case Western Reserve University	Univ. of Michigan	Harvard	USC/CEO
Origin	Henri Savall	David Cooperrider	Rensis Likert	Michael Beer	Ed Lawler
Research	Programmatic	Evolving	Programmatic	Developing	Programmatic
Research	Intervener-Researcher	Scholar-Practitioner	Academic	Researcher/Consultant	Applied Research
International/ Global	Widespread Applications	Widespread Applications	Some Degree	Some Degree	Some Degree
Primary Concept	Hidden Cost	Organization Strengths	4 Systems	HCHP	Research/Practice
Approach	Selective Inclusion	Comprehensive Inclusion	Inclusive	Inclusive	Varies
Approach	Diagnosis-Problem Oriented	Opportunity Based	Diagnosis/Action Plans	Strategic Fitness Process (SFP)	Problem Focused Research
Results	Extensive Systematic Documentation	Culminating Documentation	Extensive Documentation	Extensive Documentation	Extensive Documentation

ADVANCING RESEARCH
THAT MAKES A DIFFERENCE: FIVE APPROACHES

Advancing research that makes a difference refers to research that is helpful in understanding and improving life in organizations and improving organization performance. Advancing research that makes a difference is an approach to organizational research that is associated with a number of traditions related to the concepts of AR and the scholar-practitioner. These traditions include, but are not limited to, the work at University of Southern California's Center for Effective Organizations, the high commitment-high performance (HCHP) work of Michael Beer (2009) at Harvard Business School, AI at Case Western University and Benedictine University, the work at the University of Michigan Survey Research Center with Rensis Likert, and the SEAM and Qualimetrics approach at ISEOR and University of Lyon 3. A common thread among all these approaches is AR associated with the work of Kurt Lewin (1946, 1951).

There are a number of factors that characterize Lewin's AR concept, but the most fundamental characteristics and objectives are learning and the application of that learning to a specific situation, as well as the contribution to a broader body of knowledge, specifically knowledge related to organization performance. For an extended review of the AR approach, see David Coghlan's (2011) thoughtful work.

Much of the work of Rensis Likert and the Survey Research Center at the University of Michigan also serves as an illustration of the AR Model with the integration of a number of organizational studies and field applications into a general theory of organizational performance, namely the "Four Systems of Management" (Likert, 1967). In the book, *Useful Research: Advancing Theory and Practice*, the Mohrman and Lawler (2011, p. 1) make explicit the mission of the Center for Effective Organizations, referring to *dual impact* research as they state:

> Dual-impact research has been the mission of the Center for Effective Organizations (CEO) at the University of Southern California's (USC's) Marshall School of Business since its founding in 1979.

Similarly, the work with AI has served as both the basis for field application and the development of a positive theory of organizational change. In particular, the work at Case Western Reserve University and Benedictine University have added to AI's development both in terms of experimental research designs evaluating its application, and the use of case studies to add additional insights into the AI process itself (Yaeger, Sorensen, & Bengtsson, 2005).

The work of SEAM and Qualimetrics very clearly falls within this tradition. This position is very clearly stated in by Savall and Zardet (2011, p. xxxvii):

> Researchers at ISEOR have refused to oppose fundamental or theoretical and applied research. If it is true, from an ontological point of view, that ISEOR researchers consider that academic research must be useful to society; this commitment has never stopped us from developing fundamental knowledge resulting from theory-based knowledge accumulation, which has been created by a steady stream of intervention-research projects. Scientific progress results from a continuous two-way flow between the fundamental side of research efforts and their pragmatic and empirical dimensions."

The Process of Action Research

In comparing several of the AR approaches there are clearly a number of similarities as well as some differences. The earliest approach discussed here, the work of Likert and his "Four Systems of Management" clearly reflect the fundamental characteristics of AR. These different systems (Likert, 1967) include:

- System 1: Exploitive authoritative systems
- System 2: Benevolent authoritative systems
- System 3: Consultative systems
- System 4: Participative group systems

This framework provides the basis for application to a specific situation while contributing to a more general model of organizations. It is longitudinal and characterized by the use of both quantitative and qualitative methods: the use of quantitative information in the terms of surveys based on Systems 4 theory, and qualitative in terms of survey feedback and team discussions. It also uses quantitative data in terms of assessing what Likert refers to as end-result variables—variables that measure the results of the intervention. These end-result variables include a range of variables, ranging, for example, from changes in production, quality and turnover. The fundamental basis for these four systems is data pertaining to leadership styles and employee attitudes. This basis is clearly behavioral, although end result variables may be more inclusive. System 4 is also highly inclusive and designed to involve all employees in dialogue concerning organizational performance.

The Process of Appreciative Inquiry and Dual-Impact Research

Appreciative Inquiry is also highly participatory, designed to get the "whole system in the room" (Yaeger, Sorensen, & Bengtsson, 2005). Much like the AR process, it is designed to provide a vehicle for creating dialogue among organization members. Appreciative Inquiry originated as an inclusive large group intervention, but has evolved into an approach that includes both group/team development as well as application to individuals. The approach is very clearly based on attitudes and beliefs as reflected in its strong social constructionist orientation. It is not as systematic in incorporating a longitudinal design or systematic theory building. Theory building does in fact exist, but not in the same systematic, programmatic fashion as either Likert's Four Systems of Management Theory, the work at USC's CEO, or SEAM and Qualimetrics. Appreciative Inquiry builds on identifying "the best" of the organization, creating dialogue around those characteristics and building a vision and strategy for the future. It is probably the most behaviorally oriented and least traditional management approach in its orientation.

SEAM, in contrast, is probably the most oriented toward combining in a systematic fashion more traditional management (financial data) and behavior. It is clearly longitudinal, for example, a typical contract can last a number of years. It is highly programmatic, disciplined and rigorous. It systematically continues to integrate new data, new understandings across a variety of applications into a continuously developing theory of management.

It is also probably the least inclusive and participatory in that it collects and integrates organizational information for presentation to management in a manner designed to persuade management of the problem and the preferred solution. SEAM is collaborative but not in the same sense as Likert's Four Systems. In many ways, SEAM provides the most comprehensive, complex approach to AR of the various approaches discussed here.

The work at USC's CEO, described by Mohrman and Lawler (2011) is characterized by a number of similarities: work that is collaborative with strong relationships between researchers and corporations, focused on specific problems within a process that is designed to further develop and define a more general body of theory. Another example of AR, which is particularly useful with corporate application, is Beer's (2011) framework. This work presents illustrations of individual cases representative of AR in companies, which include his work at Corning, Medford, and BD.

EDUCATION OF THE SCHOLAR-PRACTITIONER

The interface between the practitioner and the scholar is a critical component of generating research that "makes a difference." This interaction takes several forms, including researchers establishing relationships with corporations in joint research projects, implementing the concept of the scholar-practitioner, or combining both the practitioner and the scholar role into one person. This concept of the scholar-practitioner refers to a practitioner who is educated in and understands the field from an academic perspective, is able to serve as a knowledgeable bridge and resource, and is in a corporate position to collaborate. This individual may also serve as a knowledgeable member of a corporate–university research team, or as an individual practitioner invested in and capable of contributing individually to the literature and knowledge base of the field. One major approach to educating scholar-practitioners is a doctoral degree program. Two of these programs are Benedictine University and the University of Lyon-ISEOR. Although the University of Michigan Survey Research Center is not discussed here as a program designed to prepare scholar-practitioners, in fact, a number of scholars associated with this program became leading scholar-practitioners, including Ed Lawler, Phil Mirvis, and Ram Tenkasi, to name a few.

The doctoral program at Benedictine University focuses primarily on the education of corporate executives who hold responsible positions, such as managers, OD consultants, or HR corporate personnel. The program has a 20-year history with more than 200 graduates. This environment has successfully contributed to both OD practice and the knowledge base of the field. A few examples include the implementation of OD practices in an organizational change of historic nature at one of the largest global automotive manufacturers and documentation and theory development related to these initiatives. A second and award-winning project was a field experiment testing the results of different approaches to turnover reduction at 90 field sites using Appreciative Inquiry. A third illustration is another award-winning field experiment using Appreciative Inquiry in the implementation of lean manufacturing in a global manufacturing organization in nine different countries. Another award-winning project involved a field experiment using a recent significant AI addition. All of these application research projects were reported at both practitioner and academic conferences. For a very useful discussion of the education of the scholar-practitioner doctoral level education see Tenkasi (2011).

ISEOR and SEAM provide an additional illustration of scholar-practitioner education at the doctoral level. The work at ISEOR is truly an impressive example of the potential of scholar-practitioner doctoral education. Insights into the SEAM scholar-practitioner PhD is provided in the following quote from Boje and Rosile (2003, p. 13):

SEAM PhDs are more than process consultants, they consider themselves qualitative researchers, and financial researchers; in short, intervener-researcher, who carefully collect and code qualitative interviews into a text-retrieval computer system to persuade clients to commit to major interventions. This means that PhD candidates are trained at ISEOR to do semi-structured interviews and observation studies as part of their training.

This quote addresses the role of the Action-Researcher in terms of addressing a specific situation. The following quote illustrates AR's second role—the contribution to generalized theory development: "...research across client projects is generative in its continued refinement of grounded theories of SEAM" (Boje & Rosile, 2003, p. 16).

PUBLISHING: THE DISSEMINATION OF ACTION RESEARCH FINDINGS

In *Useful Research,* Mohrman and Lawler (2011) discuss the learning derived from the collection of articles presented. One of their comments is related to publishing and disseminating knowledge, as they argue that a key learning is the use of nonacademic pathways to disseminate research findings to the world of practitioners (Mohrman & Lawler, 2011, p. 410). The contributors to AR mentioned here do this quite well—illustrating the use of nonacademic pathways. All are major contributors to academic outlets but to practitioner outlets as well. For example, Likert was a master at using both avenues of research dissemination. Likert and his colleagues were regular contributors to academic conferences, such as the Academy of Management and academic publications, but Likert's *New Patterns of Management* (1961) is a classic in the presentation of considerable academic research to a practitioner audience, which helped to identify it as a bestselling book on management. Likert also contributed to *such practitioner oriented publications as Personnel and the Michigan Business Review,* and the American Management Association Personnel series, among others.

In a similar fashion, members of the Center for Effective Organizations have followed a like pattern with regular ongoing contributions to the academic literature and conferences as well as books for a practitioner audience, books like Lawler and Worley's (2006) *Built to Change* (2006) and Cummings and Worley's (2009) bestselling OD text, which has helped educate legions of MBA managers and aspiring managers.

Michael Beer certainly fits this tradition as well and may be the most outspoken advocate of writing directly for the practitioner. Examples include works like his most recent book *High Commitment, High Performance* (2009), articles in the *Harvard Business Review* and *Sloan Management Review.* Beer also is a major contributor to academic sources with regular presentations at the American Psychological Association and the Academy of Management.

Appreciative Inquiry is also a model for communicating theory and applied concepts, as evidenced by AI's record in "boundary spanning," illustrated by awards from both the American Society for Training and Development and the Academy of Management, as well as a special issue of the *OD Journal*, which is dedicated to both the practitioner and the academic.

The work at ISEOR and SEAM is very much part of the tradition described above. Savall and Zardet, for example, have authored a number of books designed for both the practitioner and scholar, including *Mastering Hidden Cost and Socio-Economic Performance, Work and People: An Economic Evaluation of Job Enrichment, Reconstructing the Firm,* and *The Qualimetrics Approach: Observing the Complex Object.* The work at ISEOR and SEAM is also shared regularly through the annual meeting of the Academy of Management, annual conferences at the University of Lyon, special conferences, for instance, the one focused on SEAM at the University of St. Thomas, and the Journal *Revue Sciences de Gestion,* as well as U.S. Journals such as the *OD Journal.*

INTERNATIONAL APPLICATION

Three of the approaches discussed in this chapter provide data on international applications. As examples, Likert (1967) reports the successful implementation of System 4 Management in Japan, India, and Yugoslavia, and Yaeger, Sorensen, and Bengtsson (2005) and a later article by Yaeger, Sorensen, and associates (2010) report successful AI applications in a wide range of countries including the U.K., Canada, Brazil, Africa, Nepal, Australia, the Netherlands, Mexico, Japan, Taiwan, Denmark, and India. The extent of the global activities using SEAM is reflected in its use in 1,200 companies and 50,000 field interviews in 35 countries. In addition teacher-researchers trained at ISEOR can be found in France, Tunisia, Brazil, Morocco, Burundi, Angola, Mexico, Switzerland, and the United States.

More recently, an important addition to the AR literature is the experience with SEAM in the Middle East, as illustrated by Patrick Tabchoury's (2012) work that describes some of the difficulties in consulting in this area of the world. Tabchoury identifies "possible solutions" through Socio-Economic Consulting with cultural and social aspects that include: (a) helping create a sound work environment including greater involvement of local workers; (b) maintaining local traditions and cultures; (c) promoting skill management and long life training; (d) insuring equal balance between economic and social issues; (e) using management consulting that reduces cost and improves quality; (f) applying socio-economic management tools that can be customized to any setting, balancing short-term and long-term

178 ■ P. F. SORENSEN and T. YAEGER

economic results; and (g) enabling the involvement of each and every actor in the development process.

THE FUTURE OF MEANINGFUL RESEARCH

The future of AR depends on the opportunity to share individual studies and the development of a general body of knowledge through academic publications. The current and future of sharing opportunities to contribute to the building of a general body of knowledge are characterized by a variety of views and opinions. Beer (2011, p. 164), for example, notes that:

> Being a boundary spanner has been a challenge. While practitioners welcome practical knowledge, I have found that academics are much less welcoming. The dominant normal science paradigm makes it hard to publish my findings and ideas in the most prestigious academic journals.

In a similar vein, Cummings (2011, p. 333) identifies and discusses the forces shaping business school research, examining the characteristics of research useful for theory and practice and lamenting that "...the kind of managerial research predominant today has almost the opposite characteristics." In their work, Savall and Zardet (2011, p. 69) voice related concerns, stating:

> Could it be possible that a hierarchical relationship exists, on the scale of academic criteria, between quantitative and qualitative measures? Could qualitative measures be less scientific than quantitative measures?

An alternative view of the current state and future opportunities for contributing to the academic literature is presented by Rynes (2011, p. 353), who suggests that increased emphasis is being placed on application, as evidenced by research involving AR, SEAM, AI , Beer's (2009) High Commitment/High Performance approach, and USC's CEO.

In her argument Rynes presents evidence to support this position including:

1. Increased citations in the material of business schools
2. An increase in specials forums concerned with the integration of research and practice
3. New sources of funding
4. Journals are changing
5. Young academics want to do relevant work

CONCLUSION

In the first chapter of their book, *Useful Research,* Mohrman and Lawler (2011, p. 18) raise a series of questions for researchers who desire to influence organizational practice:

> How might my research impact organizational practice? What kind of research questions should I ask? How can the knowledge from my research reach and influence practitioners? How do I learn to do this kind of research?

This chapter was framed in terms of the AR concept, an approach which is at the core of each of these questions. Each one of the programs cited in the chapter provides an answer to these questions, although each program answers them in its own unique way. There can be no question that each of the AR approaches discussed here have made major and significant contributions to the knowledge and practice of improving organization performance. They have done so through sophisticated methodologies, the development and implementation of the concept of the scholar-practitioner, and the dissemination of knowledge through both academic and practitioner publications and conferences. The work of SEAM and Qualimetics at ISEOR is unquestionably an important part of the rich tradition and contribution of Action Research.

REFERENCES

Beer, M. (2009). *High commitment, high performance: How to build a resilient organization for sustained advantage.* San Francisco: Jossey-Bass.

Beer, M. (2011). Making a difference and contributing useful knowledge: Principles derived from Life as a scholar-practitioner. In S. Mohrman, E. Lawler & Associates (Eds.), *Useful Research: Advancing theory and practice* (pp. 147–168). San Francisco: Berrett-Koehler Publishers.

Boje, D. (2011). Preface to the 2004 Edition: Qualimetrics contributions to research methodology. In H. Savall & V. Zardet (Eds.), *The Qualimetrics Approach: Observing the complex object* (pp. xiii–xix). Charlotte, NC: Information Age Publishing Inc.

Boje, D., & Rosile, G. (2003). Comparison of Socio-Economic and other trans-organizational development methods. *Journal of Organizational Change Management, 16* (1), 10–20.

Burke, K. (1937). *Attitudes towards history.* Berkeley, CA: University of California Press.

Coghlan, D. (2011). Action research: Exploring perspectives on a philosophy of practical knowing. *Academy of Management Annals, 5* (1), 53–87.

Cummings, T. (2011). How business schools shape (misshape) management research. In S. Mohrman, E. Lawler & Associates (Eds.), *Useful Research:*

Advancing theory and practice (pp. 331–350). San Francisco: Berrett-Koehler Publishers.

Cummings, T., & Worley, G. (2009). *Organization development & change.* Mason, OH: South Western Cengage Learning.

Derrida, J., & Derrida, A. (1991). *Reader: Between the blinds.* New York, NY: Columbia University Press.

Fairclough, N. (1992). *Discourse and social change.* Cambridge, UK: Polity.

Gebhardt, R. (1988). *Ethnostatistics: Qualitative foundations for qualitative research.* Qualitative Research Methods Series #12. Newbury Park, CA: Sage.

Lawler, E., & Worley. C. (2006). *Built to change: How to achieve sustained organizational effectiveness.* Jossey-Bass.

Lewin, K. (1946). Action research and minority problems. *Journal of Social Issues, 2* (4), 34–46.

Lewin, K. (1951). *Field theory in social science.* New York: Harper & Row.

Likert, R. (1961). *New patterns in management.* New York: McGraw-Hill.

Likert, R. (1967). *The human organization.* New York: McGraw-Hill.

Mohrman, S., Lawler, E., & Associates, Eds. (2011). *Useful research: Advancing theory and practice.* San Francisco: Berrett-Koehler Publishers.

Rynes, S. (2011). Counterpoint: Now is a great time for conducting relevant research. In S. Mohrman, E. Lawler & Associates (Eds.), *Useful Research: Advancing theory and practice* (pp. 351–368). San Francisco: Berrett-Koehler Publishers.

Savall, H., & Zardet, V. (2011). *The Qualimetrics Approach: Observing the complex object.* Charlotte, NC: Information Age Publishing Inc.

Sorensen, P., Yaeger, T., Savall, H., Zardet, V., Bonnet, M., & Peron, M. (2010). A review of two major global and international approaches to organizational change: SEAM and Appreciative Inquiry. *OD Journal, 28* (4) 31–40.

Tabchoury, P. (2012, August). Experiences consulting in the Middle East. Panel presentation within MC Symposium entitled "Consulting in the Middle East: Recent Experiences and Alternative Models, Academy of Management, Boston, Massachusetts.

Tenkasi, R. (2011). Integrating theory to inform practice: Insights from the practitioner-scholar. In S. Mohrman, E. Lawler & Associates (Eds.), *Useful research: Advancing theory and practice* (pp. 211–231). San Francisco: Berrett-Koehler Publishers.

Yaeger, T., Sorensen, P., & Bengtsson, U. (2005). Assessment of the state of appreciative inquiry: Past, present and future. In R. Woodman & W. Pasmore (Eds.), *Research in organizational change and development* (pp. 297–319). London: Elsevier Ltd.

CHAPTER 14

CONTRIBUTION OF THE SOCIO-ECONOMIC APPROACH TO MANAGEMENT TO UPDATING JOSEPH WHARTON'S LEGACY

Gilles Guyot

Today, the universal paradigm of business schools doesn't date back to the founder of the first business school, Joseph Wharton, in 1883, at the college of liberal arts of the University of Pennsylvania, the place where, as "ironmaster," he was heading one of the largest industrial companies of that time. In fact, it dates back to the dawn of the fifties, when the situation of business schools was a success for the Master's programs, which had been growing from 110 students in 1910 to 4,335 in 1949 (Daniel, 1998). At that period of time, a failure of academic research had been observed, because professors were mainly involved in vocational education and consultancy.

Facilitating the Socioeconomic Approach to Management, pages 181–192
Copyright © 2014 by Information Age Publishing

THE IMPLEMENTATION OF THE CURRENT PARADIGM

Due to the growing inadequacy between the knowledge imparted to the students and the changing business world (Schlossman, Gleeson, Sedlak, &Allen, 1994, p. 4, quoted by Mintzberg, 2004, p. 25), two large studies were ordered by the Ford foundation, (the Gordon & Howell report) and the Carnegie corporation (the Pierson report). Both studies proposed a new paradigm, based on the model of the Graduate School of Industrial Administration, at the Carnegie Institute of Technology in Pittsburgh. It is important to remind readers of the very influential role played by the Dean of G.S.I.A., George Bach, in both committees. In fact, he convinced them to adopt the so-called "Carnegie Model."

The Carnegie Model

This model, created and set up by George L. Bach, economist and GSIA Dean, has been summarized by Henry Mintzberg (2004) as follows:

- Systematic research matters; teaching follows. «Research was their fundamental engine of progress» (Gleeson & Schlossman, 1995, p. 14).
- Research must be descriptive above all, especially to understand business and organizations; prescription could follow, in practice.
- Such research should be rooted in a set of underlying disciplines, notably economics, psychology, and Mathematics. These should also be central to masters-level courses as well as being the foundations of such business functions as finance, marketing, and accounting.
- The classroom is a place to train students in the skills of analytical problem solving, in the style of operations research, or "management science."
- Particular attention should be given to doctoral studies, to stimulate research and have the graduates carry these ideas to other schools.

This approach was implemented by a group of very smart people, including future Nobel Prize honorees in economics, recruited by Bach, as well as in the other social sciences and mathematics. The most promising output was about "organization theory," which was an attempt to link all disciplines.

From the Practical to the Academic

Mintzberg (2004, p. 28) explains that "the pendulum thus swung with a vengeance, from the practical to the academic- indeed to the very place

where Joseph Wharton had tried to secure it almost a century earlier."
Quoting Pierson, in his 1959 report, Mintzberg (2004, p. 30) underscored:

> If business schools in increasing numbers move into the...direction [pre-
> scribed], the charge will doubtless be made that their work will soon become
> too academic, and thus lose much of its value in terms of specific career train-
> ing. Again, viewed against the record to date, the likelihood that this will oc-
> cur is remote indeed.

In fact, it is the situation today, at least for the mainstream of business
schools all over the world. Indeed questions can be raised about the extent
to which this paradigm is meeting Joseph Wharton's expectations as Mintzberg seems to believe.

WHARTON'S LETTER TO THE TRUSTEES
OF THE UNIVERSITY OF PENNSYLVANIA

The analysis that the above quoted opinion of Mintzberg is not exact is
based on two reasons. First, even though Wharton spoke German and "a
cultured *Germanophile* who had long considered professional training in
Germany as a proper model for America" (Sass, 1982, p. 84), he never took
part in the battle between academic chapels at the University of Pennsylvania, focusing his role (and money) on his Wharton School's model.

Second, everything started in 1876, when John Hopkins University was
founded on the model of the German research design (Sass, 1982, p. 55).
From that time, the German model had rapidly conquered the American
higher education system and both W. Peppper (the provost) and professor Bolles (in charge of recruiting new faculty for the Wharton School in
1883) "had realized that the future success of the Wharton School required
that [they] find some way to join with the dynamic new university system"
(Ibid). For that purpose, they recruited Edmund J. James as professor of
public finance and administration. Trained in German economic thinking (*Cameralist* school), James had received a Doctorate at the university
of Halle, in Prussia. He played a Central role in organizing a German-style
research-oriented graduate school at the university [of Pennsylvania] (Sass,
1982, p. 62). As dean of the Wharton School (1887–1895), he conceived
and implemented a "German Style Wharton School with a Halle trained
faculty at work on the major issues of reform. He was also active in spreading the new academic learning across the nation" (Sass, 1982, p. 79).

The Wharton Model

As described in the letter to the trustees of the University of Pennsylvania, Wharton wanted a program based on "a new relation between the business world and the college of Liberal Arts, leading to a new class of university educated business men." In fact, Wharton has designed his school to fit "a young man...for an efficient civil service as well as for the struggle of commercial life. He would let the students have...what they will of fine college fare but let them do have potatoes" (Sass, 1982, pp. 35–39).

- As a first course, the project specified instruction in accounting and mercantile law.
- As a second course, Wharton identified three different areas of economics: taxation, money and industry, and commerce and transportation. The ironmaster conceived of economics as a policy tool, not as abstract speculation for its own sake.

Wharton also spelled out series of measures to insure that graduates of his school would have a vigorous and conservative character:

> Lazy or incompetent students must be dismissed...elocution should be taught. The general tendency of instruction should be such as to in calculate and impress upon the students...The immorality and practical inexpediency of seeking acquire wealth by winning it from another rather than by earning it through some sort of service to one's fellow-men." (Sass, 1982, p. 21)

Around 1885, James presented a plan to reorganize the Wharton School into a School of political and social science" (Sass, 1982, p. 66). By organizing the intellectual components of particular occupations into a curriculum and setting up a research program to develop this "knowledge," he hoped to bring the enlightenment and dynamism of the university to all practical affairs (Sass, 1982, p. 66). Such was the promise, according to James (1885), of Germany's academic innovations and their diffusion into society. Sass (1982, pp. 68–69) explains that "Joseph Wharton looked with cold jealousy on James' effort to redesign his newborn school. [He] also saw in James' scheme a purpose for the school different from his own. "My object," he pointed out, was simply "to provide if possible a way for young men to fit themselves for the management of affairs—to acquire sound knowledge of the principles of what is called business." And he refused to provide money for this change which then collapsed.

This anecdote, among others, clearly shows that Joseph Wharton's goals were far away from the principles of the Carnegie model. Then, it appears that the mainstream of the current paradigm has betrayed Wharton's teaching goals.

CONSEQUENCES

The myriad consequences of the new paradigm began to appear as early as the beginning of the 1960s, both in teaching and research.

Teaching Management: The MBA

The current MBA was totally reorganized in the sixties as a consequence of both the Gordon & Howell report and the Pierson report, "faculty at Columbia, Chicago, Harvard, and Wharton recommending more tightly structured, more broadly based and more academically rigorous programs" (Hunt & Speck, 1986, p. 160). By the same time, "the effect on undergraduate programs was delayed and their program directors were unable to respond rapidly because of the poor almost marginal quality of the students they were able to attract." As Murray (1988, p. 71) further explains:

> by the desire of the business schools to enhance the quality of their student intake... Another motive was the desire of graduate business school academics to improve their status vis-à-vis academics in the other parts of the parent university.

In fact, we are certainly approaching the real explanation of the success of this new paradigm with the faculty: the fundamental and universal complex of professors in management towards their colleagues of the other disciplines and their thirst for academic respectability. It is true that, from the very beginning, their students were not among the best, and their link to practice was not well considered by the other disciplines.

Whatever were the reasons, it appeared that in the 1980s the broad MBA was not very good. We have seen the doubts of Pierson, in 1959, who argued that, "too much academic work [will] lose a large part of its value in term of training for a specific career." One of the coauthors of the other report published in 1959, Howell (quoted by Murray, 1988, p. 71), wrote: "...the current paradigm of business education, the MBA, which has worked quite well for a long period of time, twenty-five years or so, isn't going to work much longer. You can see it breaking down at the edges. That's inevitable, that the way it should be (Schmotter, 1984, p. 14)."

It is clearly documented that, since the mid-1980s, a lot of criticism has been written on the MBA, from Porter and Mc Kibbin (1988, p. 64) to Mintzberg (2004). The former criticized the business schools for focusing too much "on analytics, with insufficient emphasis on problem finding as contrasted with problem solving and implementation" and the latter, quoting Leavitt (1989, p. 40), reckoned that "80% of the MBA curriculum in top-rated American business schools [was] concerned with just the analytic problem solving." He also emphasized the splitting of business schools into a set of hermetic silos and the coming down of social science disciplines. Even at GSIA, by 1973, the integrative "administrative theory" completely disappeared (Mintzberg, 2004, p. 31).

Consultants (e.g., McKinsey, Boston Consulting Group) who appointed graduates in philosophy, wrote that they were as good as MBAs (sometimes better), with a three weeks training instead of two years (Pfeffer & Fong, 2002, p. 81). The impact on salaries was not significant, except for the best students graduating from the best schools (parable of the banana tree: what matters is the selection process at the entrance of the program, which supposes that you get enough top students). Some people could object that MBAs may have improved since the eighties but many authors (Mintzberg & Gosling, 2002, p. 28) have shown that, even though new subjects have been added, "the basic structure of courses and the basic concepts are remarkably similar" (Pfeffer & Fong, 2002, p. 84).

The major issue remains the very nature of management, which has been thoroughly analyzed by Mintzberg (2004, p. 2):

> What I call conventional management programs, which are mostly for young people with little if any managerial experience ("Wrong People"...) because they are unable to use art or craft, emphasize science in the form of analysis and technique (Wrong Ways...). That leaves their graduates with the false impression that they have been trained as managers, which has had a corrupting effect on the education and the practice of management as well as on our organizations and societies in which it is practiced (Wrong Consequences...).

For Mintzberg, synthesis, not analysis, is the very essence of management, and conventional management courses teach only analysis. As he concludes, "Management education must be based on experience. Managers cannot be made in vitro" (Brown, Crainer, Dearlove, & Rodrigues, 2002, p. 162).

Mintzberg (2004, p. 6) has also clearly defined the very nature of management, noting:

> It's not a science, merely an art and, above all, a craft. What MBA students get in their classes is knowledge of functional analysis (often reduced to technique) and systematic assessments...Art encourages creativity and leads to "ideas," to a "vision." Craft, based on tangible experience, try to establish connections.

Due to a strong commitment to academic approach, MBA programs are unable to prepare students for managing people in their individual singularity and to handling a decision-making process.

Much of what business schools impart—theory and analytical techniques of various sorts—is readily learned and imitated . . . Communication ability, leadership, interpersonal skills, and wisdom . . . "the ability to weave together and make use of different kinds of knowledge" (Mintzberg & Gosling, 2002, p. 28) are, at once, less easily taught or transferred to others, but . . . have more value in the competition for leadership positions. (Pfeffer & Fong, 2002, p. 84)

Quoting Bailey & Ford (1996, p. 9), Pfeffer & Fong (2002, p. 85) further note that "the practice of management is as best taught as a craft, rich in lessons derived from experience and oriented towards taking and responding to action." In fact, as pointed out by Leavitt (1989, p. 40), "the lack of fields for practice is a dramatic weakness in this teaching process."

Last (but not least) the silo system, which has been developed in all American business schools since the 1960s, has destroyed all cooperation between disciplines. If management were (and indeed it is) a discipline of synthesis between functions, in order to find and implement the best possible action, since the failure of "administrative science" and the cancelling of the business policy course, replaced by the new "strategic management" silo, all sorts of "horizontal course" has disappeared from the curriculum (Mintzberg, 2004).

Research in Management: The Pretence of Knowledge

By the 1960s, business schools, in order to gain academic recognition] took on the "traditions and ways of mainstream academia" (Crainer & Dearlove, 1999, p. 40 quoted by Pfeffer & Fong, 2002, p. 79). Quantitative, statistical analysis gained prominence, as did the study of the science of decision making. In both their teaching and research activities, business schools "enthusiastically seized on and applied a scientific paradigm of precision, control and testable models" (Bailey & Ford, 1996, p. 8). Of course, the contribution of this research to knowledge has been fruitful and decisive, but management is not economics and cannot be reduced to a world only populated with *homo economicus*.

In fact, even in economy, the desire to reduce research to a scientist approach (like in physics), has been very much criticized. In his Nobel Memorial lecture, given on December, 11th, 1974, Friedrich von Hayek (1989, p. 7) explained:

our capacity will be confined to such general characteristics of the events to be expected and not include the capacity of predicting particular individual events. That corresponds to . . . the mere pattern predictions to which we are increasingly confined as we penetrate in from the realm, in which relatively simple laws prevail, [i.e., Physics] into the range of phenomena, where organized complexity rules...Of course, compare with the precise predictions we...expect in the physical sciences, this sort of...predictions is a second best with which one doesn't like to have to be content. Yet the danger of which I want to warn is precisely the belief that, in order to have a claim to be accepted as scientific, it is necessary to achieve more. This way lies charlatanism and worse...

That is the pretence of knowledge, which is a consequence of a "scientistic" attitude. And Hayek had expressed it even more in his introduction (Ibid, p. 3). The "scientistic" attitude—an attitude which, as I defined it some thirty years ago, "is decidedly unscientific in the true sense of the word, since it involves a mechanical and uncritical application of habits of thought to fields different from those in which they have been formed. I want today to begin by explaining how some of the gravest errors of recent economic policy are a direct consequence of this scientistic error.

Note: given in 1974 in Stockholm, the lecture has been published in December 1989 by the American Economic Review.

Management, unlike economics, is a crowded world. There, every individual person, in his or her own singularity, is an actor of the firm. All the time, the individual makes decisions (or not, which is similar), and this reality makes management apart from the other social sciences. To manage well requires one to get the best from everyone and the best game from the team.

Because of the pressure exerted by economists on management, mainly in finance, the actors have been replaced by *homines economici*, driven by their personal interest. Pouring from finance, great theories have contaminated all management's functional silos.

> Rejecting what we saw as the "romanticism" of analyzing corporate behaviors in terms of the choices, actions and achievements...we have adopted the "scientific" approach of trying to discover patterns and laws and have replaced all notions of human intentionality with a firm belief in causal determinism for explaining all aspects of corporate performance. In effect, we have professed that business is reducible to a kind of Physics. (Ghoshal (2005, p. 77)

and he goes further:

> I argue that academic research has had some very significant and negative influences on the practice of management. More specifically, I suggest that, by propagating ideology inspired amoral theories, business schools have freed their students from any sense of moral responsibility.

This "gloomy vision (Hirshman, 1970) has led management research increasingly in the direction of making excessive truth-claims based on partial analysis and both unrealistic and biased assumptions." And Ghoshal claims that, because—in social sciences—theories are self-fulfilling (Gergen, 1973, p. 313), it has had dramatic consequences on management practices. For example, theory implies that:

> the manager's task is to use hierarchical authority to prevent the opportunists from benefitting at the costs of others...The outcome of such [an] approach...is: Instead of controlling and reducing opportunistic behavior of people, it is likely to create and enhance such behaviors. (Ghoshal & Moran, 1996, p. 25)

"As there is a degree of depravity in mankind which requires a certain degree of circumspection and distrust, so there are other qualities in human nature which justify a certain proportion of esteem and confidence," wrote James Madison in the Federalist Papers (1788, February 13th), and he concluded: "were the picture which have been drawn by... some among us faithful likenesses, the inference would be that... nothing but the chains of despotism can restrain [men]... from destroying... one another." That is why, applying certain models, due to their implicit ideas, conducts companies to large internal conflicts and underachievement.

The result has been clearly diagnosed by Harold Leavitt (1989, p. 39): "We have built a weird, almost unimaginable design for MBA level education that distorts those subjected to it into creatures with lopsided brains, icy hearts and shrunken souls." We are now light-years from Wharton's moral philosophy. And the result is awesome. The Enron/Andersen case is the most emblematic, but there are many other ones. It may also explain the poor international performance of many companies.

ALTERNATIVE "QUALIMETRICS" MODELS

Among the various reasons emphasized to explain why the current paradigm remains in place, in spite of the strong critics it faces since a quarter of a century, is the lack of credible alternative models. As an example of contribution to bridging the gap between theory and practice in management science we will present the socio-economic approach to management.

Among models that can be used to revamp the management education system, Mintzberg mentions several schools of thoughts, mostly drawing on the action-research stream. We propose to examine in particular the example of the Socio-economic approach to management and show how it might contribute to tipping the scale of the Wharton's model. This socio-economic theory has been developed through a long-standing process of interaction between researchers and company actors over the past decades. The research process is referred to as qualimetrics intervention-research (Savall & Zardet, 2011), a kind of action-research which consists in discovering concealed variables on company performance through experimenting organizational innovations with company actors. The epistemological underpinnings of this approach consist of a hybrid constructionist and positivistic epistemologies. Indeed, the scientific objective is to create generic contingency knowledge—scientific laws, which are independent from any settings, *and* context specific knowledge, which is useful for a given company or industry.

The socio-economic theory contributes to both research and teaching in the management sciences.

Contribution to Research

Socio-economic theory is based on "scientific observation of the complex object" (Savall & Zardet, 1984), consisting of organizational metamorphosis. Indeed, the Wharton model might have been relevant in a time when variables were not as numerous as today. In essence, there was not as much interaction at global level and people were considered as obedient and submissive human resources. It is not the case anymore, and the paradigm of complexity, as developed since March and Simon's (1958) seminal book on "Organizations" has been largely ignored by quantitative research methodologies, even when trying to fine tune structural equations with moderator variables, because of the heap of unveiled variables.

Many attempts at capturing the complexity of dynamic phenomena, in particular in the field of action-research, fell through getting academic recognition because they mostly produce context-specific knowledge as opposed to knowledge that can be relevant in any kind of organization. In contrast, the socio-economic generic contingency principle enables sorting out those variables that are context specific and the generic ones. An example of an outcome of generic contingency implementation is the dramatic increase of hidden costs when dysfunctions are observed, whatever the kind of industry.

Contribution to Academic Curricula

In the field of management education most curricula include not only the underpinnings of management science (e.g., law, sociology, psychology, statistics, economics) and various subdisciplines such as finance management and management control, marketing management, strategic management and human resource management. As a follow-up to all the seminars taught in those various domains, a kind of "cap-stone" seminar is offered to help students make sense of the various "spare parts" of management know-how they have been trained in. Such seminars often consist of case studies presenting the different pieces of a jigsaw and students have to work together in teams to design full-fledge business plans. However, no robust scientific theory is provided, which Mintzberg considers as an art that requires reflexivity that only seasoned managers can get hold on. A different stance is proposed by the socio-economic approach to management, because it is designed to be a silo-breaker theory of management and sets up a common language for management throughout the organization to enable cooperation between the different departments and projects as well as throughout the hierarchical line.

CONCLUSION

Today, many authors share our diagnosis, but whisper that the stream of quantitative research is just unstoppable. The question doesn't lie there. In fact, we believe that the "scientistic" quantitative research, based on theoretical economics (mainly econometrics), will continue to develop in relevant fields, likely in Finance or Macro-Economics. But, similarly, the development of qualitative action-research methods, not only based on economics, but also on social approaches, taking account of the real complexity of management today (and of the nature of human beings), should create an alternative in certain fields where the current paradigm, clearly, has failed, likely human resource or public management.

This focus would allow people, not only academic publishers, but also business reviews and professional publications, to see which approach is of real interest to their concerns and to the needs of scholarship but as well as to business development, the ultimate goal of Joseph Wharton. Then, in any given class of issues, the "market" will ultimately decide what is relevant and what is not.

REFERENCES

Bailey, J., & Ford, C. (1996). Management as science versus Management as Practice in Postgraduate Business Education. *Business Strategy Review, 7*(4), 7–12.

Brown, T., Crainer, S., Dearlove, D., & Rodrigues, J. N. (2002). *Business minds: Connect with the world's greatest management thinkers.* Englewood Cliffs, NJ: Prentice-Hall.

Crainer, S., & Dearlove, D. (1999). *Gravy Training: Inside the business of business schools.* San Francisco: Jossey-Bass.

Daniel, C. A. (1998). *MBA: the First Century.* Cranbury, NJ: Associated University Presses.

Gergen, K. J. (1973). Social Psychology as History. *Journal of Personality and Social Psychology, 26,* 309–320.

Ghoshal, S. (2005). Bad Management Theories are Destroying Good Management Practices, *Academy of Management Learning and Education, 4*(1), 75–91.

Ghoshal, S., & Moran, P. (1996). Bad for Practices: A Critique of the Transactions Costs Theory. *Academy of Management Review, 21*(1), 13–47.

Gleeson, R. E., & Schlossman, S. (1995). George Leland Bach and the Rebirth of Graduate Management Education in the United States, 1945–1975. *Selections: The Magazine of the Graduate Management Admission Council, 11*(3), 8–46.

Hayek, F. A. (1989). The pretence of Knowledge, *American Economic Review, December,* 3–7.

Hirshman, A. O. (1970). *Exit, Voice and Loyalty: Response to Decline in Firms, Organizations and States.* Cambridge, MA: Harvard University Press.

Hunt, S. D., & Speck, P. S. (1986).Specialization and the MBA. *California Management Review, 28*(3), 169–175.

James, E. J. (1885). *Instruction in Political and Social Sciences.* Philadelphia, PA: Philadelphia Social Sciences Association.

Leavitt, H. J. (1989). Educating our MBAs: on teaching what we haven't taught. *California Management Review, 31*(3), 38–50.

Madison, J. (1788). *Federalist Papers no. 55,* Wednesday, February 13.

March, J. G., & Simon, H. A. (1958). *Organizations.* New-York, NY: John Wiley and Sons.

Mintzberg, H. (2004). *Managers, Not MBAs.* San Francisco, CA: Bennett-Koehler Publishers.

Mintzberg, H., & Gosling, J. R. (2002). Reality Programming for MBAs. *Strategy and Business, 26*(1), 28–31.

Murray, H. (1988). Management Education and the MBA: It's Time for a Rethink, *Managerial and Decision Economics, 9*(5), 71–78.

Pfeffer, J., & Fong, C. T. (2002). The End of Business Schools? Less Success Than Meets the Eye, *Academy of Management Learning and Education, 1*(1), 78–95.

Porter, L. W., & Mc Kibbin, L. E. (1988). *Management Education and Development: Drift or Thrust in the 21th Century?* New-York, NY: McGraw Hill.

Sass, S. A. (1982). *The Pragmatic Imagination: A History of the Wharton School, 1881–1981.* Philadelphia, PA: University of Pennsylvania Press.

Savall, H., & Zardet, V. (1984). Outils expérimentés de la gestion socio-économique des organisations : impacts croisés des systèmes d'information et des comportements organisationnels [Experienced tools of socio-economic approach to management of organizations: crossed impacts of information systems and organizational behaviors]. In *Développement des sciences et pratiques de l'organisation. Les outils de l'action collective* [Development of organizational sciences & practices. Collective action tools]. AFCET.

Savall, H., & Zardet, V. (2011). *Qualimetrics: Observing the complex object.* Charlotte, NC: Information Age.

Schlossman, S., Gleeson, Sedlak, M., & Allen, D. (1994). *The beginnings of Graduate Management Education in the United States.* Santa Monica, CA: Graduate Management Admission Council.

Schmotter, J. W. (1984). An interview with professor James E. Howell. *Selections,* (Spring).

CHAPTER 15

DELIBERATING COST

Deliberative Practices in Qualimetrics and the Socio-Economic Approach to Management[1]

Robert P. Gephart, Jr.

CONFERENCE REMARKS:
Chapter Prologue

Robert Gephart

This presentation is about "deliberating cost." It represents what I wanted to look at in the practices of qualimetrics and the socio-economic approach to management (SEAM). This paper is based on a five-year research project that came to a close at the end of March. This project was looking at and taking a broader view of the theory of sensemaking and how sensemaking works in society. It was based on studying how people really understand, interpret or even know the signs in the world. By understanding and interpreting, they are giving meaning to and making sense of signs. My own approach is sociological and not based on any mathematical methodology. I was really interested in the public hearing context because there are lots

Facilitating the Socioeconomic Approach to Management, pages 193–207
Copyright © 2014 by Information Age Publishing

of studies that use hearings as sources of data to study topics such as energy issues but do not look at the sensemaking per se that actually constitutes discourse and deliberation during hearings.

DELIBERATIVE DEMOCRACY AND ORGANIZATIONS

If we look at the public hearing context, we can see this is often the only opportunity that people have to really get included in the policy-making process. At the government level, you have the discourses about public policy. By involving other people in hearings these discourses can become more democratic. The concept of deliberative democracy is seen from both the masses of workers and government actions. It is very important to encourage citizens to be involved in hearings as a means to encourage democratic processes in society since public hearings are a visible sign of democracy.

The Deliberative Democracy

By "to deliberate," I mean to "do democracy." It is something that happens when you involve people in discussions of policies. It happens every day in every conversation, even when in past centuries we invented our country and our freedom; everything is an ongoing conversation basic to democracy. I was wondering if that goes on in this context of SEAM interventions and I started from there. One of my problems is that I am an outsider to the SEAM approach. I can read the materials in SEAM-based books but I have not seen interaction between the discourses and the practices. I am a little bit distant from this, it is like I am driving around the outside of the phenomenon, and I would rather be in the middle exploring it.

Deliberation is the best means of discussion to produce a reasonable wealth of insights from opinions. People are invited to understand new information. One of the philosophers who developed much of this idea is Habermas. If you have people in an interactional mode, listening to the others and debating things then, when people change their opinion based on the new information, you have deliberative democracy. It is a normative theory in political science based on Habermas' ideas. It addresses how we could strengthen democracy, by criticizing the institutions and adopting the standards of a democratic decision-making process.

This depiction of deliberative democracy addresses the state level of analysis and moves analysis down to include the organizational level. This state level interacts with the organizational level in some research including my own. In the management area, we can observe the critical theory of Habermas. We have critical management studies in groups such as the

Academy of Management that do not focus heavily on Habermas. There are other kinds of visions of critical theories but I am a "Habermasian" and I think that Habermas is one of the most well written critical thinkers. He is publicly a preeminent "thinker" and he is still alive. We want to use his ideas to explore decision making in organizations and this is a largely unexplored domain.

Production of Sense in Organization

We want to sit, observe, and understand proper decision making processes and creation of democratic "will"—the desire for democratic processes in society that involves cooperation among different parties and groups. People can create and use those democratic and cooperative forms, and we want to explore these deliberative relationships more deeply. This could mean creating reasonable policies and the production of sense in organizations. We are asking about the relationship of Habermasian critical theory with qualimetrics and SEAM. SEAM is a critical theory and offers critical practices.

I am wondering how the deliberative products could be used as a cost testament. Also, how are the deliberative practices operating in SEAM? I don't address the methods used in the research or touch on them today. My current interrogation or research question is on the way to improve these deliberative practices in organizations. This is a great agenda for future research. I think that through the intervention process we can create deliberation through communication and make organizations more democratic and effective.

To people, democracy is basically done through communication: private meetings and public forums, which is deliberation. "To deliberate" means to find and discuss reasons for decisions and to support views with rational arguments. It is a process in which democracy can occur. I will say that democracy has too many constraining influences; we just have to look at insights from political sciences, which are studying that. Features of deliberation involve public talk among citizens. They are invited to develop shared views, and create these views in formal and informal settings. That is the feature needed to establish valid communication.

COMMUNICATION IN SEAM

Communication: it is the thing that occurs when people make commitments and talk, accepting the obligation for validation of their statements.

Links Between Principles of Communication and SEAM

In some cases we could have a list of things that have to be done and a boss saying: "You do that because I am the boss." This is not really a deliberative starting point or a good way to proceed. We could identify 4 types of speech acts: communicative, representative, regulative, and constitutive. You could stay deliberative if the rationales of people using these speech acts and deliberation seem to sustain democracy—that is, if they are motivated to offer and accept arguments and act on them in a rational manner.

The socio-economic approach to management is a well-tested methodical approach and has been used for a couple of decades. This approach associates observed costs and hidden costs with human potential using qualimetrics principles. SEAM researchers have addressed communication with principles that quickly resolve into something I considered similar to principles of effective sensemaking. First, for example, the idea that "*We have partners in our activity*" is the idea that we challenge reactions and feedback to get quality information and thus engage in the principle of cognitive interactivity. Second, the principle of *contradictory intersubjectivity* means that you have to get different subjectivities, you feed diverse perceptions to get more objective foundations for consensus. Third, *generic contingency* is the conception that an idea is found in many situations and has universality.

SEAM process steps and qualimetrics principles are similar to practices of valid communication. Even in quite direct activities we need training to produce valid communication. Thus you need to regulate or direct appropriate talk. For example, if you try to talk about what you are teaching in class, and a person responds "no, my vacation was great," then you need to keep communication on track. Also, I am wondering how sense is made with representative truth, which seems to me to be the key challenge for a critical theory perspective. I can see in SEAM how the focus is on the processes of intervention seeking to grasp the entire communication process and to ask: is that talk knowledge? Is it appropriate? Is it rational and what knowledge in relationships will legitimate a need to engage in concrete operations?

The relationships between people through communication should be considered a core of democracy. Deliberation works well with a subordinate and a supervisor. It is better with coworkers who need to be with other employees to understand each other's work experiences. There is a challenge in ensuring deliberation and I think those challenges, by the use of practices of valid communication, may be value added. Without valid communication, work practices won't be as effective.

Application in Organization Practices

In the chapter, we chose to introduce the idea that subjectivity is embedded in numbers and tried to understand some different perceptions of costs transforming these different views of effective cost management in the context of objective cost. It was an occasion to improve the conception of knowledge. The challenge is to define the way that you create truth to assure the intent of sense added communication. You can see here that with intent, the key idea of *generic contingency* can be pursued. Searching for truth, the key challenge is the way you determine the nature of truth. By what method do you legitimate knowledge? There could be a proper way or there could be ways to force someone to go along with you and accept this truth, in which case your intent won't accord with a deliberative or democratic method.

In an organization today, the correct answer to the question of "what is 2 + 2?" is the answer that the boss accepts and sometimes it could be 1 or 2! In contrast to such deformed conceptions of truth, we are wondering what type of sense-making practices underlay communication that produces truthful and valid content that generates generic contingency. We want to look at the process that designs the player in negotiation. By this, I want to change our conception of truth and sincerity. Will people really disclose things? The people actually negotiating often don't disclose things when their interest is better served by nondisclosure. Further, the contract negotiation process restricts the involvement of people by increasing legal and rather formal social relations. It could make people evolve their ideas in a particular way that it is not the way one needs. In addition, top management plays a strong role in framing innovation that often produces an institutional power structuring with a political tension and a narrow focus on explicit costs. Such an institution does not create legitimate talk and will feel the challenge of irrational actions. I can see in my organization what would happen if we tried to use and truthfully disclose the mirror effect—this is something that would be difficult for people to accept.

People in normal practice implicitly show the importance of valid communication and also use some of the practices and fundamentals of SEAM and qualimetrics intervention. Basically I think that SEAM has taken a step forward with the principles of valid communication. SEAM actually works when practitioners consider, address and anticipate many of the principles of valid communication and deliberative democracy. One of the possible ways to advance SEAM and deliberation in organizations is thus to develop valid communication in organizations. I would like to observe cases where this occurs and to work on understanding the political aspects of communication practices. The future challenge is to uncover valid communication practices used in the SEAM intervention process. In particular I am interested in discovering North America's structuring and communication processes that relate to fundamental aspects of hidden costs and benefits. It is a democratic process that still needs to be more fully developed in organizations others consider important. Through democratic processes, we may have much better organizations.

INTRODUCTION

Deliberation "is debate and discussion aimed at producing reasonable, well-informed opinions in which participants are willing to revise preferences in light of discussion, new information, and claims made by fellow participants" (Chambers, 2003, p. 309). It is distinct from other forms of talk including bargaining and rhetoric. Deliberation emerged as a topic in political theory that addresses public deliberation and deliberative democracy. *Deliberative democracy* is a normative theory of how we can strengthen democracy and criticize institutions that do not meet normative standards of democratic decision-making. *Deliberative democracy* focuses on "the communication processes of opinion and will-formation" undertaken in public settings where this communication is prior to or separate from voting in elections (Chambers, 2003). Public deliberation is essential to democracy and it involves discussion, judicious argument, critical listening and earnest decision (DelliCarpini, Cook, & Jacobs, 2004).

Political theory discussions of deliberative democracy focus on the macro-level of society and address public law, international relations, social policies, and identity politics (Chambers, 2003; DelliCarpini, et al., 2004). In the organizational area, empirical research (Gephart, 2007, 2008) has focused on public forums for deliberation. These interorganizational settings include formal public hearings, public information sessions, and town hall meetings where actors from different organizations and groups meet to discuss and debate policy formation related to important infrastructure projects such as pipelines, gas wells, and oil sands mines.

The current paper explores the under-explored level of deliberation within organizations. We treat the corporation or organization as a "political actor" (Scherer & Paluzzo, 2007, p. 1108) and seek to explore deliberative practices at the organizational level. That is, we seek to understand "corporate decision making in processes of democratic will formation" (Scherer & Paluzzo, 2007, p. 1109) and democratic decision-making processes involved in corporate will formation. This leads us to address how deliberation in organizations "shapes preferences," enhances "integration and solidarity," creates "reasonable opinion and policy" and leads to consensus (Chambers, 2003, p. 309). We explore these issues in the context of qualimetric interventions into organizations where financial numbers are constructed by groups of employees and then used to represent hidden costs of operations (Savall & Zardet, 2011; Savall, Zardet, & Bonnet, 2008). Our general question is, "what is the role of deliberative practices in qualimetrics and the socio-economic approach to management?" More specifically, we ask: (a) how are deliberative practices used in producing estimates of hidden costs in organizations?; (b) what deliberative practices are absent or uncommon?; and (c) how could deliberative practices be extended and strengthened to improve estimates of hidden costs and make the socio-economic approach more effective? In the sections that follow, we address deliberation and valid communication in organizations, describe the SEAM perspective and qualimetric approach to estimating hidden costs in organizations, and then explore deliberation involved in hidden cost estimation.

DELIBERATION AND VALID COMMUNICATION IN ORGANIZATIONS

The concept of deliberative democracy is often closely associated with the work of Jurgen Habermas (1979, 1984, 1989, and 1996) and his work on the public sphere. Democratic theory has generally been voter-centric and views democracy as an area where public preferences and interests compete by fair mechanisms that aggregate preferences (e.g., voting).

In contrast to traditional democratic theory, deliberative democracy is a communication-centric theory of democracy that focuses on how communicative processes lead to opinion and will formation in a wide range of social settings (Chambers, 2003) in the public sphere. Deliberation requires public talk (DelliCarpini, et al., 2004) that is reflective, reasonably open ended, and that occurs under conditions of general equality (Button & Mattson, 1999, p. 610). Deliberation is widespread. It occurs any time a citizen justifies or accounts for, or defends, their views (DelliCarpini et al., 2004, p. 318). This view of democratic theory moves deliberation from an occasional phenomenon done in institutional settings centered around elections and voting to an ongoing communicative process common in everyday life situations (Bakardjieva, 2008; Gephart, 2008). For example, spirited conversations about important organizational and social policies can take the form of deliberation and these instances of deliberation can occur in backstage private settings such as organizational meetings as well as in public forums such as public hearings (Bakardjieva, 2008). Thus deliberation is "the process through which deliberative democracy occurs" (DelliCarpini, et al., 2004, p. 317). "Most fundamentally, deliberative democracy affirms the need to justify decisions" (Gutmann & Thompson, 2004, p. 3).

Deliberation as explored in this chapter has several features. First, it involves (public) talk and conversation among citizens. Second, it allows people to develop views on issues, to express these views, to learn views of others, and to reach agreements based on shared interests. Third, deliberation can occur in both formal and informal settings and these can be public or private settings. Fourth, a range of media can be used to enact deliberation (DelliCarpini, et al., 2004).

A key feature of democratic deliberation is that it seeks to both use and produce features of valid or undistorted communication (Habermas, 1979). Valid communication occurs when speakers make commitments in conversations and accept the obligation to provide rational grounds for their claims. Four types of speech acts or verbal practices produce 4 types of validity claims. Communicatives claim to be comprehensible and function to create an environment where conversational statements will be recognized. Representatives claim to be sincere or truthful and operate to disclose the subjectivity of the speaker. Regulatives are claims that statements are appropriate to the context and these practices work to establish acceptable and legitimate interpersonal relationships. Constatives claim to be true and thus to represent facts. The assumption is that if the stated claims can be substantiated, the hearer will be motivated to accept the claims of the speaker (Habermas, 1979, p. 63). If the claims are not substantiated they will be less likely to produce action motivating meanings and may meet resistance.

THE SOCIO-ECONOMIC APPROACH AND QUALIMETRICS

The chapter examines the compatibility between the deliberative democracy view of deliberative processes that take place in organizations and the Socio-Economic Management (SEAM) approach to organization. We are concerned with understanding the impact of deliberative practices on the SEAM approach and to gain insights into where and how we can strengthen deliberative practices in qualimetrics to make the SEAM approach more effective.

The Socio-Economic Approach to Management was developed in the mid-1970s by Henri Savall, a French management researcher who is based at ISEOR (Socio-Economic Institute of Firms and Organizations Research). SEAM theory integrates the social and economic sides of the organization. The assumption of SEAM is that there is an "ongoing interaction between the organization structure and the employees' behavior" (Savall, 2003, p. 33). This interaction stands behind the life of organization, and is responsible for both the effective functioning of the organization and the dysfunctions that arise during the life of any firm. The frictions between organization structures (which include physical, demographic, technological, and mental structures) cause dysfunctions classified in six categories: working conditions, work organization, communication–coordination–cooperation, time management, job training, and implementation of the strategy. "These dysfunctions result in wasted resources (loss of value added) which can be spotted by means of five symptom indicators: absenteeism, work accidents, personnel turnover, lack of quality (products and services) and direct productivity losses" (Savall, 2003, p. 33). These hidden costs significantly impact the sustainable performance of organizations. The dysfunctions, organization structures, hidden costs, and behaviors are interconnected: "The relative degeneration (atrophy) of structures and behaviors leads to bloated dysfunctions and hidden costs, which handicaps the sustainable economic performance" (Savall, 2003, p. 34–35).

Another important assumption for the SEAM theory is that the social complexity within organizations leads to the operation of contradictory forces: autonomy and integration. This occurs because social complexity increases due to the finer division of labor and the further specialization of skills of actors. This complexity provokes actors into undertaking scattered behaviors in multiple forms: they search for autonomy but lack coordination needed to accomplish work which leads to absenteeism or staff turnover (Savall, 2003, p. 36). Thus the production process requires integration through the cooperation of actors whose work must be coordinated. At the same time, workers seek independence and autonomy (escape).

Researchers who are working within the SEAM approach also developed a methodology of intervention in order to help organizations attain higher efficiencies in their work. A socio-economic intervention "can be considered a 'machine for negotiating' innovative solutions, with the underlying goal of reducing the dysfunctions experienced by the enterprise" (Savall, 2007, p. 3). In contrast to the more traditional approaches to management that concentrate on the financial performance of the firm, "the socio-economic approach, factors both people and finances into analysis. The result is an intervention that works with the whole organizational system" (Conbere & Heorhiadi, 2011, p. 6). An important part of the intervention is the work done to locate and decrease hidden costs. "SEAM offers a methodical, tested way to assess the hidden costs in an organization" (Conbere & Heorhiadi, 2011, p. 6).

Qualimetrics is the methodical means used to assess hidden costs (Savall & Zardet, 2011). From the point of view of SEAM, dysfunctions in organizations are hidden costs (Savall & Zardet, 2008, p. xix) that are collectively produced. Hidden costs are implicit and can be evaluated by associating each of the 6 components of hidden costs with the 5 indicators of dysfunctions (Savall & Zardet, 2008, p. 29).

Three principles are basic to qualimetric intervention (Savall, 2007). *Cognitive interactivity* involves an interactive process between researcher and organizational actors. This process produces knowledge through successive feedback loops with the goal of enhancing the value of significant information produced by scientific work (Buono & Savall, 2007, p. 424). *Contradictory intersubjectivity* is the technique qualimetrics uses to create consensus from varying subjective perceptions of different organizational actors. This consensus provides more objective foundations for collective work (Buono & Savall, 2007, p. 423). *Generic contingency* postulates there are invariants that exist and these constitute generic rules embodying core knowledge that exhibits stability and universality (Buono & Savall, 2007, p. 4). The management of hidden costs identified through intervention is done by identifying investments needed to overcome the dysfunction (Savall, et al., 2008, p. 58).

The SEAM intervention process begins when an organizational member or interested party contacts ISEOR about a dysfunction that needs to be addressed. This triggers a negotiation process between the organization and ISEOR (Savall, 2007, p. 16) that concludes with a written contract or agreement stipulating terms of the intervention. The negotiation phase is a client-driven process initiated by a member of the organization referred to as the introducer who has a delicate role to play since a top manager or "decider-player" with financial authority to allocate funds and formal authority to authorize the intervention needs to be recruited quickly (Savall, 2007, p. 17).

After the "decider-player" is located, a semi-structured interview is set up to identify and formalize the intervention. Through the negotiation process and phase, researchers seek to understand whether their understanding of the enterprise's view is the same as the enterprise's view in part through use of a "mirror effect" (Savall, 2007, p. 18). Thereafter, a series of meetings are held that lead to refinement and validation of the intervention agreement as well as validation of the cost estimate for the intervention. Horizontal actions by directors are initiated and managers are initiated and it is through these actions that estimates of hidden costs are produced.

The process of hidden cost estimation involves a researcher-intervener who meets with managers of an organization to address a dysfunction that has been identified. Using a process similar to a focus group, the intervener encourages a group discussion to clarify the nature of the dysfunction, to identify the frequency of the dysfunction, to uncover the reasons for the dysfunction, and to estimate components of financial consequences (Savall, et al., 2008, p. 32–34). Collaborative training sessions are held and personal coaching is provided to top and middle management in use of SEAM tools that emphasize both training in the SEAM method and exchanges or conversations among members that create resolutions and resolution charts to guide changes to team practices.

In addition, vertical actions are taken to bring in lower-level workers (Savall, 2007, p. 20). This involves creating a focus group supervised by the department head and this group is hierarchically structured with a core group, project leader, and task groups, using employees at all levels (Savall, 2007, pp. 25–26) to evaluate costs of proposed changes and to estimate value added due to reduction of dysfunctions and hidden costs.

DELIBERATING COSTS

This section of the chapter examines how practices of deliberation and sensemaking are involved in and/or needed for analysis of hidden costs. First, we address how principles of valid communication are implied by and necessary for operation of the 3 basic principles of qualimetrics and SEAM. Next, we explore how practices of valid communication are necessary for qualimetric processes to function effectively. We pose questions that need to be answered to insure communication involved in estimating costs is valid and address evidence regarding constraints on free and open communication.

Qualimetric Principles

Cognitive interactivity brings researchers and organizational members (managers) together to coproduce knowledge with the intent of improving scientific information on dysfunctions, hidden costs, and resolutions of hidden costs. Through training and coaching members to understand and use the SEAM approach, the process allows members to develop and produce communicatives—comprehensible statements that use key terms. It is a critical part of SEAM work to teach these key terms to organizational members while researchers learn the world views of managers. Regulatives that establish legitimate relations and contextually appropriate talk can emerge over time and meetings. Further, normative patterns of communication within group settings can be negotiated and can emerge. The goal is to improve the quality of scientific knowledge and this requires representatives or truthful and sincere communication oriented to producing constatives or facts. The key questions needed to ascertain whether or not the communication is democratic and deliberative are: (a) regarding communicatives, what knowledge is taught and needed to participate in deliberation between the researcher and the employees?; and (b) regarding regulatives, what knowledge is contextually appropriate to hidden cost deliberations? What interpersonal relationships are needed and legitimate for deliberation?

Contradictory intersubjectivity seeks to understand different perceptions of managers related to dysfunctions that create hidden costs and to create a consensus on the nature of dysfunctions and measures of hidden costs out of diverse perceptions that members have. This seeks to transform different views of the world into a shared and more "objective" estimate of costs. Through training and coaching, managers can improve conceptual knowledge of SEAM practices and theory. Through meetings, managers can learn what is contextually useful and acceptable in intervention contexts and can improve the intervention process. Thus the key question for effective contradictory intersubjectivity is how truthfulness is enacted in deliberation such that the intent of valid communication and sincerity among parties is demonstrated. Generic contingency postulates and seeks to uncover invariant, stable and/or universal rules and core knowledge in organizations.

Uncovering generic contingencies is a search for truths and thus the key questions related to whether or how deliberative practices underlay the discovery of generic contingencies are: (a) how is truth determined and legitimated in communication?; and (b) what sense-making practices, including provision of scientific evidence, underlay and produce consensus on generic contingencies? Determination of truth in SEAM relates to construction and interpretation of qualitative, quantitative, and financial information.

Valid Communication

Analysis of the processes for determining dysfunctions, estimating hidden costs, and anticipating investments to resolve dysfunctions show there are at least 3 constraints or challenges in the process that produce constraints on democratic deliberation and valid communication. First, the emphasis on (and need for) a decider player who is a senior authority in the organization and the fact this person selects the goals and features of the intervention mean that participation in setting up the intervention is left largely to senior authorities and does not get input from other employees. Thus a narrow context for validating knowledge is created, one that may restrict the need to be truthful or sincere since authority rather than reason could drive claims about one's motives and make self-interest, not rational deliberation by managers, a key basis for decisions. Further, it may be hard for other managers and in particular lower level employees to challenge intervention objectives and practices they view as ineffective.

Second, the negotiation process and the use of a contract related to the intervention means that only a limited range of personnel, as well as the research team, are involved in forming the agreement. This again limits the quality of information used in the intervention, restricts many people from involvement in the process, and it establishes a fixed and formal legal basis for the relationship among parties as opposed to an informal, ongoing and consensual relationship that evolves over time.

Third, the formal SEAM process focuses heavily on input from top management related to cost estimates and general implementation of the intervention. By using a relatively hierarchical structure with a manager/leader, core team and other teams, the process creates a differentiated power structure in a potentially restrictive institutional form that can limit communication to utterances that are acceptable to superiors within such hierarchical settings. Thus pre-existing status relationships and authority related norms can transform the rational process of deliberation into a politically driven process where distorted communication is produced and democratic processes fail.

CONCLUSION

This chapter has explored the role of deliberative practices and valid communication in the SEAM approach to organizational intervention. The paper has described the SEAM approach and explored how assumptions of the 3 core qualimetric principles incorporate concerns over features of valid communication. We uncovered constraints on valid communication in organizations that could emerge during SEAM interventions. And we suggested questions to be posed to identify and to overcome constraints on valid, democratic communication during qualimetric interventions into organizations.

One limitation of the chapter is that the current SEAM literature provides general discussions of the process of estimating hidden costs but does not provide rich, ethnographic literature that captures the situated communication that occurs during the process of constructing numerals. Future research needs to include fine grained studies of numeral construction practices in SEAM interventions to better understand how practices of democratic deliberation can be more fully instilled in contemporary organizations.

NOTES

1. This research was supported in part by a grant from the Social Sciences and Humanities Research Council of Canada and a Winspear Research Fellowship provided by the University of Alberta Research Awards Committee.

REFERENCES

Bakardjieva, M. (2008). Making sense of broadband in rural Alberta, Canada. *Observio, 2*(1), 33–53.

Buono, A. F., & Savall, H. (2007).Glossary. In A. F. Buono & H. Savall (Eds.), *Socio-economic intervention in organizations: the intervener-researcher and the SEAM approach to organizational analysis* (pp. 421–436). Charlotte, NC: Information Age Publishing.

Button, M., & Mattson, K. (1999). Deliberative democracy in practice: Challenges and prospects for civic deliberation. *Polity, 31*(4), 609–637.

Chambers, S. (2003). Deliberative democratic theory. *Annual Review of Politics, 6,* 307–326.

Conbere, J., & Heorhiadi, A. (2011). Socio-economic approach to management: A successful systematic approach to organizational change. *OD Practitioner, 43* (1), p. 6–10.

DelliCarpini, M. X., Cook, L. F., & Jacobs, L. R. (2004). Public deliberation, discursive participation, and citizen engagement: A review of the empirical literature. *Annual Review of Politics, 7,* 315–344.

Gephart, R. P. (2007). Hearing discourse. In M. Zachary & C. Thralls (Eds.), *Communicative practices in workplaces and the professions* (pp. 239–263). Amityville, New York: Baywood Publishing Company Inc.

Gephart, R. P. (2008, March). Organizational sensemaking and deliberation in public settings. Paper presented at the Annual Meeting of the Western Academy of Management, Kona, Hawaii.

Gutmann, A., & Thompson, D. F. (2004). *Why deliberative democracy?* Princeton: Princeton University Press.

Habermas, J. (1979). *Communication and the evolution of society.* (T. McCarthy, Trans.). Boston: Beacon Press.

Habermas, J. (1984). *The theory of communicative action.* T. McCarthy, Trans.). Boston: Beacon Press.

Habermas, J. (1989). *The structural transformation of the public sphere: An inquiry into a category of bourgeois society.* (Trans. T. Burger with the assistance of F. Lawrence). Cambridge, MA: MIT Press.

Habermas, J. (1996). *Between facts and norms.* (W. Rehg, Trans.). Cambridge, MA: MIT Press.

Savall, H. (2003). Socio-economic approach to management. *Journal of Organizational change management, 16* (1), 33–48.

Savall, H. (2007). ISEOR's Socio-Economic Method: A case of scientific consultancy. In A. F. Buono & H. Savall (Eds.), *Socio-economic intervention in organizations: The intervener-researcher and the SEAM approach to organizational analysis* (pp. 1–31). Charlotte, NC: Information Age Publishing.

Savall, H., & Zardet, V. (2008). *Mastering hidden costs and socio-economic performance.* Charlotte, NC: Information Age Publishing.

Savall, H., Zardet, V, & Bonnet, M. (2008). *Releasing the untapped potential of enterprises through socio-economic management.* Geneva, Switzerland: International Labour Office.

Savall, H., & Zardet, V. (2011). *The qualimetrics approach: Observing the complex object.* Charlotte, NC: Information Age Publishing.

Scherer, A., & Paluzzo, G. (2007). Toward a political conception of corporate responsibility: Business and society as seen from a Habermasian perspective. *Academy of Management Review, 32* (4), 1096–1120.

APPENDIX:
Conference Dialogue

Conference Participant: Talk is a simple way of doing things and at the same time I am asking if it is legitimate. Would you say that it is taking people from other forms of democracy to deliberate democracy, enabling them to avoid that tyranny of the majority? When you shift from normal democracy to deliberative democracy, you are getting away from the potential pitfall of the tyranny of the majority.

Robert Gephart: I think it's a different way of approaching things we have seen. Now, we have an accountant effect that does structure power relations. By accountant effect, I mean we have financial professionals and practices of accounting that drive communication about costs in organizations. To move beyond the accountant effect we need to continue, embrace, and enhance democracy where it is a factual event so that these processes are related to and help uncover the hidden costs of organizational operations. And all of this democratic discourse does seem to be going on even when people are going to lunch or take coffee or just talking they often complain about how organizational actions create hidden costs that accountants do not acknowledge. Even President Obama did this today at one level; also the Republican Party council did this today and this is good. From their ideas, they automatically see their vote, which is a number or measure of success, influenced by the verbal interactions they have with one another and with constituents. The point is not to simply use numbers created by professionals to avoid everyday interaction. Rather, the point is to involve citizens and even different political parties in reflections on how to create meaningful and truthful numbers. I think it is a very important shift to encourage and respect this involvement but this shift probably has some limits.

CHAPTER 16

ANTE-NARRATIVE SPIRAL APPROACH TO SEAM

Rohny Saylors and David Boje

CONFERENCE REMARKS:
Chapter Prologue

Rohny Saylors

What is the ante-narrative approach? It is the analysis of identity narrative in the present as a process that integrates past and future. A narrative draws on everything that has happened, the past story, and everything that we place bets on happening, the future ante-narrative. For example, when one asks "why am I standing at this moment in this particular situation" this is a linear narrative that looks to the future. All lived experiences from a story from which identity can be drawn. The reasons particular lived experiences are integrated into a linear narrative are the ante-narrative bets placed at the time. Looking at things from an ante-narrative perspective means looking for bets that are placed on new beginnings, beginnings similar to those experienced before. Ante-narrative is the prenarrative bet, story is everything that has happened, and narrative is a linear beginning–middle–end based on the interaction between these two.

Facilitating the Socioeconomic Approach to Management, pages 209–226
Copyright © 2014 by Information Age Publishing

EPISTEMIC AND PHYSICAL INTERPRETATIONS

David Boje speaks about the essence of process as he studies SEAM from an ante-narrative perspective. In this we try to understand what is going on in SEAM processes where people are not ready for SEAM. In such cases we coach them at the phenomenological, ontological level (c.f. Rosile, Boje, Carlon, Downs, & Saylors)

When we observe an object there are always two aspects to it. There is the *epistemic*, what we think of the thing, and the *ontic*, the physical that we assume is the basis of our epistemic conclusions. The ontic, for example, is that when I step in front of a bus, I am hit or the bus misses me. There is neither question nor word game as to whether or not I will be crushed by the bus.

On the other side of sense making, there is the epistemic aspect. Its essence concerns how people think about things, about the physical reality and about where it comes from. Ontological intentionality looks at how people use the things around them transparently, not thinking about the way they act but instead just moving toward some end. We can understand the being of people in their world through their intentionality. We can change that intentionality so that it is not transparent to the worker and to the manager. Through the mirror effect, they realize they are working and that they are real people doing real things, they are not just an extension of an arm. In South Vietnam, Nike shoe factories do not provide sufficient ventilation to keep the glue that holds the shoes together from being inhaled by the village girls they recruit. The managers rape female workers. The women are fired when they get pregnant. They go home, shamed, pregnant, and jobless. When they give birth, they find out that their babies have birth defects because of the poor ventilation.

Appreciative Inquiry (AI) would work to improve these factories productivity, but do we really want to appreciate the spirit of such a practice? There is a huge danger in AI that is not critical of itself. On the other hand, these problems could be solved from meaningful social action based on a SEAM ante-narrative approach.

SEAM FROM AN ANTE-NARRATIVE APPROACH

Our work has highlighted 2 or 3 steps in the SEAM process that philosophically deepen as one gets more involved with it. In our university, in New Mexico, undergraduates are working with small businesses and family businesses. It is hard to do because these people are not ready for SEAM. In such cases, we use the ante-narrative spiral approach. We try to get into the people's hearts because there is often arrogance when it comes to talking about one's own organization. From a SEAM perspective, we do this through diagnostic, project, implementation and evaluation.

Ante-narrative is a sort of prenarrative bet. If you have a small business or a family business, it is hard to get them to appreciate the mirror effect all at once. If you do, it has the ability to create more anger than constructive shock. However, with a spiral, you get them to deliver their thoughts and to evolve. This spiral is ontologically pragmatic. The SEAM model is a way to get people to discuss things the way they are really happening. It takes into account the material conditions of the workers and the socially constructive reality that everyone lives in. These are very different anthropological assumptions about nature and reality, but a spiral ante-narrative SEAM brings them together with fantastic efficacy. The proof of this can be found in the example of the class in which we teach SEAM.

We have ten groups in an undergraduate class at New Mexico State University that uses a 23-step process built on SEAM for small and family businesses. They had great results and undertake the process in diverse climates, about 48% Hispanic. This diversity leads to a lot of uncertainty—you never know when you are going into a very different culture about what it means to be, whether it is a multi-level organization, a small business, or a flat organization. It takes the sort of personal care about others that is at the heart of SEAM to reveal to the intervener the nuanced features of these organizations.

As illustrated in Figure 16.1, there are A-B-C-D-E-F axes that are interrelated with each other. This is the basis of the process. There are project cycles, tools, choice points in decisions, and the spirals of questions punctuating the temporal ordering. The point is that whatever people say about "disseverance," "destining," or "distancing" in the organization when the intervener asks questions, the goal is to make them start thinking and giving reflective answers about what they would have never thought of otherwise. It is about breaking people out of everyday coping and allowing them to move into a more creative mindset.

People eventually get stuck in their usual cycle. Our concept of D-spiral is that, if you are in a cycle, you keep doing the same thing over and over again, which impacts intensity. But if you can figure out what has changed, then the process changes. Then, you introduce the spiral inspired from the quantum theory. All of the axes are linked together through this D-spiral. In our practical case, it allows getting into family and small businesses, and even though the mirror effect is supposed to be enough, it impulses a shock system. We sometimes go back and forth until we can get the stimulus down because there is a lot of psychologizing in large organizations. In a small organization, we have to get into the few psychologies and into the narrative itself. After storytelling the narrative, we can mirror back the stories so it reflects on the people and they will decide how to understand the story

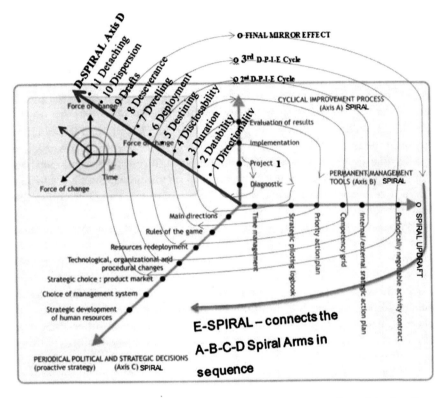

Figure 16.1 Five Dimensions of f-Spiral A-B-C-D-E Transformation of the Small Business to Apprehend the Big 'Q'-Spiral-Updraft Adapted by Boje from p. 26 of Savall, Zardet, and Bonnet (2000, 2008).

of their experiences, to restrain the identity of the organization, to change their being in the world, which will change into the physical real and help them make sense of that change.

SEAM TOOLS

SEAM has many effective tools. To understand SEAM, anyone should start with this tool baseline, for example, time management, strategic logbook, priority action plans, and internal and external strategic action plans. These tools are ante-narrative matter. For example, the competency grid helps to understand what is going on in the organization, to identify the competency owner and his situation in the organization. These are ways to help organizational members. It makes ante-narrative bets on the future that would show "this is going to become who we were." A very important tool is the periodically negotiable activity contract. At the first approach of SEAM, it is the easiest thing to ignore but it is essential to solidify the ante-narrative bet. Without this tool, one does not have the ability to make the change. It is easy to overlook, but it is critical in any intervention.

In any process—in a small or large business—there are not a lot of these macro steps to be done but a lot of human improvement. When we deal with small-size organizations, as a small business consultant, we use very simple charts that show when the process starts and the accompaniment that is done. It starts with diagnosis and, in parallel, training. This simultaneous interaction gives more strength to organizational members, allowing them to face the pain that runs through the organization at the mirror-effect stage.

INTRODUCTION: AN ANTE-NARRATIVE SPIRAL APPROACH TO SEAM

This chapter is a theoretical conception of the SEAM approach through the ante-narrative lenses. It sprung from the practice of SEAM intervention that was made by consulting students at New Mexico State University.

We take a spiral ante-narrative approach to SEAM in our consulting class. We use SEAM to accentuate the spiral processes that occur within a series of consulting projects undertaken in our course. We use these examples to show the meaning of a diagram we have derived from SEAM after integrating spiral ante-narratives. *Root–cause–analysis*, the 11 Ds, and the *mirror effect* are all exemplified through deep-descriptive quotes. This section presents an overview of this ante-narrative SEAM spiral.

The Ante-Narrative Spiral Approach and SEAM

At the beginning, we introduce the client to key consulting concepts: f and Q-spirals, storytelling, SEAM 4-leaf, A-B-C-D-E spirals for implementing SEAM (see Figure 16.2), and explain mirror effect meeting. The Socioeconomic Approach to Management (SEAM) is a spiral intervention. Four forces of change occur as the small business consulting intervention winds its way through five little f-spiral-axes (A project, B the Tools, C Strategic Context, D-Questions) as consultant and client connect them *step-by-step* in E-Spiral. The consultant tries to help the client create better processes, and those processes are spiraling, in good ways, and in bad ways. This is done by implementing 3 D-P-I=E cycles (see Figure 16.3).

.Implementing the mirror effect in an actual face-to-face meeting with the client where direct quotes from manager, employees, customers, and

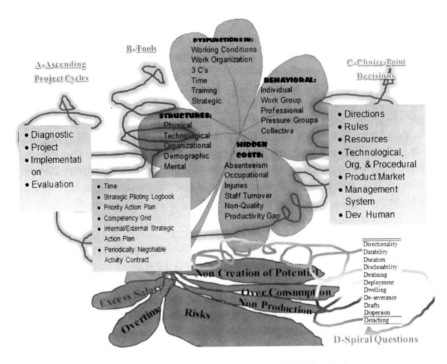

Figure 16.2 Four leaf clover diagnostic chart with A-B-C-D spirals.

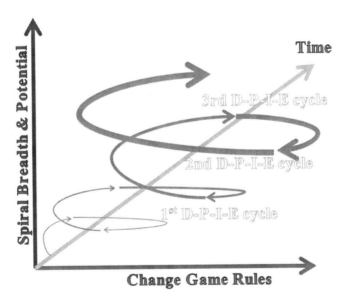

Figure 16.3 Three D-P-I-E cycles become an upward spiral of continuous improvement.

suppliers are displayed and discussed to diagnose areas that made need fixing. Particular focus is placed on stem-roots, which are the cause of surface problems that the client is talking about. The students report on this meeting at midterm. With the mirror effect, you are able to use this diagnosis to come up with solutions and recommendations. Using direct quotes from the client, you can reference them back to the problem and what the underlying cause may be. This is helpful when giving recommendations because they are better able to see why you are recommending that solution.

There are three components to mirror effect: (a) presentation of direct "storytelling" quotes (verbatim) sorted by managers, employees, customers, & suppliers (see Figure 16.4); (b) a table of hidden cost and revenue calculations, and (c) the student consultant observations and recommendations.

This is a Q-Spiral Model. A Q-Spiral is defined as a "Quantum"—spiral that has both upward and downward spiraling directions in the same enterprise (indicated by the dark and lighter-shaded arrows; see Figure 16.5). "Q" stands for Quantum, meaning the spaces, times, and mattering of the business processes. All small businesses have both upward and downward spiraling processes. There are positive upward spirals (light-shaded arrows) in the business processes where continuous expansion and improvement is happening, such as expanding production with higher quality, and hopefully lower costs, bringing on more workers with better training, and having more efficacious communication, coordination, and cooperation. This

NARRATIVE PLACES

ANTENARRATIVE FRONTIERS

PAST

FUTURE

LIVING STORY SPACES

PRESENT

STORYTELLING TRIAD MODEL

Figure 16.4 Storytelling triad.

Figure 16.5 Basic Q-spiral model of business processes.

dynamic is referred to as storytelling in words and action. And there are at the same time and place, negative downward spirals from dysfunctions in the business (dark arrows) that we can read from various measures: escalations of costs, more incivility, more conflict, less quality production, more overpayment of salaries and wages relative to production quantities, more injuries, more absenteeism, more turnover of your best people, loss of market share, unsustainable environmental waste, and more risks to everyone and everything (see Aguirre, et al., 2012).

AN INTEGRATED ANTE-NARRATIVE SPIRAL APPROACH TO SEAM COACHING

We integrate several spirals we find in Savall, Zardet, and Bonnet (2000, 2008) with a D-spiral. To keep it simple, we develop an A, B, C, & D spiral, then combine all their steps together into an E spiral of 23 steps.

A-Spiral

It is three D-P-I-E cycles from Savall and associates (2000, 2008) that together make a spiral. The D-P-I-E stands for Diagnose, Project, Implementation, and Evaluation. You coach your client by engaging in three D-P-I-E cycles that become a spiral of upward momentum in tapping untapped human potential.

B-Spiral

It is a set of management tools you coach your client to learn. Six come from Savall, et al. (2000, 2008): time, strategic piloting logbook, priority action plan, competency grid, internal-external strategic action plan, and periodically negotiated activity contract. We added a seventh tool, Q-Spiral updraft, to deal with spiral coaching.

C-Spiral

The C-spiral is all about the bigger strategy picture. It begins with the main direction of strategy, changing the rules of the game: Main Directions (also 1st of the 11 Ds of Quantum Storytelling: Directionality); Rules of the Game (games of De-severance of space-time-mattering); Resource Deployment (this is the 6th D in Quantum Storytelling); Technological, Organizational, and Procedural processes (6th D–Deployment in Quantum Storytelling); Product Market (6th D–Deployment, plus #7–Dwelling in new place in market); Management System (5th D, Destining, in a radical approach to management system futuring); and Develop Human Resources (11th of the 11 Ds of Quantum Storytelling: Detaching from thy-self to develop whole-self potential of your HR).

D-Spiral (Quantum)

The D-spiral is a set of 11 questions to ask clients in-order-to shake up their thinking, so they can think out of the box. The D-spiral is also a new language, new terms that all begin with the letter "D" that move from a linear understanding of space and time, to a spiral understanding (see Table 16.1). Sometimes we call the D-spiral by the name Quantum, since it is based upon a quantum understanding of space–time existence. The D-questions are explained in Boje's (2012) online book, *Quantum Storytelling*.

E-(A-B-C-D) Spiral

Our semesters last 16 weeks. The following 23 steps, which are provided to our students, are an integration of Savall, et al.'s (2000, 2008) textbook on SEAM with Boje's (2012) online text, in an *Integrated Spiral Pathway*

TABLE 16.1   Eleven D's of Quantum Storytelling and the Questions Asked of Blacksmith Artists

11 D's	Q to Ask Your Client	Where It Helps You Client Consultation
Directionality	1. What is the directionality of the business processes; to what future are they headed?	Axis C: Direction. This is not compass direction, it is strategic direction, arriving from the future → present.
Datability	2. What is the datability of the business process developments?	4-Leaf Structures: Important pivotal dates where technical processes, physical and other structures were acquired.
Duration	3. What is the duration of various business processes?	Axis C: Strategic Choices–helps sort out how long various strategies have been in effect.
Disclosability	4. What is the disclosability of the future business processes revealed to you?	Axis A–projects that disclose a future, Axis B–PAP and I/ESAP; SI in top leaf. The future is arriving into the present, presenting a set of potential futures, in the choice points in Axis C.
Destining	5. What is the destining of the processes unfolding in ways you can foretell? Follow up, in fore-caring, fore-structuring, fore-having, fore-conceiving.	Axis B: PAP & I/ESAP; Axis C–all items. This is weak destiny, where even where the is momentum and carved channels in the market, there are also choice-points among futures.
Deployment	6. What is the deployment of business processes, in-order-to, for-the-sake-of?	Axis B: PAP & I/ESAP; Axis C–all items. Look at existing processes of production, distribution, & consumption. How are these processes deployed. How could they be?
Dwelling	7. What is the dwelling, in-place in the world of business processes?	Knowing place in the market, in the state, etc. lets them sort out Axis B: PAP & I/ESAP; Axis C—all items.
De-severance	8. What is the de-severance (de-distancing) of space-time-mattering?	De-severing space is bringing something far close. De-severing time can be bringing a future potential into the path of SAP and I/ESAP and the Axis C choice-points.
Drafts	9. What are the drafts, updraft, and downdraft, into tighter (down) orbits, or into more open outer orbits (up), and the turning points from one draft to another?	Axis A, B, & C. This is where the client and consultant sort out strategic choice points, moving into more updraft spiral-ante-narratives, ascending into more potential.
Dispersion	10. What is the dispersion of processes, too diverse, or consolidating them?	This can free up resources to invested in more strategic processes, letting go of low-value added activities

(continued)

TABLE 16.1   Eleven D's of Quantum Storytelling and the Questions Asked of Blacksmith Artists (continued)

11 D's	Q to Ask Your Client	Where It Helps You Client Consultation
Detaching	11. What is the detaching from being drawn into they-ness, they-relations, they-self and finding a path of own most authentic potentiality-for-Being-a-whole-Self?	Following the they-crowd is not great strategy. Developing into whole-Self potentiality fits well with Axis C

approach to coaching using the methodology of storytelling. Storytelling coaching works by listening to the storytelling of the client, then helping them "restory," breaking out of the narrative routine way they understand their organization into a restoried way of developing their future and understanding their past in a new way (Cast, Rosile, Boje, & Saylors, 2013).

Step 1

Diagnostic (A-spiral: Diagnostic, Project Plan, Implementation, & Evaluation of Results) begins by you asking the 11 D-questions (spiral D) which you are to tape-record or video-record and then meticulously transcribe the verbatim answers in your Midterm and Final Report. You will also use the Axis B tool (PNAC) to negotiate your consulting contract for three "A-spiral" Projects each with a D-P-I-E cycle (Diagnostic, Project, Implementation, Evaluation).

The A-Spiral is a series of three cycles of D-P-I-E (Diagnose, Project, Implement, & Evaluate). For Step 1, meet with your client, and envision three projects, implementable in one semester, that could bring small changes about in their organization. Put these agreements in your PNAC and sign it. Pick three successive small doable projects that will result in an upsurge of momentum in the client's organization. The momentum comes from answering the eleven questions that get you in the D-Spiral. It is called a D-spiral because all the questions are about a concept that begins with the letter D, such as directionality of the momentum, datability of key moments in bringing about that momentum, and so forth. Please tape-record or video-record and then meticulously transcribe the verbatim answers to the eleven D-spiral questions for your Final Report. Other D-questions are spread out along the 23 steps. You will also use the Axis B tool (PNAC) to negotiate your consulting contract for three "A-spiral" Projects each with a D-P-I-E cycle (Diagnostic, Project, Implementation, Evaluation).

Please do not bite off more than you can chew. Three small projects and their changes can have huge ripple impacts if they become Integrated Spirals of the A-B-C-D-E spirals. Do not get too locked into the second and third project. You have not even done a diagnostic yet, or utilized the new tools (B-spiral). Be prepared to revisit the PNAC tool frequently, throughout the semester, and please choose the second and third Projects more wisely than the first ones. Get to the stem-roots of the problem. That is what problem-based-learning is all about. Be prepared to change out the second and third project that your client invited you to engage. You won't know which ones will make the real differences until you get further along the path. It's about roots, not surface symptoms. You will learn this lesson quite soon.

Step 2

The next step involves a time tool (B-spiral). What is "time"? If you answered "clock time" or "calendar time" then you don't really know too much about what time is all about. Most people assume time runs past-present-future. You asked the Duration question. Now listen to the answer. Time is *not* some sort of straight line. Or that time runs in repeating cycles. I guess if you are in a robotic rut, doing the same factory job day in and day out, that may be true. However, if you want to move beyond the linear and cyclic rut of repeating the same thing again and again, then a new "middle" pathway must be courted, some new channels that spiral upwards sorted out by you and your client, and some Q-Spiral updrafts located to attract your momentum must be found.

Step 2 is about freeing up time, but noticing the time that is not adding value, the time that is spent putting out the same old fires, again and again. Put that time wasted into time that is spent on the future. You asked the Datability question and collected a set of meaningful, highly significant datables. All dates are not equal, some stand out, and are significant in the life path of a business. Time also runs future–present–past. Since Einstienian and Quantum physics, not to mention String Theory, we know that time runs in many directions, but for a strategy person like yourself, how is time approaching, arriving, in future-ahead-of-itself?

It is the time by which the future is arriving into the present, making waves in the present. It is a meaningful time of understanding the business and its many directions. It is the first tool you will teach your client (see Figure 16.6).

Step 3

Direction (C-spiral), which is also the first D-question (Directionality in D-Spiral). Keep in mind your consulting focus: to help your client move out of many dysfunctions and poor root stems, and, using the savings and income potential, construct step-by-step an Updraft-Spiral. This means sorting out direction in the C-spiral, asking about choice-points, when at the crossroads, which way will the client be turning? Ask about the directionality, not from the past to present, but from the future. Strategy foretells the future. It is not a repetition of the past (that is aimless). Think strategically, and act it. Ask:

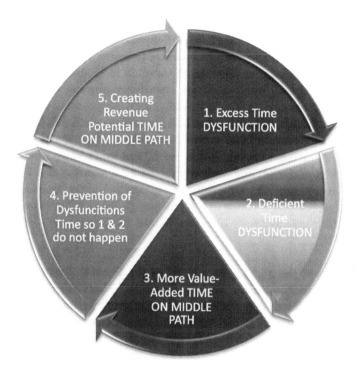

Figure 16.6 The five aspects of time.

How is the future arriving, and what is the array of futures that are potentially available? There is never just one future, except in linear/cyclical thinking. The cycle never just repeats itself exactly (silly rabbit). Even the continuous cycle time and quality improvement folks know the cycles do *not* really repeat —they spiral. It is time to notice how the last cycle is not the same as this one, to note the differences, so you notice the choices. It is all about the differences. It is noticing differences just arriving, like the customer coming in wanting a slightly different product or service configuration. Noticing the flows of action, that is the second sort of storytelling. That is what choice-making is all about. What? The action-storytelling, where there are no words said at all. So you will need to observe the direction, not just talk about it. Look at the processes in place, unfolding, and the direction of their transformation, and what transformations are arriving.

Step 4

Project planning (A-spiral) done collaboratively with your client. What project can you and the client implement quickly, without a lot of resources, by freeing up the time you found in Step 2. Teach the D-P-I-E of A-spiral, and get ready to do three of them.

Step 5

Using the Strategic Piloting Logbook tool (B-spiral) begin creating indicators with your client so you can measure progress (qualitative and quantitative indicators help to pilot the direction). Indicators are as simple as deadlines, mileposts, number of new customers, number of web hits, and so forth. Add in some sustainability indicators: power usage (a simple indicator is the electric bill, the water bill), power waste (lights left on, water wasted), power sources (find some sustainable ones), and cut the waste by recycling, reducing, reusing, and so forth. You won't know where you are going or if you have arrived, unless you create some indicators. Don't leave it to the accountant. Do some ABC or your own Activity Based Costing by figuring out the hidden costs of the business doing as it has been doing on all those four leaves of the clover (see Figure 16.2).

Step 6

The rules of the game are captured by the C-spiral. Business is a game and it is time to change the "rules of the game." There are choice points in the political and strategic decision making of every business. What game is being played in action, in the weaving of actions among the actors and the actants (e.g., things, technologies, equipment, mattering). Who is making the game rules? How can those rules be changed (ethically, See Aristotle's Nicomachean ethics)? Are the rules of the game ecologically sustainable?

Step 7

D2—Datability. What are the most important datable moments in the life story of the business? Get those living stories of what is emerging, unfolding in the now, not just the rote narrative of the past. Record them by tape and or video. This can be done on the first field visit. Most students don't pay attention to the first set of life stories the client says in that first interview. I think students have been trained not to pay attention to living stories, and look instead for the quick solution, and thereby miss the spiral altogether. A life story is primordial, from birth to death, and you are in the middle of yours, not dead yet, still alive, and already born, on some sort of pathway, even if you never thought about it. There are datable moments in your future, such as graduation, the next job, perhaps a wedding, children, and so on. Datable moments are happening in your future, and arriving in your present, just as much as the datable moments from the past are arriving in the Present. People always capitalize the Present, but not the past nor the future. I think they know that with each newness in the Present, that emergence opens up a rehistoricizing of datable moments past, and opens up futuring so what you think will be the milestones shift in your landscape, and new ones are beckoning you to approach.

Step 8

Mirror Effect meeting with client (A-spiral, part of D-P-I-E cycle). This step is where you feed back the living stories and quotes sorted by stakeholders, present a hidden costs and untapped potential revenues chart based on questions asked in the 4-leaf diagnosis; and make 3 consultant observations and recommendations. This is a long meeting, a meeting about the text, the scripts you collected from employees, clients, suppliers, and whomever you could access. And it is your observations put into field notes on all those visits. Not a note taker? OK, get a good tape recorder, one with dual microphones (stereo microphones), and start recording conversations, in meetings, in interviews, where ever you have permission. By the time your midterm arrives, you are advised to have the Mirror Effect face-to-face meeting with your client. It is where you point out the costs and lost revenues of behaving, structuring, etc. and how much dough they can have, and peace of mind, if they find what Aristotle (350 BCE) calls the "middle path," the one between excess and deficiency, which is by the way the definition of all those dysfunctions you analyzed in the upper leaf of the 4-leaf.

Step 9

Implement project in collaboration with your client (A-spiral). Good advice, but many a student consultant has ignored it. Implementing a Project that the client is not on board with will lead to many headaches, even hard feelings. Clearly the spiral updraft is tugging you in a more amenable directionality. You did the Diagnostic, the Project plan, and now it is time to Implement—collaboratively, please. You are not here to be a slave. You are consulting, so they can do this on their own, with their own resources. This is first of three Projects (check your PNAC, and may be time to renegotiate, so you have three small changes in projects that are doable).

Step 10

The Priority Action Plan tool (B-spiral) lay out three goals, an action plan, and who implements what for the next year. With the first project, you have some basis for setting the PAP in motion.

Step 11

Resource Deployment (C-spiral). This step focuses on making priorities, cutting back here, and expanding in the implementation of project (Step 9). PAP gets implemented with the cost savings and enhanced revenues you promised in the Mirror Effect meeting. Deployment is part of the Q-Spiral set of questions, so go back and listen to your recording.

Step 12

D3 and D4 (D-Spiral: Durability and Disclosability). Ask about durability of the various processes of production and distribution. Then ask about disclosability of the future arriving at their doorstep, to tell what sort of processes need to be fore-structured.

Step 13

Evaluation (A-spiral)—evaluate results of the project using the Piloting Logbook indicators you have to date. Then renew the Diagnostic, and Project Number 2 gets planned and implemented.

Step 14

Competency Grid (B-spiral). It is time to assess the existing competencies of each person in the firm, and do a second grid of what competencies are needed to get the business in uplift to their PAP and second Project Implementation. This also helps prepare them for the longer-range strategy coming up.

Step 15

D5, D6, D7 (D-Spiral: Destining, Deployment, & Dwelling). Time to ask the big quantum questions: What destining are they courting? How are they deploying to meet it? What is their place (dwelling-in-the-market-place and in sustainability with the natural environment)?

Step 16

Evaluation (A-spiral) Evaluate Project 2, Diagnostic, Project plan for the third project, and get into Implementation, where the client is implementing and you are doing quite little activity.

Step 17

I/E SAP (Internal/External Strategic Action Plan) (B-spiral). Now that you have two projects completed, and a third underway, it is time to take a turn in the path. This is a five-year strategic plan with three long-term objectives, action plans, who does what when, with more logbook indicators set up to measure their progression. The PAP was one year of the 5 years. This is the big game change.

Step 18

More D's (D-Spiral: Deseverance & Drafts). The de-severance removes distance so the far in space and time and mattering are near (ready-to-hand in the business processes). Drafts are force fields in the spiral-ante-narrative. It is like a glider-plane, where you float looking for new updrafts, and avoid the downdrafts. If the business has been in a downdraft, descending, then they will welcome the updraft. Your job is to help the client find the updrafts, and make the moves in the processes to get in place, to take that uplift pathway.

Step 19

Complete the Evaluation (A-spiral) of the third project. Adjust the Logbook indicators, PAP, and Competency Grid, so there is a smooth passageway to the I/E SAP.

Step 20

The PNAC (Periodically Negotiable Activity Contract) A-spiral. This process takes place at several levels. It is a PNAC between consultant and client, so expectations stay eye-to-eye over course of the three projects. Second, it is a PNAC training that you do with the client so PNACs are used in the business with all the employees. And it is about compensation. If the employee helps move the firm into updraft, into more money, more customers, more revenue, or less waste, what is going to be the reward, the payout for them. How do they participate in the good times? Yes it is profit-sharing, but also accountable for any of those six root-stems under the 4-leaf. By now the client should be familiar with all 6 tools and using them to pilot their business on the upward spiral-ante-narrative path. If they are just repeating the same old business cycle, then your consulting has not worked.

Step 21

Technological, product market, management systems, and develop human resources C-spiral. Now is the time to make some choices, some are political and others are strategic. To change C-spiral is also lead Q-Spiral (which is also the 11th D of Quantum Storytelling) is quite the accomplishment.

Step 22

The D-Spiral: Dispersion & Detaching. As the business enters new up-paths there is dispersion of processes, some of which are not all that helpful in the road ahead. And you as a consultant are detaching, getting ready to end your engagement with the client. And the client is achieving potentiality-for-being-a-whole-self, not imitating competitors, not doing the "they-self" walk (Cf., Boje, Helmuth, Saylors, 2013). Finding that unique sense of freedom in the updraft is a major result that you and your client can be proud of.

Step 23

Q-Spiral-Updraft. Submit your final Report to the client and instructors. What value- added did your work with the client lead to in terms of up-draft-Q-Spiral? You are done. Make your presentation; get along on your pathway.

CONCLUSION

Throughout this chapter we have looked at the 23 quantum spiral consulting steps. We have gone through a triple iteration of the DPIE cycle, each one building momentum from the last. This has been couched in a future looking antenarrative perspective. While many have had trouble implementing SEAM for small businesses, family businesses, or gaining traction over a short period of time, the theories laid out here, and their concomitant 23 steps, help to overcome many of these troubles. SEAM is the most important advancement in managerial socio-technical systems since accounting, and in following these steps, we have seen literally hundreds of organizations benefit in terms of both sustainability and profitability.

REFERENCES

Aguirre, G., Boje, D. M., Cast, M. L., Conner, S. L., Helmuth, C., Mittal, R., Saylors, R., Tourani, N., Vendette, S., & Yan, T. Q. (2012).University sustainability and system ontology. *International Journal of Organization Theory & Behavior, 15* (4).

Boje, D. M. (2012). *Quantum Spirals for Organizational Consulting.* Pre-Press Version, PeaceAware.com.

Boje, D. M., Helmuth, C. A., & Saylors, R. (2013). 23. Cameo: Spinning authentic leadership living stories of the self. *Authentic Leadership: Clashes, Convergences and Coalescences,* 271.

Cast, M. L., Rosile, G. A., Boje, D. M., & Saylors, R. (2013). Restorying a hard day's work. *Research in Occupational Stress and Well-being, 11,* 257–281.

Savall, H., Zardet, V., & Bonnet, M. (2000, 2008). *Releasing the untapped potential of enterprises through Socio-Economic Management.* Geneva, Lyon: International Labour Office for Employers' Activities (ILO).

Rosile, G. A., Boje, D. M., Carlon, D. M., Downs, A., & Saylors, R. (2013). Storytelling diamond: An antenarrative integration of the six facets of storytelling in organization research design. *Organizational Research Methods, 16* (4) : 567–580.

CHAPTER 17

SEAM ONTOLOGICAL THEORY

Debra P. Hockenberry

CONFERENCE REMARKS:
Chapter Prologue

Debra Hockenberry

I believe in symbolic messages. When I entered the front doors looking for this conference, I was greeted by somebody asking if I was looking for the women entrepreneurship program. At that moment, I asked myself, "How could she know that?" Many of you know, I advocate for entrepreneurs. As Dr. Heorhiadi said, I like to engage individuals and I research aspects of creative deviance within entrepreneurs and intrapreneurs and their ability to introduce innovation. I would like to take a few moments to present what I consider to be a representation of some of these aspects of innovation and entrepreneurship. What it is like to be there in that "aha" moment of invention? I believe that SEAM is a method that can address our culture and can bring forth more of the entrepreneurial potential.

I want to focus in on those individuals who look into the future, who have some kind of innovative topic that would categorize them as entrepreneurial outliers. SEAM taps into that unrevealed talent that lies within, oftentimes unrevealed until that moment of invention. SEAM is based on a belief system that includes an inclusive approach and enables talents to be

Facilitating the Socioeconomic Approach to Management, pages 227–237
Copyright © 2014 by Information Age Publishing

revealed, which I think is the key to tapping into the entrepreneurial spirit, or creative deviance, of individuals.

Ontological theory reveals hidden potential through a variation of time consciousness. The kind of futuristic entrepreneurial innovation occurs, not through a strategic process, but instead, through an understanding that time is present, past and future all at the same time. In this way, the view becomes a universal view looking through time all at once rather than linearly. It is the understanding of "knowing" what it is going to be. It is that "gut feeling" that we know what is going to work. We don't know how, we don't know when. It is not an equation or formula that you can give to a person in order to make them entrepreneurial. You can't give a person so many experiences, offer creative seminars and brainstorm a little bit, and expect them to develop this kind of potential. This kind of potential can't be created. So what are we missing? We are missing the propensity toward futuring™.

The dynamic aspects, the phenomenon of revelation allows for innovation to appear. It is not a form of strategic creation. When I look at the research, it appears this creative deviance can follow two different ways of looking at time. If we are looking at a business curve, strategically, it's a linear timeline. We bet that this technology, this new innovation is going to work and the result is almost 50% hit or 50% missed because the market is suspected to do something at a certain time. When we are talking about that kind of innovation that is timeless and universal or creatively deviant—that kind of being, that individual who has the time concept of past, present, future, all going on at once—we are looking through that business cycle. We are not looking at the business cycle in a strategic linear way. It is an experience of the time all at once.

When we embrace this kind of potential and bring it into the business environment, it works well for us. It is an act of prediction, not of shaping. We ask this question to SEAM, "Do hidden costs include this kind of innovative predictive and outlying potential?" When we look at the typical American business structures and behaviors, we end up throwing these kinds of individuals out into a self-employed entrepreneurial world instead of incorporating them within an intrapreneurial environment.

The future depends on innovational entrepreneurship. Many businesses say that they want to include entrepreneurship, and expect people to be entrepreneurial. In fact, they are expecting people to be strategic and, once they reveal their propensity toward futuring™ in this predictive fashion, they are often thrown out of the environment to create on their own. I do mean, thrown.

If we look at the physical dynamics within a working environment, creative deviants generally are physically all the way down the hall. Technologically, if you have an engineer who is really on target, we don't attempt to give him more technology to use. Organizationally, the department is not separated; instead, all engineers are put together. The assumption is that they can work together, because they understand each other. The entrepreneurial engineers are expected to be entrepreneurs. They may be focused on making their little gadget or chemical explosion or whatever it is, but they may not be futuristically entrepreneurial. How can we distinguish this value?

The same approach exists when we deal with behavior. There are some stigmas to outliers. The work group doesn't always include a creative deviant without emotional intelligence. In fact, these individuals may not be considered emotionally intelligent because of their differing viewpoint. When someone displays so much difference or deviance, but their talent remains obvious, companies decide to make them contractors. They send them off into a business world of their own, forcing them to work on business aspects and thus, no longer completely focused on using their creative potential.

These actions symbolize a big comment on how we talk about and embrace innovation within our culture. This is not just within the business world but in our culture itself. Why expect entrepreneurs not to be engaged with other businesses or require them to be independent businesses?

Through SEAM's socio-technical view, this hidden potential outside business industry and environment can be embraced and incorporated intrapreneurially. SEAM embraces and includes this unrevealed value that remains the key to innovation.

INTRODUCTION:
Revealing the Unseen, Recording the Unheard, Enhancing the Intangible—The Ontological Aspects of Primordial Entrepreneurial Social Norms and Entrepreneurial Invariants

The socio-economic research of an entrepreneur or intrapreneur becomes restricted when assuming that the entrepreneurial process occurs in a linear fashion. Individuals do not always think linearly, nor do the social or cultural environments always respond with consistent results. The preconceived notion of the business cycle does not assure the unfolding of the business cycle. Therefore, using strategic or analytic equations or diagrams limit our full understanding of the process and the state of being that makes up the essence of entrepreneurial endeavors. However, this is what most entrepreneurial theory includes.

Directional Anomalies in Entrepreneurial Theory

The entrepreneurial process is usually described as an orderly and linear process beginning with discovery and recognition of an opportunity, followed by resource acquisition, strategy development, organization, and execution (Shane, 2003). The ideation process, as described by Mintzberg, includes a strategic perspective, interpreting experimentation results (Mintzberg, Ahlstrand, & Lampel, 2005). "If the stories of past business cycles could predict the future there would be no surprises, and by that fact no business cycles" (McCloskey, 1990, p. 96)

The linear view of the entrepreneurial personality also dominates. When it comes to describing the personality of those who characterize innovative thought, research seems to focus on defining various industries or areas of entrepreneurship. Kolb (1984) notes that domain experts usually favor analytical and conceptual processes. However, can we define someone like Ben Franklin or Thomas Edison as a domain expert? And by doing so, are we restricting the emergence of what we would like to have revealed through this kind of definition?

Goffman (1967, p. 2) reminds us that it "is not the individual and his psychology, but rather the syntactical relations among the acts of different persons mutually present to one another" that is important. Scenario thinking, peripheral vision and intuitive logic are some of the creative methodologies intrapreneurs have incorporated into their practices. These methods of gaining knowledge still include an assumption that future knowledge is a tangibly attainable entity, thus the linear depiction of time.

Heidegger illuminated the unnoticed dynamics between the economical, political, sociological, technological, and scientific associations when including measurement and calculations (Heidegger, 1977, p. 111). Without understanding these dynamics, there could be hidden meanings and states of being that distort the statistics. Heidegger (1962, 1991, 1999) focuses on directionality. This corresponds to the unseen and intangible flow. Statistics conceal the nonlinear and the noncyclical processes by using a general linear modeling of the world. "As the battle continues to subjectify the objective (epistemic) and objectify the subjective (ontic), what gets unnoticed or concealed is the third paradigm, an ontological approach" (Boje, 2012).

Retrospective sense-making pressures the practitioner to invent rationalities based on recitation of rules and principles already preconceived and possibly not currently in use. The actual character of a practice can be missed by this approach (Chia & Mackay, 2007, p. 234). Heidegger does not dismiss sense making, but instead, adds the primordial fold to account for the difference between being-in-the-world and the in-Being. It is the in-Being that is the primordial conception of "spacetimemattering." Polanyi (1957) calls this "indwelling," a kind of tacit knowing (Boje, 2012).

An invariant is something or someone whose change or absence would alter or destroy itself. In order to reduce an experience to its essence, we have to obtain pure objectivity and see ourselves with such distance that all the implications of sensory or thought withdraw to the bottom of nothingness.

Every ideation, because it is an ideation, is formed in a place of existence that must turn back into itself in order to find there again the same idea.

The variants are actually the possibilities because they can be replaced and be determined as inessential. There is therefore something inessential, a hollow or a zone, where what is not inessential, not impossible, assembles. There is no positive vision that would definitively give me the essentiality of the essence (Ponty, 1969, p. 110–112).

Social Norms in Entrepreneurial and Intrapreneurial Environments

Three significant social norms among entrepreneurial and intraprenerial environments include the lack of business plans, the reliance upon the sole proprietor for comprehensive skill and the misnomer that the individual is creative when they are strategic. Taking these social norms and acting as though they are acceptable assumptions only leads to a delusional study of entrepreneurship. By assuming the individual serves as the means and not the end, the state of an individual's being and experience remains disregarded.

Limiting Through Definition

If the recognition of an entrepreneur or intrapreneur becomes limited by the definition of their expertise, barriers toward entrepreneurial invariance can emerge. When the system itself does not engage in opening up to sources beyond itself, the full individual potential cannot be complimented. By engaging outside themselves, entrepreneurs can engage in new avenues and possibilities. Seeking complimentary connections without expectation opens up to opportunities for primordial entrepreneurship. An entrepreneurial invariant becomes necessary as the molecule of change, allowing the untapped potential to become uncovered.

An entrepreneurial invariant changes things through their being. However, if an individual is unable to freely be themselves at all levels of potential, they cannot offer their abilities to the organization. Whether an individual's entrepreneurial endeavor, or an intrapreneurial endeavor that emerges within an existing organization, the ability to change things comes from a juxtaposition of an individual and the dynamics of the whole. Defining the culture of that whole can limit the inclusion of full or complete creativity. Expecting a specific level of emotional intelligence as a requirement within the social norms places a restricted definition for the entrepreneurial invariant.

Some recent findings concluded that technology entrepreneurs rely on strong ties to their perceived "inner group." Even though they generate ideas on various interdisciplinary domains, they almost exclusively pursue ideas within their core domain. From there, they quickly document the research, analyze, and generate an active experiment to validate and develop their ideas (Gemmell, Boland, & Kolb, 2012).

In bureaucratic corporations, it is the respective functional department that serves as the area that gives permission to get something done within that field. The sales force holds the reigns for selling something as marketing would dominate in marketing decisions. Bureaucratic systems are based on the assumption that the power is within the functions, products and services, markets, and technologies; and these departments are the most efficient way to promote innovation and change. Characteristic of a monopoly, complacency, bloat, and stagnation can be promoted and bring about a system that interferes with freedom, choice, and competition. Most organizations will act this way because they cannot see an alternative (Pinchot, 1985).

Even though both technical and creative jobs may exist within a company, emotional intelligence and social skills become part of the psychological contract for success. For example, in the case of engineers or IT specialists, the most important aspect of their job relies on technical skills and does not necessarily emphasize social skills or creative skills. Yet, those engineers who are more emotionally intelligent are considered to be the ones who move up the ladder of success within the organization.

In the case of people working in public relations, arts or creative departments the social skills are more important for the direct duties, but once again, emotional intelligence determines their success with regard to promotion and job stability (Goleman, 1995). In reality, these companies establish a strict set of norms and codes of conduct that leave little room for employees' creative expression.

The perceptions of new venture legitimacy have been examined, and both entrepreneurial and intrapreneurial results show that the credential and behaviors are positively related to legitimacy perceptions (Nagy, Pollack, Rutherford, & Lohrke, 2012). Results confirm the importance of psychological stamina, extroversion, and attention to detail as factors influencing leader effectiveness, and suggest that the social judgment aspects of emotional intelligence remain most important. Results also show that the Big Five personality factors usually influence leadership in different organizational contexts (Bartone, 2009).

A Rhizomatic Business Plan

To date, a rhizomatic or spiraling business plan does not appear to exist, even though the tendencies and actions of typical entrepreneurs include such actions. Defining themselves as a "jack of all trades," a visionary with multiple interests and skills, or even a serial entrepreneur that cannot be bothered by rules, many entrepreneurs rely on themselves for comprehensive skills. Oftentimes, they will start without a business plan because they are impatient. The psychological attributes of "risk taker" stems from this urgency to get on with their ideas and get things done.

Most entrepreneurs rely on themselves for comprehensive skills. This urgency to get things done can parallel a sense of "knowing."

> But this essence of being is not primary, it does not rest on itself, it is not it that can teach us what being is; the essence is not the answer to the philosophical question, the philosophical question is not posed in us by a pure spectator: it is first a question as to how, upon what ground, the pure spectator is established, from what more profound source he himself draws. (Ponty, 1969, p. 109–110)

"Many people have trees growing in their heads" (Deleuze & Guattari, 1994, p. 160). This visual depicts a linear and progressively ordered mental structure (Linstead & Pullen, p. 1290). With this unfolding plan already solidified and agreed upon as a clarification toward achieving the entrepreneurial goal can oftentimes serve as a substitute for a business plan. Practically sanctified by the internal calling of the vision, the need for a usual business plan seems to place a barrier on the differentiation and outlier qualities necessary for a new venture. However, this visionary unfolding does not parallel the strategic plan that most organizations customarily use.

Creativity vs. Strategy

A severe difference exists between those strategic entrepreneurs and those who are creative or intellectual outliers. An individual who may improve a product, recognize a hole in the market or find an alternative to an existing product or service merely utilizes various strategic forms of innovation. Brainstorming, projections, and even futuring™ is called applied history. These are systematic phenomena that use efficacy, sense making, and intentionality within a holistic network of intentional states, tacit belief systems and values. This kind of action provides explanatory adequacy for accounting and the meaning of action (Chia & Mackay, 2007, p. 228).

The foreseeing, forebelieving, and foreknowing of creative and intellectual outliers occurs through intuition or clairvoyance and not an equation of epistemological elements. Clairvoyance is the ability to see, hear, and feel the nonvisible, intangible, and unheard, in a timeless state of consciousness by being—or in the ontological state. Intuition, on the contrary, deals with perceiving the unknown. In addition, it was found that clairvoyance and intuition were either independent of each other or intermingled. Still, clairvoyance is practiced as a profession and seen separately from the intuition described as needed for innovation. Although soothsayers, prophecies, and astrologers played a separate but integral part of historic strategic planning, they are not encompassed within the current strategic literature. The ontological underpinnings of intuition and clairvoyance indicate that it is present as a transcendental component as well as an essential element of the living system, with philosophical and neuroscience underpinnings. This systemic phenomenon presents itself beyond the dualistic and linear causality models of directionality (Hockenberry, 2012).

The distinction between creative deviance and strategy emerges as a defining element of innovation. This distinction can illuminate hidden potential that can be tapped into. These unseen, unheard, and intangible elements play a key role in the ontological theory of primordial aspects of entrepreneurial invariants.

FUTURE POSSIBILITIES USING SEAM
AND THE ONTOLOGICAL THEORY

In order to explore why some organizations incorporate spirals of entrepreneurial movement more effectively than others, it is important to look at the proponents of the propensity toward futuring™. Clarification of the concepts of futuring™ need to be reviewed through qualitative and socio-economic methods, extracting the ontological view of entrepreneurship and intrapreneurship. Futuring™, or venturing, itself is idea based, not always secured by a tangible outcome. It is directional and moving, assembling through various waves of experience and opportunity. Gathering information from time, space and matter in order to determine a meaning, the intrapreneur defines, interprets and designs from the already predesigned and envisioned market exchange and status quo (Magala, 2009, p. 122).

Untapped potential can be uncovered using seam to define the ontological aspects of entrepreneurship. The core beliefs of seam include tapping into the potential of an organization's employees and engaging in changing the organization systemically to enhance potentiality and decrease hidden costs. These values are consistent with OD values, but add an organizational change approach (Conbere & Heorhiadi, 2011). SEAM was created to monitor the time needed to transform an enterprise into a new competitive environment because expectations and actual reality always differ. (Savall & Zardet, 2013, p. 16).

Deserverance (overcoming the dualisms), allows the ontological primordial process and practice to take place. By looking beyond the linear causality model to an assembling spiral and dynamic causality, the depth of a dynamic system emerges (Boje, 2012). The first support for the ontological dimension of time, space and matter lies within the cognitive analysis of knowledge in organizations by referring to individuals within the organization, its groups and the organization as a whole (Nonaka & Takeuchi, 1995, p. 57). The second refers to the various contributions of the organization and the economy. Interpreting becomes the externalization stage of knowledge that occurs between the ontological group and organizational levels (Akehurst, Rueda-Armengot, Lopez, & Marques, 2011, pp. 184–188).

It appears that the trend is to look for qualities of the invariant entrepreneur; however current entrepreneurial theory and the social norms of entrepreneurs lead us to looking at the variants for answers. Once an ontological theory is created that focuses on the aspect of a coposited nonlinear timespacematter consciousness, a more detailed and comprehensive definition of innovation within entrepreneurship can continue. Details concerning the primordial aspects of the invariant can bring about an emergence of necessary attributes to an entrepreneurial future.

REFERENCES

Akehurst, G., Rueda-Armengot, C., Lopez, S. V., & Marques, D. P., (2011). Ontological supports of knowledge: Knowledge creation and analytical knowledge. *Management Decision, 49* (2), p. 183–194.

Bartone, P. T., Eid, J., Johnsen, B. H., Laberg, J. C., & Snook, S. A. (2009). Big five personality factors, hardiness, and social judgment as predictors of leader performance. *Leadership & Organization Development Journal, 30* (6), 498–521.

Boje, D. M. (2012). Ethnostatistics and Ontological Storytelling Feb 5, 2012; Revised Feb 16. Working paper on line at http://peaceaware.com.

Chia, R. & Mackay, B. (2007). Post-processual challenges for the emerging strategy-as-practice perspective: Discovering strategy in the logic of practice. *Human Relations, 60,* 217–242

Conbere, J., & Heorhiadi, A. (2011). Socio-economic approach to management: A successful systemic approach to organizational change. *OD Practitioner, 43* (1), 6–10.

Deleuze, G., & Guattari F. (1994). *What is philosophy?* London, UK: Verso.

Gemmell, R. M., Boland, R. J., & Kolb, D. A. (2012). The socio-cognitive dynamics of entrepreneurial ideation. *Entrepreneurship Theory and Practice, 36*(5), 1053–1073.

Goffman, E. (1967). *Interaction rituals.* Garden City, NY: Hawthorne, Aldine.

Goleman, D. (1995). *Emotional intelligence.* Broadway, NY: Bantman.

Heidegger, M. (1962). *Being and time.* New York, NY: Harper San Francisco.

Heidegger, M. (1977). *The question concerning technology.* London: Garland Publishing.

Heidegger, M. (1991). *The principle of reason.* Trans. Reginald Lilly. Bloomington, IN: Indiana University Press.

Heidegger, M. (1999). *Ontology: The hermeneutics of facticity.* Indianapolis, IN: Indiana University.

Hockenberry, D. (2012, June). *A co-posited approach to time, space, and matter within intrapreneurship.* Paper presented at AOM/ISEOR conference, Lyon, France.

Kolb, D. (1984). *Experiential learning: Experience as the source of learning and development.* Englewood Cliffs, NJ: Prentice-Hall.

Linstead, S., & Pullen, A. (2009). *Management and organisation: A critical text.* London, UK: Palgrave Macmillan.

Magala, S. (2009). *The management of meaning in organizations.* London, UK: Palgrave Macmillan.

McCloskey, D. (1990). *On narrative: If you're so smart—The narrative of economic expertise.* Chicago, IL: University of Chicago Press.

Mintzberg, H., Ahlstrand, B., & Lampel, J. (2005). *Strategy safari: A guided tour through the wilds of strategic management.* New York. NY: The Free Press.

Nagy, B. G., Pollack, J. M., Rutherford, M. W., & Lohrke, F. T. (2012). The influence of entrepreneurs' credentials and impression management behaviors on perceptions of new venture legitimacy. *Entrepreneurship Theory and Practice, 36* (5), 941–965.

Nonaka, I., & Takeuchi, H. (1995). *The knowledge creating company: How Japanese companies create the dynamics of innovation.* New York, NY: Oxford University Press.

Pinchot, G., III. (1985). *Intrapreneuring.* New York, NY: Harper & Row.

Polanyi, K. (1957). *The economy as instituted process: The sociology of economic life.* Boulder, CO: Westview Press.

Ponty, M. M. (1969). *Visible and invisible: Studies in phenomenology and existential philosophy.* Evanston, IL: Northwestern University Press.

Savall, H., & Zardet, V. (2013). *The dynamics and challenges of tetranormalization.* Charlotte, NC: Information Age Publishing.

Shane, S. (2003). *A general theory of entrepreneurship: The individual-opportunity nexus.* Cheltenham, UK: Edward Elgar.

APPENDIX:
Conference Dialogue

Conference Participant: If I understood correctly what I have heard, people are their own entrepreneurs, sometimes excluded from the organizational core and it sounds to me like SEAM is a way to include them in ways that they had been otherwise wandering examples.

Debra Hockenberry: I think certainly if you are going to look at existing businesses, there are outliers that can be incorporated into the corporate world. My sense is that we may also want to look at this on a larger scale. If we are looking at the businesses themselves, they may want to take into consideration the entrepreneurs outside of the business who are part of that industry or that movement. Maybe we are excluding that population. Just because of our culture, we throw them out of business because we believe entrepreneurs want to be independent and business owners. We may want to think in a larger and broader sense, and support the creative deviant so that they do not have to worry about the business end and can focus on innovation.

Marc Bonnet: According to the ISEOR experience, the SEAM process consists of enhancing entrepreneurial aspects of change and making them actors of that transition. But needing to develop an agreement with what we called a Periodically Negotiable Activity Contract that enabling projects that don't contradict the current work in progress. Otherwise, some of the entrepreneurs will develop their project outside the company. It results in loss of skills and loss of energy for the company.

Henri Savall: Do you know that SRC stands for socially responsible capitalism? The link is the entrepreneur and there is a hidden theory in SEAM. An individual is a frustrated entrepreneur. That is the root cause of hidden costs. And SEAM develops and gives the opportunity to develop entrepreneurship which is hidden in any individual. A proper social responsibility comes to a socially responsible capitalism. It is what I observe when an organization implements SEAM.

CHAPTER 18

SEAM AND CRITICAL THEORY

Chato Hazelbaker

CONFERENCE REMARKS:
Chapter Prologue

Chato Hazelbaker

In this presentation my objective is to demonstrate some key linkages between critical theory and the Socio-Economic Approach to Management (SEAM). As I have studied both of these topics I have found that there is a shared ideology as well as agreements at the core of both theories and the ways in which these theories lead to action. The objective of linking these two approaches is that the study of both might be furthered as they inform each other.

I also want to recognize that this work has been shaped and informed by many individuals. I have been very fortunate to learn about SEAM with Marc Bonnet, Vincent Cristallini, Alla Heorhiadi, and John Conbere.

Facilitating the Socioeconomic Approach to Management, pages 239–251
Copyright © 2014 by Information Age Publishing

239

THE ORIGIN OF SEAM

SEAM has its roots in the 1970s when its founders wanted to merge the classical human relations school of management and the technical view introduced by F. W. Taylor. SEAM sought to recognize and integrate the human factor, particularly the need to quantify human potential. A key aspect of SEAM included developing a process to find dysfunctions within the organizational that were leading to hidden costs.

Critical theory emerged in the 1930s, in Germany with the Frankfurt school. The school was displaced from Germany by World War Two. The goal of critical theory at this time was to interpret, criticize, and reframe Marxist theory for contemporary society. Critical theory, sought to be both practical and normative. These two words also describe SEAM.

In the view of the founders of critical theory, they were charged with becoming social diagnosticians and therapists whose aim was nothing less than the elevation of the individual and the society. In this goal there are some parallels with SEAM. In the combination of the social and technical, I also see linkages between critical theory and SEAM.

SEAM in Organizations

In the Horivert process, which is the way that SEAM works across the organization, we see actions that match up with the concept of democratic language in Critical Theory. That is SEAM in action. The mirror effect, which is a key part of a SEAM intervention, is reflexive learning—a key concept in critical theory. This idea is founded on the fact that you do not simply learn something, you also have to understand and reflect on what occurred during an action. According to Brookfield (2005) the preeminent task in critical theory is learning and I think that this concept is embedded in the SEAM concept.

A key to SEAM is that a consultant is not just coming into an organization and executing a predetermined plan. In the Horivert process, the consultant spends specific time with the leaders, training them how to undertake the SEAM process. They have to be part of the learning process, and it is also part of critical theory. The learning is the tool for change, and you cannot change an organization without changing the way it thinks and developing the organizational capacity to become a learning organization. This is one of the key linkages between SEAM and critical theory. I am fascinated by that, particularly since we do not hear a lot of unsuccessful SEAM projects.

BRIDGES BETWEEN SEAM AND CRITICAL THEORY

There are many places where the theories and values at the core of critical theory and SEAM are in harmony. When you look at critical theory, you could observe that it is actually informed by sociology and business scholars. It could sound unpopular in the Academy but Freud, for instance, had a big impact on the development of Critical Theory.

Brookfield (2005) said the core concept of critical theory was questioning ideology. SEAM identifies ideology as part of the organization problem. Cristallini works from the analogy of a virus, which is called TFW in reference of Frederick Taylor, Henri Fayol, and Max Weber (see Chapter 2). If you do not correct that ideological problem, your organization cannot become better.

This one small example indicates that there are many factors that are worth exploring. In my context, I could say that actually a better world exists and is still reachable. I do not think that SEAM or critical theory necessarily agrees on what that better world looks like, but they do agree that a better world exists. Both critical theory and SEAM agree on the fact that it exists, not only for individuals but also in organizations.

Values

These elements suggest that there is value in combining the research findings and the methods of both theories. Both SEAM and critical theory reject the dominant ideology and that may explain a part of the resistance in organizations.

As an analogy, picture a princess kissing a frog in the hope it will become a prince. I only say that in my small context, you have to kiss a lot of frogs to find a prince. SEAM and critical theory are both frogs according to the academy. It is going to take some effort to get these adopted in the academy and turned into the metaphorical prince.

I think that SEAM is being introduced in the United States at a very critical time. Critical theory offers a very international element. The linking between the values of SEAM and critical theory and the way that they could match are the areas that I would like to explore in further research. The international application of SEAM could inform critical theory on issues of diversity in a remarkable way. Critical theory deals specifically with race and gender theory. SEAM does well across different contexts and countries which can inform critical theory.

With regard to issues of power and emancipation, critical theory is in some way obsessed by this idea and SEAM is an approach that seems to release power throughout the organization in an equalizing way. If we look at the SEAM databases through the lens of critical theory, we may gain additional explanations and understanding of the power in organizations. The shared value of honoring and considering each individual could transport the theories from SEAM to critical theory and vice versa.

One of my goals is to more fully understand how SEAM works through the perspective of critical theory. As Savall has noted, SEAM is a geopolitical project and Critical Theory is a geopolitical process. I love the idea that SEAM is a geopolitical process as it means more than just improving companies—it is about improving the world. It may be that critical theory is a start and SEAM is the action.

INTRODUCTION: THE HARMONY
OF CRITICAL THEORY AND SEAM

In the process of discovery, when a phenomenon occurs or a solution is discovered it takes time for the theory to adequately explain why or how. In exploring the why and how, the field of study is advanced and greater leaps can be made. Ancient Greeks and American Indians used various molds to cure disease but it wasn't until 1877 in France that Louis Pasteur built on the work of other scientists to postulate that bacteria could kill other bacteria. By adding to the theoretical understanding of how antibiotics worked, Pasteur was able to launch a field of study that made leaps and bounds and is still being expanded today.

The Socio-Economic Approach to Management (SEAM) is a change management approach that has been tremendously successful in helping organizations thrive, improve the lives of workers, and improve economic returns. Its success is partly rooted in the fact that it is one of the most closely studied change management programs (Conbere & Heorhiadi, 2011). The body of knowledge is expanded through ISEOR, the institute which houses SEAM. ISEOR maintains an extensive database that comes from SEAM interventions, and contributes to an ongoing field of study through conferences, articles, and books.

Critical theory has emerged during the same period to help a group of scholar practitioners, particularly in fields like adult education, explain the world and provide areas of inquiry research (Brookfield, 2005). It too has an expanding body of knowledge moved forward by contemporary scholars such as Stephen Brookfield, Cornell West, and many others.

In taking a look at these two approaches and their corresponding bodies of knowledge, it appears that critical theory and SEAM contain important parallels that deserve exploration. Many of the underlying assumptions and values of critical theory and SEAM are in harmony, and even some of the interventions suggested by critical theory seem to be played out in the activities of those conducting SEAM interventions in organizations. This harmony of values and actions between SEAM and critical theory may provide interesting future avenues for development and exploration in both fields of study, and more globally in the overall field of Organization Development (OD).

The Socio-Economic Approach to Management

The Socio-Economic Approach to Management has its roots in the 1970s as a change management program in France. A group of researchers including Henri Savall looked at the classical theories of organizations established by Taylor and others and sought to integrate this learning with the human relations school (Savall, 2010). The goal was to recognize and integrate the human factor, which according to SEAM founders was overemphasized by the neoclassical human relations school and underappreciated by the traditional proponents of Taylorism.

What emerged was SEAM, which found its home at ISEOR around 1973 (Savall, 2010). There are many distinctive elements of the SEAM approach and many foundational values that make it different from other approaches to change management. SEAM is carried out by a team of consultants, who are referred to as intervener-researchers, reflecting their role as both a consultant in the change process and continuing the research work of ISEOR. Like other change management programs there is a defined process and an extensive set of tools, but the underlying assumptions and values in the SEAM process are quite different when compared to other change management programs.

Key to SEAM is the concept of hidden costs (Savall, Zardet, & Bonnet, 2008), those economic inefficiencies that come from what SEAM researchers define as dysfunctions. These dysfunctions can be defined as places where the organization or its members do not work as well or productively as possible. SEAM classifies dysfunctions into six categories: working conditions, work organization, time management, communication–coordination–cooperation, integrated training, and strategic implementation. By finding these dysfunctions and revealing their hidden costs, SEAM finds additional revenue that can be returned to the bottom line. Here SEAM shows how it is tied to its earliest thinking of matching the human factor with the technological elements, as dysfunctions are often uncovered where the human actors and the processes meet.

Another key to SEAM, where it seems to differ from other change management programs, is the focus on developing human potential. SEAM chooses the term "actors" to describe employees as a reflection of the value that, "By focusing on people, management can develop new income through reducing hidden costs and performance (Conbere & Heorhiadi, 2011, p. 7) As an example, Conbere and Heorhiadi (2011) make clear that SEAM largely rejects lay-offs instead focusing on how to build the potential in the workforce.

SEAM is grounded in a type of action research, with intervener-researchers both participating in change projects and being responsible for the ongoing addition to knowledge about change management through ISEOR's SEAM database and other academic contributions. SEAM has proven to be highly profitable in the companies where it has been implemented. Because of the ongoing additions to the database, SEAM intervener-researchers can demonstrate the effect of their interventions across a variety of industries in many international settings. The SEAM data base has been developed for 33 years, with over 1,000,000 hours of research work making it an incredibly well studied form of change management (Savall, 2008). Today, SEAM intervener- researchers can look at companies as diverse as bakeries and town councils and make a fair prediction prior to the intervention of what the percentage of hidden costs are in the organization.

An Overview of Critical Theory

Critical theory can be traced to Germany when the Frankfurt School was originally formed at the Institute for Social Research in 1923. The central figures of the Institute for Social Research were Theodor Adorno, Max Horkheimer, Herbert Marcuse, Friederick Pollock, Leo Lowenthal, and Walter Benjamin (Aggers, 1991). There are many others who furthered the theory, among these Jurgen Habermas. This group of philosophers and social scientists based their early work in orthodox Marxism, which some members began to turn away from as early as the early 1940s.

To understand the development of critical theory one must understand Germany and Europe at the time the Frankfurt School began doing its work. As Brookfield (2005, p. 22) stated, the original mission of the Institute for Social Research was "to interpret, critique, and reframe the relevance of Marxist thought for contemporary industrial society."

All around them, critical theorists were seeing institutions change and many of their theories regarding how the social order would unfold were being challenged. Authoritarian institutions like the Nazi party were on the rise forcing the Institute to move to Geneva by 1933. As the work progressed into and beyond the 1930s and 1940s much of the work became about exploring the economic, ideological, and cultural factors that prevented the Marxist revolution that some in the Frankfurt School assumed would occur (Aggers, 1991).

As World War II raged and then ended, the "critical theorist became a social diagnostician and therapist, whose aim was nothing less than the liberation of the individual and society" (Farrell & Aune, 1979, p. 96). Sigmund Freud was an influence that further explains this statement. The Frankfurt School took inspiration from Freud and his diagnostic approach of psychoanalysis. Habermas is credited with most explicitly looking to Freudian theory for guidance (Conbere, 2010). This multidimensional and multidisciplinary approach is an important element of critical theory even as it has moved beyond studying Marxist writings or thoughts.

Horkheimer stated that the three essential elements of critical theory were that it must be explanatory, practical, and normative (Bohman, 2010). He also wanted the development of critical theory to include not only diagnosing social problems, but also naming the actors. Most importantly, Horkheimer wanted a theory that was prescriptive in terms of coming up with solutions. In this early description of the importance of critical theory, Horkheimer strongly rejects the positivistic stance of the neutral researcher and calls for a researcher that is an active part of finding solutions.

Brookfield (2005) laid out his own five distinctive characteristics of critical theory. Based on his analysis of the work, particularly of Horkheimer, Brookfield notes first that this approach is closely tied to political analysis and the tension among social classes. This dynamic is strongly tied to economics and the exchange of goods and services. Secondly, Brookfield (2005, p. 25) stated critical theory at its core should "provide people with knowledge and understanding intended to free them from oppression."

A third characteristic is another important departure from positivism. Critical theory recognizes and breaks down the wall between the researcher and the research subject. Fourth, this approach is defined by its goal of a fairer and better world. The final distinctive aspect is that one cannot prove critical theory until it has worked. In Brookfield's (2005, p. 29) words, "Verification of the theory is impossible until the social vision it inspires is realized."

The Harmony of SEAM and Critical Theory in Theory and Values

There are strong connections between the development of critical theory and SEAM in history and influence. Both are multidisciplinary in approach and development, both look to ideology as a source of problems, and they share values and a vision for the future.

As he founded the SEAM paradigm, Savall (2008) took a multidisciplinary approach similar to critical theory, which was informed by sociologists, economists, and psychologist among others. The field is interdisciplinary, being best known by those in philosophy, aesthetic theory, literary criticism, and women's studies (Aggers, 1991). It continues to be highly interdisciplinary today in terms of the fields that employ and add to its body of knowledge.

In the case of both SEAM and critical theory there is a desire to look at ideology as the source of problems. Ideology can be stated as "A coherent set of beliefs that describes the worldview held by members" (Mir, 2003, p. 735). More than that, both approaches are suspicious of dominant ideologies that go unexplored and their detrimental effect on the society as a whole.

SEAM intervener researcher Vincent Cristallini (2011) suggested that organizations are not looking deeply enough to find the solution to their problems. He made the case that many of the problems that organizations try to solve are symptoms of a systematic failure that stem from a flawed ideology. Only by looking at the flaws in the ideology can we understand why organizations are behaving in ways which are counterproductive.

Critical theory makes a similar case. According to Brookfield (2005, p. 40), "The first, and arguably preeminent, learning task embedded in critical theory is that of challenging ideology." Critical theory looks at the ideology of the whole system, recognizing from the outset that something is not functioning correctly that is preventing a better system from occurring.

It is important to note here that both SEAM and critical theory envision a more hopeful future where things are objectively better than they are today. Again, there is harmony here. "A core belief of SEAM consultants is that organizations do not exist only to make money, they exist to serve society in general and all the employees in particular" (Conbere & Heorhiadi, 2011, p. 6). Similarly, Habermas grounds critical theory in the goals of the Enlightment, setting out a vision of what some have referred to as a utopia, but he goes further. "His own description of modernity's 'unfinished project' of democratic Enlightenment indicates a real appreciation of diverse modernizing trajectories" (Johnson, 2005, p. 113). To me, this suggests progress, a foundational desire to improve things for people that is core to both approaches.

What is important about this is that both SEAM and critical theory may not agree exactly on what a better future looks like, but they are at their very center committed to the idea of a better future. This seems to bond them as approaches, and separate them from a number of other approaches. Brookfield (2005, p. 27) calls this the normative grounding of critical theory, noting "Not only does the theory criticize current society, it envisages a fairer, less alienated, more democratic world."

Using the analogy of a virus, Cristallini (2011) argues that the entire organizational system is infected. He asserts that business is carrying a hidden virus, and this virus is causing all kinds of problems. It is going undiagnosed as a systemic problem, and other organizational change efforts are treating symptoms rather than the core illness. The virus is passed from generation to generation, and organization to organization. As defined by Cristallini, the virus is essentially a flawed ideology.

Cristallini (2011) and his colleagues at ISEOR named the virus TFW for Taylor, Fayol, and Weber, the three individuals they credited with promoting the thinking that is now at the heart of the virus. Taylor and Taylorism is well known to Americans with background in manufacturing. Taylor was one of the first to undertake time studies in factories near the turn of the previous century. He is credited with developing the idea of hyper-specialization, and separating the management of the task from the individual performing the task (Cristallini, 2011). American readers do not as commonly recognize Fayol and Weber as Fayol is French and Weber is Austrian. "Fayol promoted the idea of specialization and separation of business function" (p. 3). A sociologist, Weber built an ideal model for organizations based on rules, a system that largely mirrors the modern idea in America of a legal bureaucracy. Interestingly, in Fayol, both critical theory and SEAM find argument. In their shared rejection of part of what has become the plan/control theory (French, 2009) there is yet more evidence of a harmony between the two.

Key to the virus are two concepts that Cristallini (2011) argued are promoted by these three men—depersonalization and submission. Cristallini (2011, p. 3) defines the term depersonalization to mean that the individual must give way to the needs of the organization. Submission is related, "The submission assumes that the individual complies with the requirements, because it accepts the principle of subordination, it is docile and waives his freedom and his aspirations."

There are two important points here where SEAM and critical theory cross. The first is that the virus is closely tied to the ideology of capitalism, one of the ideologies that critical theory rejects. The second is that the rejection of depersonalization and submission are specific areas where SEAM agrees not only in theory but in action.

As stated above, critical theory has a firm foundation in Marxist thought. "Marx argued that the capitalist labor process was a complex combination of neutral techniques, which would increase the output of labor under any relations of production, and biased techniques, which increase output solely by repressing the antagonisms of class societies" (Gartmann 1999, p. 384). At the core of critical theory is the rejection of capitalism, because according to the definition of Marx it specifically relied on the oppression of the working class in order to benefit the ruling class. While other definitions of capitalism may exist in modern America, the initial definition as put forward by Marx was relatively specific.

In discussing the differences between SEAM and traditional management approaches, Conbere and Heorhiadi (2011, p. 6) stated, "Therefore SEAM rejects the idea that employees are human capital, a term that degrades employees into nonhuman commodities." Again, as stated above, the focus on SEAM is in unleashing human potential rather than subordinating it.

As noted above, two parts of the virus that Cristallini places at the core of dysfunction are depersonalization and submission. Critical theory has much to say about these two concepts. Erich Fromm, who wrote extensively about alienation, a term that I believe closely matches Cristallini's concepts of depersonalization and submission. While recognizing the advances of the modern age, Fromm (1994) pointed out that the overall affect is that individuals are largely judged by what they contribute economically the system, and what has been lost is the use of production to benefit the salvation or happiness of the worker. As SEAM says that depersonalization and submissions are not optimal in an organization, critical theory loudly agrees, calling for democracy, and particularly in its exploration of racial and gender issues systems to overcome alienation (Brookfield, 2005).

The conclusion of SEAM, that a flawed ideology is at the heart of dysfunction and gets in the way of organizations functioning at a higher level, is similar to the conclusion reached by critical theorists as they challenge ideologies in organizations. As Ogbor (2001, p. 590) stated, "Corporate culture, if uncritically examined, remains an ideology, which is socially constructed to reflect and legitimize the power relations of managerial elites within an organization and society at large." Working from the work of Marcuse and others, he notes that by not challenging ideology corporations become one dimensional in their thinking and therefore are prone to reduce the number of options and build and promote dysfunctions.

The Harmony of SEAM and Critical Theory in Action

There is an element beyond theory and values that SEAM also appears to be in agreement with critical theory—action. One of Brookfield's distinctions about critical theory is the breakdown between the researcher and the environment. In SEAM, the interventions are carried out by intervener-researchers (Savall, 2010). They go into the environment with the clear goal of changing it. Those processes are based on previous research and the outcomes are fed into a database of research that is intended to improve the process in the future. Critical theory has at its core the belief that the researcher changes the situation by entering it, and more importantly as stated above critical theory is prescriptive, with the researcher having the goal of creating change.

Particular elements of SEAM also appear to be the embodiment of critical theory in action at key moments during the intervention process. One of the first steps in the SEAM process is for the intervener-researchers to gather data, and then present that data back to the organization. Rather than doing interpretive work with the data, the intervener-researchers present the data in what is called the mirror effect (Cristallini, 2011), using the actual quotes which participants gave during the data gathering sessions and grouping them into themes. This process appears to almost force the participants into the mode of reflexive learning, which according to Brookfield (2005) is learning that includes discussion of conflicting evidence and evidence that may run contrary to stated goals or the status quo. By not prioritizing the data into existing buckets of knowledge, and by presenting it as people have stated it, the mirror effect appears to force people to look at the information critically and forces them to decide how to react to the information.

Through the SEAM process HORIVERT the team of consultants seeks to engage the entire organization in a way that gathers actionable input from all involved (Savall, 2010). While there may be disagreements about whether the HORIVERT process truly accomplishes this, the aim and goal is very close to seeking democracy as sought in critical theory. This is particularly tied to components of democracy promoted in critical theory, including the idea that all people should be allowed to take actions that are motivated by their own desires and interests, not in submission to an authority, but motivated by the accomplishment of a common good (Brookfield, 2005).

In the HORIVERT process there is a horizontal action, which is a diagnostic of dysfunctions with the board of directors and the management team. There is also a vertical action aimed at workers in at least two departments, in order to enhance empowerment at all levels. It focuses on integrated training to improve the skills of the personnel. Over time this action involves every department, its entire hierarchical line of command from the CEO to line personnel (Savall, Zardet, & Bonnet, 2008).

I can see this process as an attempt to put in place Habermas's conditions for ideal speech, which he puts at the very heart of creating a truly democratic process (Brookfield, 2005). It also seeks to gain input across the organization in a way that minimizes some of the power dynamics that are of particular concern in critical theory.

Another way that SEAM and critical theory agree in action is in the role of learning. The SEAM intervention process is really a learning process, where during several stages participants are taught different ways to participate and manage. Managers are a particular focus of this learning: "Management's commitments in the intervention process may be considered as a learning experience" (Savall, Zardet, & Bonnet, 2008, p. 153).

Critical theory also relies on both the capacity and willingness of individuals to learn and by extension for organizations to learn. "At its root, living democratically was seen by Lindeman as an adult learning process" (Brookfield, 2005, p. 62). As Brookfield further explains, one of the goals of critical theory, to bring about a more democratic society, can only be accomplished when individuals learn and practice democratic disciplines and became more and more competent in practicing those disciplines. Learning is at the core of critical theory and it is as that core of SEAM.

FINAL THOUGHTS AND SUGGESTIONS FOR ACTION

As I look at critical theory and SEAM and discover places where they are similar, I feel as though I have only scratched the surface. There is a great deal of room for a research agenda to look more carefully at how critical theory and SEAM can both help provide evidence for each other and spur further development in the fields. As an example, critical theory has a great deal to say on the subject of power, and there are instances where SEAM in action tries to minimize power dynamics. Looking at the SEAM database a researcher may be able to come up with a deeper theoretical understanding of how people react in these power situations and that may in turn inform critical theory. In a similar way, SEAM has been used internationally, which could provide interesting information to critical theory in terms of race and culture, areas where critical theory is often applied.

It is also possible that by combining the research efforts in SEAM and critical theory each may gain wider acceptance, particularly in the United States where both are little known or understood. I owe this insight to John Conbere (personal communication, September, 2012) who first pointed out that perhaps the underlying cause of this is that both critical theory and SEAM challenge the ideology of the dominant culture, and as he stated, "And, so are rejected in spite of the data."

An ongoing conversation between those practicing critical theory academically and as change agents and SEAM intervener-researchers would undoubtedly lead to a rich discussion. The discoveries that may come from that would likely propel both fields for the foreseeable future.

REFERENCES

Aggers B. (1991). Critical theory, poststructuralism, postmodernism: Their sociological relevance. *Annual Review of Sociology, 17,* 105–131.

Bohman, J. (2010). Critical Theory. In E.N. Zalta (Ed.), *The Stanford Encyclopedia of Philosophy.* http://plato.stanford.edu/archives/spr2010//critical theory.

Brookfield, S. (2005). *The power of critical theory: Liberating adult learning and teaching.* San Francisco, CA: Jossey-Bass.

Conbere, J. (2010). *What is truth? An introduction to epistemology in the social sciences.* Working paper. Minneapolis, MN: University of St. Thomas.

Conbere, J. & Heorhiadi, A. (2011). Socio-economic approach to management. *OD Practitioner, 43*(1), 6–10.

Cristallini, V. (2011, March). Rôle de la gouvernance dans la lutte contre la pandémie mondiale du virus techno-économique [The role of governance in the fight against the global pandemic of the techno-economic virus], paper presented at the 8th Annual Conference of the ADERSE [Association for the Development of Education and Research on Corporate Social Responsibility]). Paris, France.

Farrell, T. & Aune, J. (1979). Critical theory and communication: A selective literature review. *The Quarterly Journal of Speech, 65*, 93–120.

French, S. (2009). Critiquing the language of strategic management. *Journal of Management Development, 28* (1), 6–17.

Fromm, E. (1994). *Escape from freedom*. New York: Holt Paperbacks.

Gartman, D. (1999). Comments on 'Marx and the labor process': An interpretation. *Critical Sociology, 25* (2/3), 384–386.

Johnson, P. (2005). Habermas: A reasonable utopian? *Critical Horizons, 6*, 101–118.

Mir, A. (2003).The hegemonic discourse of management texts. *Journal of Management Education, 27*, 734–737.

Ogbor, J. (2001). Critical theory and the hegemony of corporate culture. *Journal of Organizational Change Management, 14* (6), 590–608.

Savall, H. (2010). *Work and people: An economic evaluation of job-enrichment*. Charlotte, NC: Information Age Publishing.

Savall, H., Zardet, V., & Bonnet, M. (2008). *Releasing the untapped potential of enterprises through socio-economic management*. Turin, Italy: International Training Centre of the ILO.

CHAPTER 19

WHY SEAM?

Susan Huber

As I entered the restaurant, I quickly scanned the buzzing room crowded with evening diners. I wondered if I would recognize the celebrated French scholar midst all of the clientele hunched in quiet conversation. Henri Savall and I were not acquainted, however, the doctoral faculty in the Organization Development program at the University of St. Thomas knew him well, and the students talked about him in the hushed tones of respect typically reserved for a celebrated scholar. I zeroed in on a table with two gentlemen engaged in intense conversation and a woman with panache, and walked toward it at the same time the St. Thomas faculty hosts were arriving.

We had introductions around the table, with Savall apologizing because he spoke little English. I laughingly assured him we would get on famously because I had lost most of the spoken French I had laboriously practiced as an undergraduate student. After some small talk about the November chill in Minnesota, Savall adroitly switched the topic to the discussion of the evening—the Socio-Economic Approach to Management or SEAM. He and two University of St. Thomas faculty members hosting the dinner were clearly interested in striking a partnership agreement and I was invited to give the provost's blessing to the idea.

Henri Savall, the founding father of SEAM, who actually speaks impeccable English, began to explain his approach to management to me in a most

Facilitating the Socioeconomic Approach to Management, pages 253–255
Copyright © 2014 by Information Age Publishing
253

unusual way. As we ate he would periodically pass me a tiny, inch square, post-it note with a drawing on it. Sometimes he asked me what I understood the figure to mean; sometimes he just slid the note in front of my plate. Initially I was clueless and a bit flummoxed on how to respond. I began to think this might be a very long evening.

I finally decided to put my administrative role aside and just enjoy the conversation with our French guests. I could feel myself settling into my old and comfortable student role, trying to pick up the intermittent French phrases and learn something about an approach to management that was not familiar to me. With a bit of embarrassment, I realized the post-it notes were starting to make sense. I started questioning Henri and his wife, Dr. Veronique Zardet, and his colleague, Dr. Vincent Cristallini and realized the post-it procedure, curious in its own rite, was a brilliant, scholarly shorthand that graphically documented a complex philosophical approach to management.

I am not a scholar of organizational management, but I became fascinated with the intersection of leadership and work cultures as I explored the work culture of air traffic controllers for my doctoral research many years ago. Organizational frameworks bridge multiple types of organizations and the SEAM process focuses on organizational diagnosis and interventions using many of the qualitative research methodologies I had learned and taught over the years. I found myself quickly invested in my newfound knowledge and eager to learn more about the SEAM philosophy and methodology.

In June of 2013, I met with Savall, Cristallini and Marc Bonnet at ISEOR (Socio-Economic Institute of Firms and Organizations) headquarters in Ecully, France. They offered me an individualized and intensive seminar on SEAM and we rapidly progressed from post-it notes to white boards and textbooks. As we explored real-time case studies of economically troubled businesses that had implemented strategic changes in their work setting as a result of partnering with SEAM consultants, I began to understand more about the transformative power of the SEAM methodology. The type of change management embedded in the SEAM philosophy taught business leaders how to preserve and enhance their organizations by learning how to reduce hidden costs.

I learned how the organizational analysis that undergirds SEAM views the work culture of the organization alongside the economic performance of the organization. SEAM links the behavior of employees in the workplace to organizational output. The socio-economic tension that the SEAM philosophy addresses leads managers to take corrective action in the workplace. It allows them to build a workforce that believes in itself and offers them the confidence and skills to do what it takes to make the organization successful.

So much of the SEAM approach correlates to what students learn about leadership in their graduate studies at the University of St. Thomas, that discussing the notion of collaboration seemed like belaboring the obvious. I was already convinced that learning about the SEAM process would be beneficial for our students. I had even started to reconsider the idea, initially raised by John Conbere and Alla Heorhiadi, of establishing a SEAM Institute in Minneapolis that would be headquartered at the University of St. Thomas. Yet, midway through my seminar training, when Savall seemed to be reasonably pleased with my learning progress, I felt compelled to ask the critical question. I asked him to compare SEAM to other managerial approaches that still hold a historical place in management textbooks and with business leaders. I wanted him to help me understand what made SEAM different.

For a moment I regretted the question while his professorial silence filled the room.

I feared I had insulted him, which was certainly not my intention. With a quick nod to his colleague, he exploded in laughter. He drew a post-it from his jacket pocket and wrote on it "SEAM works."

The breakthrough moment for me came with those two words. I knew I was drawn to the philosophy because of its solid research-base, but research and reality are not always 100% compatible. I mentally asked myself whether I was captivated by the innovative practitioner component of SEAM and wanted to believe that would make the approach work because I personally thought it was a missing component from some of the historical approaches to management consulting. I could honestly answer yes to that question, but what held my attention most closely was the skillful use of data gathering that SEAM consultants employed in their case studies. The organizational case studies that I read appeared to be built on solid qualitative and quantitative data. The consultants analyzed the human side of organizational effectiveness along with the economic constraints of the business. Then they worked strategically and collaboratively with management to diagnose and resolve the problem. I view this as a departure from the norm. Management consultants typically give short shrift to gathering qualitative data because of its time consuming nature. It is much easier and more efficient, perhaps, for consultants to offer a formulaic solution to managerial leaders that can be applied almost as a logarithm.

From my perspective, a genuine socio-economic approach to management would necessarily have to gather and analyze both qualitative and quantitative data from an organization in a scientific manner to build an authentic case study that would provide useful insights to understanding the dynamic that caused the problem under study. Methodologically connecting the qualitative and quantitative aspects of organizational life links research to intervention. That is precisely why SEAM works.

CHAPTER 20

CONCLUSION

Final Conference Dialogue

Conference Participant: I want to talk about an experience I had two years ago when I was called in by the department of management studies from the University of Delhi. It was a full online MBA Information Technology program in cooperation with another business school from Singapore. It contained two semesters of Information Technology and two others on Information Technology Management. In this part, there were courses called Organization Dynamics which were, in fact, Organization Development and Change. They asked me to teach this course and I had no experience in teaching online and also I was not a specialist of Organization Development. I worked with a basic support document called protocol about group management, a very traditional Organization Behavior course.

I had been working with the help of Marc Bonnet on the accessibility of some chapters from the book *Mastering Hidden Costs and Socio-Economic Performance* and other books written under the direction of Henri Savall. I have made this experience due to the amount of hidden costs and I have to say that it was useful resource.

In this MBA program, courses were taught as sequences, and I had the opportunity to teach two times this course, each during five weeks.

Facilitating the Socioeconomic Approach to Management, pages 257–265
Copyright © 2014 by Information Age Publishing
257

The time devoted to hidden costs in these sequences was between three or four weeks and the final focused on these concepts. What we asked the students, who were executives from very large companies such as HSBC or leader companies in software system or industry, it met with a very good reception. The provider in charge of development in this program has been, from the beginning to the results, a very positive proposer. I think that the students, who were working at the time, were very happy and really loved that approach, probably due to the fact that a good number of them were from the largest part of India, Pakistan, or Indonesia (80%). The rest of them came from all over the world (China, Hong-Kong, Singapore, UK, United States). A good number of Indian students seem to give a voice to that system because they always have a significantly holistic approach, even though it is sometimes more political. They became, at the end, almost ready to play with the idea of hidden costs.

The philosophy of the SEAM method was very well accepted and viewed as very original, interesting and positive. The final exam consisted of making a basic analysis of hidden costs and proposing a strategic plan with ideas on how to implement it. It was difficult to ask them more even if they were smart people. I think this experience was a very positive step and the university asked me to develop it for its international MBA program—which suggests that there is a hope.

Conference Participant: I am wondering if SEAM would be better taken into account if we separated the method from the philosophy. My concern is not to defend my core subject, I just want to introduce some of these concepts to the next generation of our students who take care implementing SEAM just care about its philosophy. They don't have to apply the method. Does SEAM have to make the philosophy and the method collaborate, or would it be better to separate those tools?

Conference Participant: If I may ask a final question, with SEAM we have seen an intervention system, a series of management tools which those roll out into proactive decisions. This approach is based on an underlying belief system about people and about management. My understanding of SEAM is to really take action. If you are focusing on this, somehow you are getting the beliefs across. I have two questions. First, how do you really do this? Second, in the programs that use a bit of SEAM, are they really doing an intervention system or is it more of an art that comes from beliefs about values, beliefs about human beings, and beliefs about the [TFW] virus?

Henri Savall: Most of our clients discovered the philosophy ten to twenty years after the beginning of our intervention. They lived the philosophy through the tools, the process of change strategy, and eventually discovered there was an underlying idea. This philosophy goes back to SEAM's origin, in 1973, but I hid it to make it suitable in the management of organizations. Looking back over two decades, we initially brought in philosophy but then we stopped—the philosophy embedded in SEAM is very subversive when it refers to mainstream paradigms.

Conference Participant: From an organizational perspective, they are learning through this [SEAM] process and the intervener-researcher needs to know this. He has to know that we can expect it is a critical theory question. How do we teach something that is very subversive when it is too easy to simply say, "Yes, I get it"—and then continue with operations as usual?

Henri Savall: It is their philosophy. It is no longer about money.

Conference Participant: I appreciate the point that SEAM's underlying philosophy could have subversive aspects. As I understand what that means, even if they had studied critical theory, participants are still asking about the principles of critical theory.

When I first read this one [a critical theory article], I thought "Oh my God, I should not be reading this because it is Marx's incarnation!" Even if it wasn't exactly based on Marxism, you want to convey the philosophy through the intervention methodology. As a practitioner and a leader in the social sector, the up-hill battle was the influences on human potential. If I had not been introduced to the intervention and the other aspects of SEAM, I am not sure that I would have connected the interaction and what I believe SEAM brings into our organization.

In our organization, we have values and beliefs because of the mission we are driving. What I had learned in my doctoral studies is that it's not enough to have people who have values. I have to understand more about the association of their beliefs and values. In the context of all these influences, what could create a belief? I am excited about SEAM and I think it could offer great opportunities. One of the things that came to me yesterday is how do we look at that aspect of human potential? How do you create metrics that give us empirical information on what happens through these experiments with SEAM?

I put this concern on the table because from another perspective that is not SEAM related, there are other system approaches for our community to apply. One of them is looking at the way that institutions, across public sectors, support the academic achievement of our children. Especially, kids who are not achieving a great level on standardized tests. This process is named "S-Drive." It brings a lot of potential to provide academic support for our children. It concerns the institutions,

the businesses, and everybody who is getting behind what we had identified by metrics. The educational assessment standards based on children do not develop sufficient empirical information as suggested by
social sectors at the table. They support that old goal based on the will
to get 100% per kid from the standardized tests. My question is, how do
we plan that aspect of human potential through SEAM?

Conference Participant: From my perception also, we are in front of a metric
standpoint. It seems to me that one of the key considerations consists
of qualifying the context. What is the variance of the population we
are measuring? We want to measure human potential, so we have to
measure the potential of the society as a whole, which seems to be
quite difficult.

With regard to your organization [in reference to the previous
questioner], you have to consider the children who are helpless. That
is a small variance; we can have proper metrics. If we stand with this
context, we can work with proper measures that are more effective.

Conference Participant: In looking at our accomplishments, what we have is
to say: "for each dollar invested in our kids, there is a 16% global rate
return." When we look at SEAM, we are talking about engagement.
I am reminding of what some of the participants said these past two
days. By the way they had implemented SEAM we can say that they are
moving forward. Something happened following their participation
with the different management tools and their achievements.

Conference Participant: I am an OD academic and also an entrepreneur.
I think when we talk about human potential, it is important to define what kind of potential we are referring to. We can talk about
human economic potential, production potential, and so forth, but
I think about the Human Being. If we think in terms of mind potential, there is no limit to that conception, to what could be accomplished. I am wondering if we want to try to measure something which
is immeasurable.

There could be a significant danger in trying to put into metrics
something which is so secret, so variable. But I think that this challenge
provides an opportunity, given the tension polarities to measure things
in a physical world. It has the potential to reach and accomplish great
things but sometimes I think that we have the sacrament of our essence
and it has to be respected. We have also the responsibility to take care
of that principle about polarity to reach producing more parts.

I would love to hear more about economic potential or productive
potential. When I think about the human potential, I think it is a very
special opportunity.

Conference Participant: The point I would like to draw is the closest analogy that I know: teaching consultants the way to implement change. The content of our teaching program is not only both philosophy and a set of values, but also a system. It depends on a series of tools fitting in that system. This is not probably what we think of as a consultant, but I admit that the SEAM program matches these two parts very well.

When you separate the three parts of the diagram (see Figure 20.1) there is a lot of potential consequences. People learn the tools very well and after study the philosophy. They learn an intervention system but they don't understand the "whys and wherefores" of each piece. The lesson I have learned by teaching consultants is that you have three pieces (philosophy, values and tools) somehow in disruption.

Henri Savall: Measurement may be the core concept in SEAM. What are we doing when we are walking? We are measuring. I measure when I walk outside. The individual is a machine to measure. Life is measuring. These are local relative measures.

If this group says "is this measure true?" it may not be but it is useful! When people are interacting, they measure everything in the world. These are qualimetric measures: qualitative, quantitative and financial.

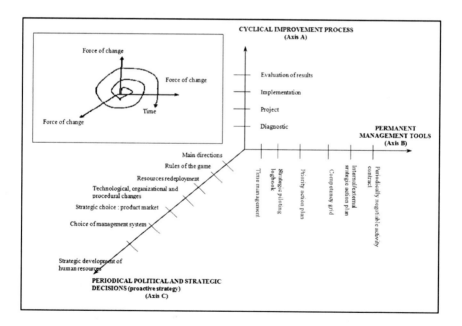

Figure 20.1 The three axes of the Socio-Economic Intervention Dynamics (called the "SEAM Trihedron").

The traditional economic models are not true because they do not measure hidden costs and performance. What represents a 1% increase in the price or salary, when compared with $20,000 to $80,000 per year and per person of hidden costs? It is crazy to lean on that traditional model. Here is the amount and this can be converted from costs into performance through interaction and cooperation. There is no other way. Through experimentation, we know that there is a way. If people in a group wish to convert costs into performance, they will succeed. If they don't, nobody in the world can convert these hidden costs. That is good news!

John Conbere: Would it be fair to say that through diagnosis of dysfunctions, tools and creating the interaction, SEAM belief is to release the human potential? In another sense, the human potential doesn't have to be measured does it?

Henri Savall: They are hidden entrepreneurs and also they are able to measure their evolution.

Conference Participant: An individual in the new economy might think this model is a little bit industrial. It is pretty much based on capital, like in the case "Das Kapital." Professor Savall, you are writing about the traditional performance function of capital and labor. What would happen in an economy where knowledge and innovation are more important?

Henri Savall: Knowledge theory is a fad.

Eric Sanders: In some models, this is expanding the basic model of the "production function." If you expand these models you will see that:

- $Y = f(E, N, K, L, H) + r$
- Y for production value,
- E for efficacy,
- N for natural resources,
- K for capital,
- L for labor,
- H for human capital, including knowledge entries and skills from people
- r for the residual.

Using this model, you can explain more things, but you still have a residual. This expanded model explains more about the production function so the residual maybe a little bit smaller, but it stills remains. That is where Dr. Savall's work helps explain the residual. Capital may he try to make the residual disappear but we have to qualify what is going to be constant in the model, what we cannot explain. There will always be things that we cannot explain. There are some multiple variables in multianalysis and when some of those are gone, then hidden costs appear.

Conference Participant: You are talking about hidden costs. Hidden costs are bigger, and they are bigger because knowledge is created with value. For example, for a company like Apple, every employee is a high tech engineer. So for a company like that, the amount of hidden costs is around $20,000 per employee because they do not have that many physical tangible assets.

Conference Participant: Are you saying that people infuse more value per capita?

Conference Participant: They are the knowledge producers.

Conference Participant: There are also dysfunctions in their performance. For example, the amount of email we receive is one of the biggest causes of dysfunctions in the workplace. It is a great tool, but people spend 1, 2, or 3 hours on email instead of spending time on productive work.

John Conbere: To what extent is this discussion relevant to your experience?

Jean Caghassi: For me it is totally relevant. I may not be an academic, but I am interested in human potential. I remember my first contact with management; it was in the early 80s. Academic management professors were reading Michael Porter and his fellows, but I could not find personally the way of doing what he was describing in his books. Porter's prescriptions only really apply to large corporations—they are miles away from my day-to-day life as a manager. So, my religion was not to do what managers were doing—that was wrong to me. And this belief was my single management tool.

   The fact that SEAM is based on research, this back-and-forth relationship with people, for instance, with what happens during the mirror effect. You can observe much critical instincts. The way that knowledge is spread in the company is very important. I don't think it would not work. I know other management tools, but I don't know other management systems as holistic as SEAM.

Conference Participant: For me the application is in the measurability. We can qualify the effects of what is going wrong. Behind the measure, I think there is an idea. Developing the measure could be useful in companies, even in the education industry. I heard precious little about measuring at the end; however there is measurability in bringing much information in terms of knowledge. Through SEAM's processes, in education, we could be able to measure hidden potential and perhaps we could change the model we have. All I know is that we need it. I am wondering how we get that and do we have time.

Conference Participant: We do have an advantage. We decide the nature of the gage, the way to use it, and finally the objects that we are measuring. We could measure something one day and another one due to daily activity. It is irrelevant to measure something systematically.

The profit measure, contribution measure, it is the value added by the whole community when it is a nonprofit organization. You decide the content that you put into HCVAC. It's not accounting, it's economics.

Conference Participant: With the entry of new leaders in the organizations that adopted SEAM, how to make sure that each new generation who comes in gets fully developed? Do you develop SEAM training internally?

Vincent Cristallini: SEAM is an ongoing, never-ending improvement process. You have to consider the dynamics: when new people come into the company, the company organizes training sessions. There are many ways to sustain SEAM in a company. One way is through internal interveners and trainers who we support with our external maintenance training. This soft way helps them maintain the integrity of the concept.

Conference Participant: As I could understand from these cases, with SEAM, we are entering a long-term relationship through projects. Training in these tools, which had been introduced in the organization, seems to be a minimum. We are talking about a long-term relationship.

Vincent Cristallini: It is also an in-depth, long-term relationship. We consider that SEAM is a kind of equipment with clear concepts throughout the method. This equipment requires ongoing maintenance.

Jean Caghassi: Based on my experience, SEAM is a powerful method, well-structured and effective. My first contact with SEAM was when we went to a company with the CEO. I worked with Frantz Datry, and I was astonished by the quantity of information that the tool could contain. The model has become a cornerstone for me. The activity broker (the takeover group) was not able to veer the system off course in the acquired company because of this cornerstone. As long as this cornerstone existed, they were not able to divert. My concern regarding the company I managed over 16 years, after discussions with Henri Savall, is that a key cornerstone is the Periodically Negotiable Activity Contract (PNAC). Using the PNAC, the acquiring company was not able to divert the takeover [target] company.

Conference Participant: Are there cases where SEAM did not work as well? What learning could you take away from that experience?

Henri Savall: We had two cases in all our engagements. The reason is that we choose our clients. They have to take exams. We have a first meeting; we bring all the CEOs together. We come back another time. When the CEO is in a hurry we stress the need for "strategic patience." The negotiation is the fourth milestone. It lasts one year. We need to make sure they know what they are purchasing and committing to. This integrated system, which is very demanding, is the reason why negotiations are so long. We had to design a master field for negotiation. Once we begin an intervention, we want to be sure that there is no misunderstanding between us and the client. We have a "designing by doing" process. A SEAM intervention is a "learning-by-doing" process. It requires a learning curve and motivation. In other consulting firms, you first pay the fee before designing the program—only then can the people understand what they are going to do. With SEAM, we never discuss fees before making sure our clients have understood the ins and outs of the method. A new philosophy in our system is that people evaluate. They are intelligent, they measure and observe the dynamic people representing up to 95% across the board, even if 5% of people won't buy in.

Conference Participant: Dr. Savall, how many individuals are required to study a project when a prospective client wants to adopt SEAM?

Henri Savall: We need two people at least, and then others will be added as deemed necessary. There are two previous conditions before implementing SEAM. First, a general manager who wants to manage; however, we observe in many organizations that "pilots don't want to pilot. In this instance, SEAM cannot be implemented. The second requirement is that there are people in the organization who are feeling some external strategic threats. The definition of a "strategic threat" is that "tomorrow we won't be able to do our work the same way we are doing it today."

SEAM GENERAL
BIBLIOGRAPHY

Ansoff, I. (2010). Preface. In H. Savall, *Work and people: An economic evaluation of job enrichment* (pp. 19–25). Charlotte, NC: Information Age. (Original French work published 1974).

Bernácer, G. (1922). La teoría de las disponibilidades como interpretación de las crisis y del problema social [The theory of available funds as interpretation of crisis and social issue]. Madrid, Spain: Revista nacional de economía.

Bernácer, G. (1955). *Una economía libre, sin crisis y sin paro* [A free economy without crisis and without unemployment]. Madrid, Spain: Aguilar.

Boje, D. M. (2004). Preface. In H. Savall & V. Zardet, *Recherche en sciences de gestion: Approche qualimétrique. Observer l'objet complexe* [Research in management science: Qualimetrics approach: Observing the complex object]. Paris, France: Economica.

Boje, D. M. (2009, June). Storytelling, appreciative inquiry, and tetranormalization. Paper presented at the international conference organized in partnership with the ISEOR and Divisions of the Academy of Management, Lyon, France.

Boje, D. M., & Rosile, G. A. (2003a). Comparison of socio-economic and other transorganizational development methods. *Journal of Organizational Change Management, 16*(1), 10–20.

Boje, D. M., & Rosile, G. A. (2003b). Theatrics of SEAM. *Journal of Organizational Change Management, 16* (1), 21–32.

Bonnet, M., & Cristallini, V. (2003). Enhancing the efficiency of networks in an urban area through socio-economic interventions. *Journal of Organizational Change Management, 16*(1), 72–82.

Buono, A. F. (2003). SEAM-less post-merger integration strategies: A cause for concern. *Journal of Organizational Change Management, 16*(1): 90–98.

Facilitating the Socioeconomic Approach to Management, pages 267–273
Copyright © 2014 by Information Age Publishing
All rights of reproduction in any form reserved.

Buono, A. F., & Savall, H. (Eds.). (2007). *Socio-economic intervention in organizations: The intervener-researcher and the SEAM approach to organizational analysis.* Charlotte, NC: Information Age Publishing.

Cappelletti, L. (2007) Intervening in small professional enterprises, enhancing management quality in French notary publics. In A. F. Buono & H. Savall (Eds.), *Socio-economic intervention in organizations: The intervener-researcher and the SEAM approach to organizational analysis* (pp. 331–353). Charlotte, NC: Information Age Publishing.

Cristallini, V. (2009). *L'habileté managériale, réalisme et courage en management* [Managerial ability, realism and courage in management]. Paris, France: EMS.

Delors, J. (1975). Preface. In H. Savall, *Enrichir le travail humain: L'évaluation économique* [Human job enrichment: Economic evaluation]. Paris, France: Dunod.

Fernández Ruvalcaba, M. (2007). Socio-economic approach to management in Mexico. In A. F. Buono & H. Savall (Eds.), *Socio-economic intervention in organizations* (pp. 251–278). Charlotte, NC: Information Age Publishing.

Humble, J. (1973). *Social responsibility audit: A management tool for survival.* New York, NY: Amacom.

ISEOR. (2001). *Knowledge and Value Development in Management Consulting: Proceedings.* International Conference Co-Sponsored by Management Consulting Division of the Academy of Management (USA). Ecully, France: ISEOR.

Lussato, B. (1972). *Introduction critique aux théories des organisations (modèles cybernétiques, hommes, entreprises)* [Introduction to critical theories of organizations (cybernetic models, men, businesses)]. Paris, France: Dunod.

Marquès, E. (1975). *La Comptabilité des ressources humaines* [Human resource accounting]. Paris, France: Éditions Hommes et Techniques.

Martínez García, E. (2009). *Bernácer G. 'Functional doctrine of money.'* Dallas, TX: Federal Reserve of Dallas.

Ordre des Experts-Comptables et Comptables Agréés. (1984). *Comptabilité et prospective: Réponses comptables aux nouveaux besoins d'information* [Accounting and prospective: Accounting responses to new information needs]. Paris, France: OECCA.

Péron, M., & Bonnet, M. (2008). CSR in intervention-research: Example of an implementation of the SEAM model. *Revue Sciences de Gestion—Management Sciences—Ciencias de Gestión, 239*–263.

Péron, M., & Péron, M. (2003). Postmodernism and the socio-economic approach to organizations. *Journal of Organizational Change Management, 16* (1), 49–55.

Perroux, F. (1972). *Pouvoir et économie* [Power and economics]. Paris, France: Dunod.

Perroux, F. (1975). *Unités actives et mathématiques nouvelles—Révision de la théorie de l'équilibre économique général* [Active units and new mathematics—Revision of the general economic equilibrium theory]. Paris, France: Dunod.

Perroux, F. (1979). Preface. In H. Savall, *Reconstruire l'entreprise—Analyse socio-économique des conditions de travail: L'entreprise, l'équilibre rénové et les coûts 'cachés'* [*Enterprise, renovated balance and 'hidden' costs*]. Paris, France: Dunod.

Perroux, F. (1974). Économie de la ressource humaine [Economics of human resources]. *Revue Mondes en développement.* ISMEA, 15–81.

Pigé, B. (2008). *Gouvernance, contrôle et audit des organisations* [*Governance, control and audit organizations*]. Paris, France: Economica.

Reynaud, J. D., & Douard, H. (1972). *The quality of working life: A central issue in industrial relations. Proceedings of the conference on the quality of working life.* New York, NY: Harriman.

Robertson, D. H. (1940). *A Spanish contribution to the theory of fluctuations.* Paris, France: Economica.

Ruiz, G. (1983). El sistema de pensamiento de Germán Bernácer Tormo (1883–1965) [Germán Bernacér's system of thought]. *Pensamiento ibero americano: Revista de economía política*, 191–213.

Savall, H. (1974, 1975b). *Enrichir le travail humain: L'évaluation* économique [*Enriching the human work, the economic evaluation*]. Thèse Université Paris IX-Dauphine; full text published by Paris: Dunod.

Savall, H. (1974). Avant Keynes et au-delà: Germán Bernácer, économiste espagnol [Before Keynes and beyond: Germán Bernacer, Spanish economist]. *Revue Mondes en développement*, 5.

Savall, H. (1975a). *G. Bernácer: l'hétérodoxie en science économique* [*Germán Bernácer: Heterodoxy in economics*]. Paris, France: Dalloz, Collection Les Grands Économistes.

Savall, H. (1977, March). Formation et conditions de vie au travail [Training at work and working conditions]. *Revue française de gestion*, 17, 126–142.

Savall, H. (Ed.) (1978). Aspects humains et sociaux de l'économie industrielle [Human and social aspects of industrial economics]. *Revue d'Économie Industrielle*, 7–11.

Savall, H. (1978b). Article: 'Bernácer.' *Encyclopédie de l'Économie* [*Encyclopedia of Economics*]. Paris, France: Larousse.

Savall, H. (1979). *Reconstruire l'entreprise: Analyse socio-économique des conditions de travail* [*Rebuild the enterprise Socio-economic analysis of work conditions*]. Préface de François Perroux. Paris, France: Dunod.

Savall, H. (1983). *G. Bernácer: L'hétérodoxie en science économique* [*G. Bernácer: Heterodoxy in economics*]. Paris, France: Dalloz, collection Les Grands Économistes.

Savall, H. (1987). *Les coûts cachés et l'analyse socio-économique des organisations* [*Hidden costs and socio-economic analysis of organizations*]. Paris, France: Encyclopédie du management.

Savall, H. (2003a). An update presentation of the socio-economic management model and international dissemination of the socio-economic model. *Journal of Organizational Change Management, 16* (1), 33–48.

Savall, H. (2003b). Socio-economic approach to management. *Journal of Organizational Change Management.* West Yorkshire, England: Emerald.

Savall, H. (2010a). Bouleversement des normes et pilotage stratégique des organisations: Menaces et opportunités [Disruption of standards and norms and strategic monitoring of management: threats and opportunities]. In D. Bessire, V. Cappelletti, & B. Pigé (Eds.), *Normes: Origines et conséquences des crises* [*Standards and Norms: Origins and Consequences of Crisis*]. Paris, France: Economica.

Savall, H. (2010b). *Work and people: An economic evaluation of job-enrichment* (2nd ed.), Charlotte, NC: Information Age. (Original work published 1981).

Savall, H. (2012a). Petite lecture épistémologique de la responsabilité sociale de l'entreprise [An epistemological reading of corporate social responsibility].

In A. Le Flanchec, O. Uzan, & M. Doucin (Eds.), *Responsabilité sociale de l'entreprise et gouvernance mondiale* [CSR and global governance]. Paris, France: Economica.

Savall, H. (2012b). *Origine radicale des crises: Germán Bernácer, précurseur visionnaire* [Root origin of crises: Germán Bernácer, a visionary forrunner]. Charlotte, NC: Information Age Publishing.

Savall, H., & Bonnet, M. (1995). *How to keep up with high labor standards in industrial companies located in developed nations competing with low wage countries: Results of socio-economic experiments in European firms aimed at implementing new management negotiation methods.* Washington, DC: Xème Congrès de l'Institut International des Relations Professionnelles.

Savall, H., & Zardet, V. (1987). *Maîtriser les coûts et les performances cachés. Le contrat d'activité périodiquement négociable* [Mastering hidden costs and performance: The periodically negotiable activities contract]. Paris, France: Economica/ Harvard: L'Expansion Prize of Strategic Management, 5th ed. 2010.

Savall, H., & Zardet, V. (1992). *Le nouveau contrôle de gestion: Méthode des coûts-performances cachés* [*The new management control: Method of hidden cost-performance*]. Paris, France: Eyrolles.

Savall, H., & Zardet V. (1994). Performance économique et engagement social de l'entreprise: Jusqu'où est-ce compatible? [Economic performance and social commitment of the company: How far is it compatible?]. *Revue Stratégies Ressources Humaines, 9,* 30–38.

Savall, H., & Zardet, V. (1995a). *Ingénierie stratégique du roseau, souple et enracinée* [Strategic engineering of the reed, flexible and rooted]. Paris, France: Economica. Traduit en espagnol en 2009: *Ingeniería estratégica: un enfoque socio económico,* Prólogo de Solis, P. México: UAM.

Savall, H., & Zardet, V. (1995b). Management socio-économique de l'entreprise: Ou comment régénérer confiance et performances [Socio-economic management of the enterprise: Or how to regenerate confidence and performance]. In *Confiance, entreprise et société* (pp. 163–179). Paris, France: Eska.

Savall, H., & Zardet, V. (1995c). *Ingénierie stratégique du roseau, souple et enracinée* [Strategy engineering of the reed, flexible and grounded]. Paris, France: Economica, 2nd ed. 2005.

Savall, H., & Zardet, V. (1996a). Pour des stratégies d'entreprise à la fois économiques et sociales [Fostering both economic and social corporate strategies]. *Revue Personnel, 367,* 44–52.

Savall, H., & Zardet, V. (1996b). Mesure et négociation de la performance globale de l'entreprise: Éléments pour une théorie socio-économique du contrôle de gestion [Measuring and negotiating the corporate over all performance]. *IIIème Congrès Mondial de l'International Fédération of Scholarly Associations of Management.* Paris, France: IFSAM.

Savall, H., & Zardet, V. (1996c). La dimension cognitive de la recherche-intervention: la production de connaissances par interactivité cognitive [The cognitive dimension of intervention-research: The production of knowledge through cognitive interactivity]. *Revue Internationale de Systémique, 10*(1–2), pp. 157–189.

Savall H., & Zardet, V. (1996d). Who benefits from quality insurances strategies? Test of analysis of the division of the economic value. Paper presented at the 5th Conference of the International Association of Strategic Management. Lille, France.

Savall, H., & Zardet, V. (1997). Les effets des démarches qualité sur l'emploi [The impacts of quality processes on employment in certification, quality and employment]. In *Certification, qualité et emploi* (pp. 33–52). Paris, France: Economica.

Savall, H., & Zardet, V. (2004). Entreprise, normalisation et responsabilité sociale: propositions d'une théorie socio-économique de l'intégration [Business, standardization and social responsibility: Proposition of a socio-economic theory of integration]. Tunis, Tunisia: *Congrès IAS* (Mai).

Savall, H., & Zardet, V. (2004). *Recherche en sciences de gestion, approche qualimétrique: observer l'objet complexe* [Management science research, the Qualimetrics approach: Observing the complex object] Paris, France: Economica.

Savall, H., & Zardet, V. (2005). Processus participatif de changement pour une performance socio-économique durable: Cas évalués d'entreprises et d'organisations [Participatory process of change for a sustainable socio-economic performance: Cases of companies and organizations]. *Revue Gestion,* 4, pp. 78–102.

Savall, H., & Zardet, V. (2005). *Tétranormalisation: Défis et dynamiques* [Challenges and Dynamics of Tetranormalization]. Paris, France: Economica.

Savall, H., & Zardet, V. (2006). Visión europea y enfoque socioeconómico: ¿Hacia una responsabilidad social de la empresa, sustentable y soportable? [A European vision and socio-economic approach: Toward an acceptable sustainable corporate social responsibility]. In G. R. Martínez (Ed.), *Desempeño Organizacional Retos Y Enfoques Contemporáneos* [Contemporaneous approaches and challenges of Organizational Development], pp. 73–87. México: UAM.

Savall, H., & Zardet, V. (Eds.) (2007a). *Evaluación de desempeño y gestión socioeconómica* [Evaluation of performance and socio-economic management]. Mérida, México: Gobierno de Yucatán, ISEOR.

Savall, H., & Zardet, V. (2007b, June). L'importance stratégique de l'investissement incorporel: Résultats qualimétriques de cas d'entreprises [The strategic importance of intangible investment: qualimetric results of case of companies]. *Le 1'ière Congrès transatlantique de comptabilité, audit, contrôle de gestion, gestion des coûts et mondialisation* [1st Transatlantic Conference on Accounting, Audit, Management Control, Cost Management and Globalization]. Institut International des Coûts (IIC) American Accounting Association, ISEOR, Lyon, France.

Savall, H., & Zardet, V. (2008a). *Mastering hidden costs and socio-economic performance.* Charlotte, NC: Information Age.

Savall, H., & Zardet, V. (2008b). Le concept de coût-valeur des activités. Contribution de la théorie socio-économique des organisations [The concept of cost-value of activities. Contribution of socio-economic theory of organizations]. *Revue Sciences de Gestion-Management Sciences- Ciencias de Gestión, 64,* pp. 61–90.

Savall, H., & Zardet, V. (2008c). Tétranormalisation et nouvelles règles du jeu : contribution de la théorie socio-économique [Tetranormalization and new rules of the game: the contribution of socio-economic theory]. In *XIème Journée François Perroux*. Écully, France: ISEOR.

Savall, H., & Zardet, V. (2010). Tétranormalisation: Origine, cheminement et portée du concept [Tetranormalization: Origin, direction and scope of the concep]. In Bessire, V. Cappelletti, & B. Pigé (Eds.), *Normes: Origines et conséquences des crises* [*Standards and norms: Origin and consequences of crisis*] (pp. 5–7). Paris, France: Economica.

Savall, H., & Zardet, V. (2011a). *The qualimetrics approach: Observing the complex object*. Charlotte, NC: Information Age.

Savall, H., & Zardet, V. (2011b). Le management de la responsabilité sociale de l'entreprise par les indicateurs [The management of corporate social responsibility through indicators] in Trébulle & Uzan (Ed.), *Responsabilité sociale des entreprises: regards croisés Droit et gestion*. Paris, France: Economica.

Savall, H., & Zardet, V. (Eds.). (2011c). *Réussir en temps de crise: Stratégies pro-actives des entreprises* [Succeed in times of crisis: Pro-active strategies of firms]. Paris, France: Economica.

Savall, H., & Zardet, V. (2011d). Contribution de la théorie socio-économique des organisations à la poursuite et valorisation de l'oeuvre de François Perroux au XXIème siècle [Contribution of socio-economic theory of organizations in the pursuit and promotion of the work of Perroux in the XXI century]. In E. d'Hombres, H. Savall, & E. Gabellieri, (Eds.), *Humanisme et travail chez François Perroux* (pp. 21–40). Paris, France: Economica.

Savall H., & Zardet V. (2012, October). Nouvel énoncé de la théorie socioéconomique des organisations et des territoires [New statement of the socioeconomic theory of organizations and territories]. *Cahier de recherche* [Working paper], ISEOR.

Savall, H., Zardet, V., & Bonnet, M. (2000). *Releasing the untapped potential of enterprises through socio-economic management*. Geneva: ILO-BIT.

Savall, H., Zardet, V., & Bonnet, M. (Eds.). (2009a). *Management socio-économique: Une approche innovante* [Socio-economic approach to management: An innovative approach]. Paris, France: Economica.

Savall, H., Zardet, V., & Bonnet, M. (2009b). Théorie socio-économique des organisations et tétranormalisation: Perpétuer l'oeuvre de François *Perroux* [Socio-economic theory of organizations and tetranormalization: Perpetuating the work of François Perroux]. In M. Kalila (Ed.), *Les Hommes et le Management: Des Réponses à la Crise*, Mélanges en l'honneur de Sabine Urban. Paris, France: Economica.

Savall, H., Zardet, V., & Bonnet, M. (2011). *RSE et développement durable, fondements de la théorie socio-économique des organisations* [CSR and sustainable development, foundations of the theory of socio-economic organizations in CRS between globalization and Sustainable development]. In N. Barthe & J. J. Rosé (Coord.) *RSE entre globalisation et développement durable* (pp. 239–268). Brussels, Belgium: De Boeck.

Savall, H., Zardet, V., Bonnet, M., & Péron, M. (2008). The emergence of implicit criteria actually utilized by reviewers of qualitative research articles: Case of a European journal organizational research methods. *Organizational research methods, 11*, pp. 510–540.

Savall, H., Zardet, V., Bonnet, M., & Péron, M. (2009, June). Conditions to governing the performance of employment and environmental standards socioeconomic considerations and proposals based on case histories from the chemicals and food manufacturing industries. Colloque international et Consortium Doctoral en partenariat avec Academy of Management, Université Jean Moulin Lyon 3, Lyon, France.

Savall, H., Zardet, V., & Péron, M. (2011). The "evolutive" and interactive actor polygon in the theater of organizations. In D. Boje (Ed.), *Storytelling and the future of organizations: An antenarrative handbook* (pp. 137–163). New York, NY: Routledge.

Taylor, F. W. (2004). *The principles of scientific management.* New York, NY: Harper. (Original work published 1911)

Villacís González, J. (1987). Una Teoría de los Circlos a la Luz de la Teoría de las Disponibilidades [A theory of cycles through the available funds theory]. *Boletín ICE,* no. 2074, 2563–2603.

Villacís González, J. (1992). Análisis macroeconómico histórico y actual de la teoría de las disponibilidades en Germán Bernácer [A current, historic and macroeconomic análisis of German Bernacer theory of available funds]. *Revista de derecho financiero y de hacienda pública, 12,* 1323–1371.

Villacís González, J. (2009). Dynamic theory of the money market, disposable money and interest. *Journal of Business and Economics Research, 7* (9), 78–97.

Weber, M. (1922). Économie *et Société* [Economy and society]. Réédition 2007, Paris, France: Pocket.

Zardet, V. (2007). Developing sustainable global performance in small to medium size industrial firms: The case of Brioche Pasquier. In A. F. Buono & H. Savall (Eds.), *Socio-economic intervention in organizations: The intervener-researcher and the SEAM approach to organizational analysis* (pp. 45–70). Charlotte, NC: Information Age.

Zardet, V., & Bonnet, M. (2010). Intensification actuelle de la tétranormalisation: Risques et bonnes pratiques émergentes [Current intensification of tetranormalization: Risks and emerging good practices]. In D. Bessire, V. Cappelletti & B. Pigé (Eds.), *Normes: Origines et conséquences des crises* (pp. 23–34). Paris, France: Economica.

Zardet, V., & Noguera, F. (2009). *Mythe et réalité de la contractualisation de l'action publique: cas de contrats de développement territoriaux* [Myth and Reality of public policy contract agreement: The case of territorial development contracts]. Paris, France: L'Harmattan.

Zardet, V., & Voyant, O. (2003). Organizational transformation through the socioeconomic approach in an industrial context. *Journal of Organizational Change Management, 16* (1), 56–71.

ABOUT THE CONTRIBUTORS

Raúl Arceo Alonzo is a consultant in public management and strategic planning. He is the former head officer of the unit of Human Resource Policies of the Federal Government of Mexico Ministries. He is also the former head officer of the Yucatán State government and Ministry of Administration. He holds a master's degree in general administration and a master's degree in local public management and administration.

David M. Boje holds the Wells Fargo Professorship, Distinguished University Professor, and Bill Daniels Ethics Fellow in the Management Department at New Mexico State University. He also has an honorary doctorate from Aalborg University. His specialty is storytelling using qualitative methods. He advises people about several types of storytelling research methods, ranging from traditional narrative memory work, to living story emergence, to the new work in antenarrative and quantum storytelling. Presently he is working on storytelling methodologies that can tease out spiral-antenarrative processes. Boje is founder and president of Standing Conference for Management and Organizational Inquiry and the new annual conference on Quantum Storytelling. A list of his books and journal articles can be found at http://peaceaware.com/vita/

Marc Bonnet is a professor at the Institut d'Administration des Entreprises, University Jean Moulin Lyon, and the deputy director of the ISEOR. He holds a PhD in management sciences from the University of Lyon and

Facilitating the Socioeconomic Approach to Management, pages 275–282
Copyright © 2014 by Information Age Publishing
275

carries on his research, in particular, in the field of the Socio-Economic Approach to Management.

Anthony F. Buono, series editor, has a joint appointment as professor of Management and Sociology at Bentley University. He is the founding coordinator of the Bentley Alliance for Ethics & Social Responsibility, which he directed from 2003–2013. Among his many books and articles are *The Human Side of Mergers and Acquisitions* (Jossey-Bass, 1989; Beard Books, 2003) and *A Primer on Organizational Behavior* (Wiley, 7th ed., 2008). His current research and consulting interests focus on organizational change and interorganizational alliances, with an emphasis on mergers, acquisitions, and strategic partnerships, and developing organizational change capacity. He holds a PhD with a concentration in Industrial and Organizational Sociology from Boston College.

Jean Caghassi has held various executive management positions in a wide variety of fields in France, Belgium, Italy, and Spain, all with international exposure. He has applied the Socio-Economic Approach to Management as defined by SEAM for more than 10 years in his different operational responsibilities and particularly in the context of restructuring and organizational change. His current interest, as a consultant and venture capitalist, focuses on assisting managers and business owners in using SEAM to develop their organizational change capacities, with an emphasis on preparing and implementing succession processes, strategic partnerships, and mergers and acquisitions. He has participated in various seminars and conventions to promote SEAM in France, Mexico, and the United States.

John Conbere is a professor and codirector of the SEAM Institute at the University of St. Thomas in Minnesota. He is a primary developer of the SEAM Institute, which is a collaborative program between the University of ST. Thomas and ISEOR (Lyon, France) to develop academic programs and research about SEAM in the United States. Among his published articles is "Socio-Economic Approach to Management: A Successful Systemic Approach to Organizational Change," which was named "Best Article" of 2011 in the *OD Practitioner*. He holds a MDiv from the Episcopal Divinity School and an EdD in Human Resource Development from the University of Minnesota.

Vincent Cristallini is associate professor at IAE Lyon, University of Jean Moulin Lyon 3 and Research Program Manager at ISEOR. He is the author of *L'habileté Managériale—Réalisme et Courage en Management* (Editions EMS, 2009), "Seam in a Service Company: Developing Vigorous, Disciplined and Empowering Management" in *Socio-Economic Intervention in Organizations*

(IAP, 2007), and "Enhancing the Efficiency of Networks in an Urban Area through Socio-economic Interventions" in the *Journal of Organizational Change Management* (2003). Vincent holds a PhD in general management.

Martha Margarita Fernández Ruvalcaba is a professor at the Universidad Autonóma Metropolitana de México (UAM) and a partner in the ISEOR's network for research-intervention in organizations. She received her PHD in management sciences from the University of Lyon. Her current research interest focuses on the relationships between the homogeneity of public policies for higher education in Mexico and the organizational diversity of public universities; her other research focuses on the future of learning and research in Management Sciences in Latin American countries in a global context.

Robert P. Gephart, Jr. is professor of Strategic Management and Organization at the University of Alberta. He is the author of *Ethnstatistics* (Sage, 1988) and coeditor of *Postmodern Management and Organization Theory* (Sage, 1996). His research has appeared in a number of journals including *Administrative Science Quarterly, Academy of Management Journal, Journal of Management, Organizational Research Methods, and Organization Studies*. His current research interests are risk sensemaking, deliberation in organizations, and ethnostatistics. He received his PhD in Commerce and Business Administration from the University of Alberta.

Gilles Guyot is an attorney and scholar who has taught in major universities all over the world. He is regarded as a *comparatiste*, due to his strong commitment to international issues and his dedication to comparative research and scholarship in such varied disciplines as law, management, and social anthropology. He has been professor and dean at the university Jean Moulin Lyon 3 and is honorary president of the university. In 2002, he was made a knight of the Legion of Honor, France's highest decoration. His 2012 book, *L'Internationale de l'Intelligence*, argues that globalization should be driven not just by financial imperatives but by the sharing of knowledge across cultures as well.

Randall B. Hayes is currently professor of Accounting and was codirector of the Institute of Management Consulting at Central Michigan University. He has previously taught at Michigan State University and the College of William and Mary. His research is primarily in the areas of business valuation and consulting techniques. He has published numerous articles in various professional and academic journals. Hayes received his MBA and PhD from the University of Michigan.

Chato Hazelbaker is pursuing his doctorate in Organization Development at the University of St. Thomas (MN). He works as the chief communication officer at Clark College in Vancouver, WA and has served as a consultant, trainer and teacher for a variety of organizations. He currently serves as an adjunct instructor teaching Organization Development to students at Bethel University (MN) and Warner Pacific College in Portland, OR.

Alla Heorhiadi is Distinguished Service Professor and codirector of the SEAM Institute at the University of St. Thomas, Minnesota. She holds doctorates in Organization Development and Economics. She has a vast international experience by having taught and consulted in the United States, Ukraine, France, Greece, and Germany. She is licensed to do Socio-Economic interventions according to the ISEOR's standard in the United States. Since 2010 her scholarly work has focused on studying the effects of socio-economic approach to management. Her article "Socio-Economic Approach to Management: A Successful Systemic Approach to Organizational Change" that was published in the *OD Practitioner* was named "Best Article" of 2011.

Mark E. Hillon has been a civil engineer, strategic planner, and management professor. He is currently researching sustainability in organizations, agriculture, and energy in an effort to be a better global citizen. He holds a PhD from New Mexico State University with a concentration in Strategy and a PhD from ISEOR/Jean Moulin University (Lyon 3) in Management Science.

Yue C. Hillon currently teaches strategic management at Western Carolina University in Cullowhee, North Carolina. She is an innovator in undergraduate business strategy education, training students in future-oriented data-intensive strategy creation for local business clients. She teaches socio-economic management consulting to her graduate students, also in an applied business context. Her SEAM clients have spanned a variety of industries including manufacturing, aviation, restaurants, software, and education. She holds a PhD from New Mexico State University in Strategic Management, in which she pioneered the study of strategic inflections by imagery deconstruction.

Debra Pearl Hockenberry is a scholar-practitioner who focuses on innovation and entrepreneurship. She is a former legislative aide and speechwriter for a U.N. Delegate in Vienna, Austria as well as the copresident and Founder of Organizational Alchemist and VetReturns, Inc. With over 20 years' experience in marketing and publishing, she has been a business professor and published author for 30 years, teaching at universities around the world including University of Singapore, University of Heidelberg, Temple University, and Penn State University. Currently she teaches various entrepreneurship courses at Elizabethtown College. Debra has a doctorate in Organizational Development and Change from Colorado Technical University, an MBA from DeSales University, and a Bachelor of Arts in International Affairs from George Washington University. She is the author of the recent book entitled, *Novaturient Organizations and Ultraliminal Innovation.*

Susan J. Huber is the executive vice president and provost at the University of St. Thomas in St. Paul, Minnesota. She assists the president with the overall strategic direction of the university and especially its academic mission. She provides leadership and supervision to the vice presidents and associate vice presidents who staff the Office of Academic Affairs, the deans in the university's six colleges and schools and the directors of multiple academic centers. She is also a tenured faculty member and full professor in the College of Education, Leadership and Counseling, where she also served as department chair, associate dean and dean. She is the author of *The Best Dressed List: Classroom Trends and Cultural Fashions* (Rowman and Littlefield, 2003) and many other articles related to teaching and education. Huber earned a dual B.A, in Latin and English from the College of St. Teresa, Winona, Minnesota, followed by an MA Degree in Curriculum and Instruction, and an EdD in Educational Leadership both from the College of St. Thomas

Alanna Kennedy holds an EdD in Organizational Development and MBA with a concentration in world class manufacturing from the University of St. Thomas in St. Paul, Minnesota. In addition, she is certified in lean manufacturing at the bronze level by the Society of Manufacturing Engineering and is certified in Production Inventory Management (CPIM) by APICS. Kennedy has more than 25 years of manufacturing experience, which includes over 10 years of "hands on" experience in production management with direct responsibility for manufacturing operations and 15 years of experience in material management. Currently, she is employed by Emerson Process Management.

Lawrence Lepisto is a professor of Marketing and was codirector of the Institute for Management Consulting at Central Michigan University at the time of this research project. His marketing research activities have focused on the effect of aging over the life span and the impact on consumer behavior. His research in management consulting relates to the integration of consulting tools and graduate educational strategies in management consulting.

Barbara Milon is executive director of the Phyllis Wheatley Community Center (PWCC). She is also a doctoral student at the University of St. Thomas in Organization Development. Milon serves on the MinneMinds Executive and Advisory Committees, Board of MN Nonprofit Assistance Fund, MACC Alliance of Connected Communities, and member of the African American Leadership Forum (AALF). She has a Master's of Science in Community Economic Development from Southern New Hampshire University, and a Bachelor's degree in Urban Studies from Xavier University.

Thomas "Ace" Oestreich is the director of Transportation for Bloomington (Minnesota) Public Schools (2004–present). In the fall of 1999 the school district launched its own Transportation Center to control burgeoning contracted busing costs. Tom was hired as assistant director the previous spring and worked as part of a small team to ensure that every student in Bloomington would arrive safely for the first day of school on a bus owned by the district and driven by a highly trained, qualified, and licensed district employee. Tom was promoted to director in 2004, and the Bloomington Transportation Center continues to grow and thrive as they prepare for their 15th school year launch in September 2014.

Michel Péron is emeritus professor at the University of Paris III Sorbonne Nouvelle. He received his PhD from the University of Lyon. He is a researcher at ISEOR and Centre d'études et de recherches sur la vie économique des pays Anglo-Saxons (CERVEPAS, Research Center on Anglo-Saxon Economies). His research interests lie in cross-cultural management, corporate ethics, and the history of economic ideas.

Eric Sanders is an Organization Development Economist, an independent consultant who helps leaders and organizations achieve measurable results through developing their people. Sanders has degrees in psychology, economics and business administration, and is presently a Doctoral Candidate in Organization Development at Benedictine University, researching organizational learning and organizational culture. He has served as an adjunct faculty member for over 15 years at schools including Benedictine University, the Lake Forest Graduate School of Management, and Loyola University Chicago. His publications include "Financial Returns from Organizational Culture Improvement: Translating 'Soft' Changes into 'Hard' Dollars" (2005 *ASTD Research-to-Practice Conference Proceedings*, coauthored with Robert A. Cooke), "Strategic Leadership of Cultural Transformation at Advocate Health Partners," a chapter in *Strategic Organization Development: Managing Change For Success* (coauthored with Roxanne Ray, Information Age Publishing, 2009), and "An American Expatriate in China: Evidence of

Organizational Culture Crossvergence" (*Proceedings of the Southwest Academy of Management Conference*, 2013).

Amandine Savall is a doctoral student at Conservatoire National des Arts et Métiers. She is also an intervener-researcher at ISEOR, where she has carried out various interventions in French and foreign companies since 2011. Her research interests are SEAM, management control, family business, international management, and using the qualimetrics methodology. Amandine Savall has been awarded the Management & Société Award for her outstanding master's dissertation in 2012. She presented different papers at the AOM Annual Conferences (Boston, Orlando). Given her excellent knowledge in Spanish and English, she is in charge of coordinating ISEOR projects and promoting the SEAM approach overseas.

Henri Savall is an emeritus professor at the Institut d'Administration des Entreprises, University Jean Moulin Lyon, where he is the founder of the Centre EUGINOV (École Universitaire de Gestion Innovante) and the Socio-Economic Management Master's program. He is also the founder and president of the ISEOR Research Center. Professor Savall has a multidisciplinary education and his fields of interest include accounting, finance, political science, linguistics, economics, and economic history. His current research interests are socioeconomic theory, strategic management, qualimetrics methodology and tetranormalization. His research methodology is referred to as "intervention research" and "qualimetrics" as it goes beyond traditional action research. Savall and Professor Véronique Zardet were awarded the famous Rossi Award by the Academy of Moral and Political Sciences (Institut de France) for their work on the integration of social variables into business strategy. He is the founder and the editor of the *Recherches en Sciences de Gestion—Management Sciences—Ciencias de Gestión (Journal of Administrative Science)*.

Rohny Saylors is a PhD Candidate at New Mexico State University. His passion is the advancement of human creativity, hope, and authentic compassion through, and within, organizational scholarship. Accordingly, he focuses on storytelling in sustainability, the ethics of identity, and entrepreneurial sensemaking. He envisions a scholarly world where research advances human potential and a work world that values scholarship as art instead of authority. His work is a natural extension of antenarrative storytelling theory when unified with strategy as practice and rhetorical pragmatics in institutional entrepreneurship.

Peter F. Sorensen is professor and director of the PhD program in Organization Development, and the MS Program in Management and

Organizational Behavior at Benedictine University. He has authored more than 300 articles, papers and books, including a number of best paper selections. His work has appeared in the *Academy of Management Journal, Group and Organization Studies, Leadership and Organization Development Journal, Journal of Management Studies,* and *Organization and Administrative Science,* among others. He has been chair of the ODC Division of Academy of Management, and serves on editorial boards for *OD Journal,* the *OD Practitioner,* and the French journal RSDG (*Revue Sciences de Gestion*).

Therese Yaeger is professor at Benedictine University in the PhD-OD, and MS in Management and Organizational Behavior programs. Managerial and consulting roles during her more than 25-year professional career have included roles in manufacturing, small business, government, and military. Publications include *Critical Issues in Organization Development: Case Studies for Analysis and Discussion* with Sorensen and Johnson (2013), *Global Organization Development: Managing Unprecedented Change* with Sorensen and Head (2006), and *Appreciative Inquiry: Foundations in Positive Organization Development* with Cooperrider, Sorensen and Whitney (2005). Yaeger is a past chair of Management Consulting Division of Academy of Management. She is former president of the Midwest Academy of Management.

Véronique Zardet is a professor of Management Sciences at the Institut d'Administration des Entreprises (Institute of Business Administration) at the University Jean Moulin Lyon 3, when she is the director of the Center EUGINOV (École Universitaire de Gestion Innovante) and director, with Professor Henri Savall, of the ISEOR Research Center. She heads the "Research in Socio-Economic Management" Master's program. She holds a PhD in management sciences from the University of Lyon. In 2001 she received (with Henri Savall) the Rossi Award from the Academy of Moral and Political Sciences (Institute of France) for her work on the integration of social variables into business strategies. Her research is centered on the conduct of strategic change and the improvement of socio-economic performance in companies and organizations, and particularly in public services and the health industry.

Lightning Source UK Ltd.
Milton Keynes UK
UKOW04f2311140314

228163UK00002B/8/P